Letter & Spirit 9 (2014)

Christ and the Unity of Scripture

Letter & Spirit 9 (2014): 3–5

Contributors

~: William A. Bales :~

William A. Bales is an Associate Professor of Sacred Scripture at Mount St. Mary's Seminary in Emmitsburg, Maryland. A former Presbyterian pastor before his conversion to the Catholic Faith in 1990, he holds a Ph.D. in New Testament from The Catholic University of America and a Master's degree in Theology from Gordon-Conwell Theological Seminary, where he concentrated in Old Testament studies. Dr. Bales is also a Senior Fellow of The St. Paul Center for Biblical Theology in Steubenville, Ohio and Managing Editor of the Center's theological journal, *Letter & Spirit*. He and his wife Lisanne have six children and four grandchildren and live in Gettysburg, Pennsylvania.

~: Michael Patrick Barber :~

Michael Patrick Barber is Professor of Theology and Scripture at John Paul the Great Catholic University in Escondido, CA. He has authored scholarly articles for academic journals (including *Journal of Biblical Literature* and *Letter & Spirit*) and has published popular-level works on the Psalms and the Book of Revelation. He contributed the Catholic perspective to *Four Views on the Role of Works at the Final Judgment* (Zondervan Academic, 2013), edited by Alan Stanley and co-authored by James D. G. Dunn, Thomas R. Schreiner, and Robert N. Wilkin. With Senior Fellows of the St. Paul Center for Biblical Theology, John Bergsma and Brant Pitre, Barber writes for the blog The Sacred Page (www.TheSacredPage.com). He lives in San Diego with his wife Kimberly and their four children.

~: Vincent P. DeMeo :~

Vincent P. DeMeo is an associate professor of the New Testament at the *International Theological Institute* in Trumau, Austria where he teaches courses in biblical theology, patristics, and biblical foundations to marriage and family theology. His published doctoral dissertation is titled *Covenantal Kinship in John 13-17: A Historical-Narrative Approach* (Vol. 22; Rome: Ateneo Pontificio Regina Apostolorum Publishers, 2012). Among giving lectures and writing several forthcoming articles, he is currently writing a book titled *The Common Good in New Testament and Patristic Thought*. He has also taught for Ave Maria University, Franciscan University of Steubenville, and, most recently, at Kolégium Antona Neuwirtha, Bratislava, Slovakia.

~: Scott W. Hahn :~

Scott W. Hahn, founder of the St. Paul Center for Biblical Theology, holds the Father Michael Scanlan, TOR Chair of Biblical Theology and the New Evangelization at Franciscan University of Steubenville and serves as the McEssy Distinguished Visiting Professor of Biblical Theology at Mundelein Seminary of the University of Saint Mary of the Lake and as adjunct faculty at the Pontifical University of the Holy Cross in Rome. He has held the Benedict XVI Chair of Biblical Theology and Liturgical Proclamation at St. Vincent Seminary in Latrobe, Pennsylvania. Hahn is the general editor of the Ignatius Catholic Study Bible and Catholic Bible Dictionary, and is author or editor of more than thirty books, including *Politicizing the Bible: The Roots of Historical Criticism and the Secularization of Scripture 1300-1700* (2013), *Consuming the Word: The New Testament and The Eucharist in the Early Church* (2013), *Kinship By Covenant: A Canonical Approach to the Fulfillment of God's Saving Promises* (The Anchor Yale Bible Reference Library, 2009), *Covenant and Communion: The Biblical Theology of Pope Benedict XVI* (2009), *Letter and Spirit: From Written Text to Living Word in the Liturgy* (2005), and *The Kingdom of God as Liturgical Empire: A Theological Commentary on 1-2 Chronicles* (2012).

~: Leroy A. Huizenga :~

Leroy Huizenga is Chair of the Department of Theology and Director of the Christian Leadership Center at the University of Mary in Bismarck, ND. Dr. Huizenga received his Ph.D. in New Testament from Duke University. During his doctoral studies he received a Fulbright grant to study and teach at Johann Wolfgang Goethe-Universität in Frankfurt, Germany. After teaching at Wheaton College (IL) for five years, Dr. Huizenga was reconciled with the Catholic Church at the Easter Vigil of 2011. Dr. Huizenga is the author of *The New Isaac: Tradition and Intertextuality in the Gospel of Matthew* (Brill, 2012).

~: Brant Pitre :~

Brant Pitre is Professor of Sacred Scripture at Notre Dame Seminary in New Orleans, Louisiana. He holds a Ph.D. in Theology from the University of Notre Dame, where he specialized in the study of the New Testament and ancient Judaism. He is the author of several articles and the books, *Jesus, the Tribulation, and the End of the Exile* (Baker Academic, 2005), *Jesus and the Jewish Roots of the Eucharist* (Image Books, 2011), *Jesus the Bridegroom* (Image Books, 2014), and *Jesus and the Last Supper* (Eerdmans, forthcoming).

∾ William M. Wright IV ∾

William M. Wright IV is an associate professor of theology at Duquesne University, where he teaches New Testament. A specialist in the Gospel according to John and its reception in early Christianity, he is the author of *Rhetoric and Theology: Figural Reading of John 9* (Walter de Gruyter, 2009) and is co-author, with Fr. Francis Martin, of *The Gospel of John* (Baker Academic, 2015).

Introduction

The theme of this issue of *Letter & Spirit* is "Christ and the unity of Scripture." From the perspective of the hermeneutic of faith, the primary purpose of biblical narrative is to recount humanity's familial history in the light of God's covenant plan for his people. Biblical history stands in sharp contrast to the mythical view that was widely held throughout the ancient Near East. Outside Israel, time was understood in terms of a fatalistic, never-ending cycle where the gods often controlled everyone's destiny. Most of these societies exhibited a deep pessimism about both the past and the future.

The modern Western approach to history is quite different. It is, first of all, quite secular, meaning that there is little patience for the idea of gods or God controlling or superintending events. Remarkably, modern history tends to be optimistic—fueled by an ever-increasing parade of dazzling technological achievements (overlooking its colossal moral failures). Modern history is linear and progressive. When a new "age" arrives—the "industrial," the "electronic," the "information"—the old age is superseded, and, to a greater or lesser degree, simply swept away. Even core values and fundamental principles can and sometimes should be jettisoned; societal progress is the goal. Progress means moving forward, and that is generally understood in terms of bull-dozing the past, not returning to it.

Biblical history is progressive, but not supersessionist. It moves forward, but it neither forgets nor overthrows the past. What follows *fulfills* what has preceded. What has preceded will return, but with each return there is a fuller flowering, a brighter dawn. As recent Popes have noted, with the coming of Christ in the New Covenant the Old is not revoked but renewed, not taken away but transformed, not forgotten but fulfilled. "Christ is in the Old concealed; Christ is in the New revealed"—here is the very DNA of sacred scripture, from Genesis to Revelation. Not an endless, pessimistic cycle; nor an aimless, cynical post-modernism. Biblical history—the story of salvation—is what it is because Christ is there, from beginning to end. *Christ unifies all*, making the story of salvation history—like the music of a great symphony—ever-expansive, increasingly dynamic, and minutely purposeful.

In his essay "The Matthean Christ, Center of Salvation History," **Leroy Huizenga** maintains that the Gospel of Matthew stands at the center of salvation history and thus at the center of the biblical canon by describing Christian faith as a story in the four acts of creation, fall, redemption, and glory, with redemption consisting of Israel, Jesus, and the Church. The Gospel of Matthew stands at the fulcrum of the story of salvation history and is thus first in the New Testament and first among the canonical Gospels in terms of both position and importance because its Christology shows most clearly the continuities of redemption, namely, how Israel's mission to the Gentiles is fulfilled in Jesus and the Church he founds.

It is then suggested that a proper estimation of Matthean Christology rooted in the continuities of salvation history pays hermeneutical and theological dividends.

In Matthew 5, Jesus insists that he has come not to "abolish" (*katalysai*) but to "fulfill" (*plēroō*) the law (Matt. 5:17). Yet, in the following section a series of sayings, often called "antitheses" (Matt. 5:21–48), seem to do just that. Perhaps most striking is Jesus' rejection of a practice sanctioned by the law; Jesus defines divorce and remarriage as adultery, a teaching that is reiterated in Matthew 19:4–9. In his article "Jesus as the 'Fulfillment' of the Law and His Teaching on Divorce in Matthew," **Michael Patrick Barber** argues that in Matthew, somewhat like Ezekiel, Jesus explains that certain elements of the law were only given because of Israel's sinfulness. These represented "statutes that were not good" (Ezek. 20:25). Such accommodations underscored Israel's need for a "better righteousness," which biblical and Second Temple texts associated with the eschatological age. For Matthew, Jesus comes to fulfill these hopes and thus maintains God's original design for marriage without the need for such concessions.

In his article, "'These Least Brothers of Mine': A Reappraisal of the Great Judgment Scene as Apocalyptic Retribution in Matthew 25:31–46," **William Bales** contends that the popular understanding of the Great Judgment scene in Matthew 25:31–46, particularly regarding the identity of "these least brothers" of Jesus, is seriously flawed. Bales first gives an analysis of the glaring problems connected with today's popular interpretation. Then, employing Matthean parallels and a sensitivity to the apocalyptic genre of Matthew 24–25, he offers a more satisfactory understanding of the great scene, along with some implications of his findings for the church today.

The accounts of the Last Supper are often neglected by contemporary Jesus research. In his study "The Last Supper and the Quest for Jesus," **Brant Pitre** contends that the Last Supper accounts are essential for answering the four key questions in the historical quest for Jesus: What was Jesus' relationship with his Jewish context? Who did he think he was? What did Jesus expect to happen in the future? What were his intentions toward the growing community of his followers? The Last Supper accounts strongly suggest that Jesus' identification of the bread and wine with his body and blood make the best sense within a first-century Jewish Temple context in which Jesus saw himself as the Messiah. Contrary to the proposals of Albert Schweitzer and Rudolf Bultmann, the words of institution also presuppose that Jesus did not expect the immediate destruction of creation. Instead, he envisioned the community of his disciples continuing after his death during the era of the new "covenant" and deliberately instituted the Last Supper as a founding cultic rite.

Following the teachings of *Dei Verbum* regarding the hermeneutical contribution of the biblical interpretation of the Church Fathers for understanding the contents of Scripture, **William M. Wright's** article "All Things in Wisdom: Reading the Prologue to the Gospel of John with St. Augustine" examines St. Augustine's interpretation of the Prologue to the Gospel according to John (John 1:1–18). John's Prologue offers a far-reaching vision of all things in relation to the Word of God. Augustine develops the Prologue's teaching into a synthetic account of "all things in Wisdom" (Ps. 103:24 quoted by Augustine in *Tract. Ev. Jo.* 1.16) wherein all created realities, and human beings in particular, creation and redemption, revelation and reason, the Old and New Covenants, are all inter-connected with one another by virtue of their relation to Christ, the Word and Wisdom of God.

In his article "Covenant Fulfillment in the Gospel of John," **Vincent P. DeMeo** demonstrates that a covenant theology is operative in the background of John 13–17 by showing that the kinship-by-covenant rule disclosed in the Old Testament is employed as a formative and controlling principle with respect to how Jesus, and through him the Father, relates to and guides his community of disciples. DeMeo argues that in the actions and discourses of his last supper, Jesus has established the new covenant with his eschatologically gathered community and, in doing so, has formed a divine kinship relation with them grounded in familial obligations. They are the definitive covenantal children of God. DeMeo's intent is to further and deepen the recent research on the covenant tradition in the gospel by explaining how Israel's covenantal kinship relation and obligations with their God, are, according to the gospel of John, fulfilled with a realism that is heightened in an unexpected manner.

In his article "Fulfillment in Christ: The Priority of the Abrahamic Covenant in Paul's Argument against the Galatian Opponents (Galatians 3:15–18)," **Scott W. Hahn** argues that Paul's controlling argument in Galatians 3:15–18 is that the Abrahamic covenant enjoys historical priority and theological primacy over against the Mosaic covenant at Sinai. In the process, Hahn shows that the Greek word *diathēkē* in Galatians 3:15 should be taken as "covenant," which accords well with the actual statements of the verse and the "covenant logic" of 3:15–17. Hahn demonstrates that for Paul, the Mosaic covenant cannot possibly supplement or alter the conditions of the covenant-oath sworn by God to Abraham at the Aqedah (the "binding" of Isaac), in which God took upon himself the responsibility to bless the Gentiles through Abraham's seed. The background of the Aqedah also elucidates the obscure argument in Galatians 3:16: Paul sees Isaac, the "only son" of Abraham, as a type of the Christ, the "one seed" of Abraham *par excellence*, whose self-sacrifice would be completed and serve to actualize the promised blessing of the Gentiles merited at the Aqedah. Paul's argument in Galatians 3:15–18, though subtle, is coherent and persuasive when we acknowledge his contextual use and typological reading of biblical texts.

Letter & Spirit 9 (2014): 11-29

The Matthean Christ, Center of Salvation History

~: **Leroy Huizenga** :~
University of Mary

Introduction

Christian Scripture presumes and presents a coherent story, the story of salvation history. Indeed, that story is the canon's formal organizing principle, from Genesis to Revelation. But the canon's coherence has largely been lost among modern Christians, thanks largely to contemporary convictions about the competence and authority of the individual to interpret texts however he or she will. These convictions have their roots not only in intellectual currents in modern philosophy or post-Reformation theology but also in socio-cultural realities brought about by the technological revolution of the printing press.[1] With its advent in the West, inexpensive Bibles and increasing literacy went hand in hand, making for the possibility of personal and private interpretation. Further, our detailed, precise system of versification first used in the 1560 Geneva Bible has caused many of those modern Christian individuals to approach the Bible as a jigsaw puzzle of individuated pieces to be memorized as discrete units and thus often interpreted quite apart from their native context. The blessing of widely-available Bibles and a largely literate Christian population brings with it the challenge of finding some whole within which the parts make sense, of perceiving the sweep of the forest and not just the trees.

For the Bible is not an undifferentiated mass of textual signs, a cacophony of diverse and discordant voices, a random jumble of discrete Bible verses. It is not a mere collection of textual artifacts bearing witness to long-dead disparate and diverse Israelite, Jewish, and Christian communities. Rather, it is Scripture, for it has functioned as Scripture in history for very real communities who persist and thrive today.[2] Therefore it can and must be studied as such, with due attention given to its reception history and history of interpretation within those communi-

1 On the effects of the printing press on religion in Western Europe, see Mark U. Edwards, Jr., *Printing, Propaganda, and Martin Luther* (Minneapolis: Augsburg Fortress, 2004); Elizabeth Eisenstein, *The Printing Revolution of Early Modern Europe*, Canto Classics, 2d ed. (Cambridge, UK: Cambridge University Press, 2012); Lucien Febvre and Henri-Jean Martin, *The Coming of the Book: The Impact of Printing, 1450-1800*, Verso World History Series, 3d ed. (Brooklyn, NY: Verso, 2010); and Andrew Pettegree, *The Book in the Renaissance*, repr. (New Haven, CT: Yale University Press, 2011).

2 See Brevard Childs, *Introduction to the Old Testament as Scripture* (Philadelphia: Fortress, 1979), 73: "A corpus of religious writings which has been transmitted within a community for over a

ties. In this way the story of the canon of Christian Scripture may emerge, through attention to the democracy of the dead, whose descendants yet live.

In this essay I wish to show how the Matthean Christ in particular stands at the center of salvation history. First, I will delineate a simple version of the story of salvation history that reflects the structure of the Christian Bible, with the added advantage of being easy to teach in religious education and catechesis. Second, I wish to make the claim that the Gospel of Matthew stands at the theological center of that story and thus at the center of Christian Scripture. Third, I wish to expend the bulk of my energies sketching the story that the Gospel of Matthew tells. And fourth, I wish to engage in some hermeneutical reflection, asking how the Gospel of Matthew's centrality to the story of Scripture helps us perceive the unity of Scripture as we read it today.

I. The Story of Salvation History and the Structure of the Canon

Following St. Augustine, the Christian faith may be conceived as a drama in four acts: Creation, Fall, Redemption, and Glory.[3] Genesis relates how God created all things with Adam and Eve at the pinnacle, making a covenant with them, but then Adam and Eve fell, introducing both moral and natural evils into creation. Genesis then recounts how God began the process of redemption, instituting a sacred, covenantal line, a covenantal family running from Adam and Eve through Noah and Abraham to Jacob, who becomes "Israel," the father of twelve sons who become the twelve tribes of Israel. In addition to the covenants made with Adam and Eve, Noah and his family, and Abraham and his descendants, The Lord God of Israel continues the line in making covenants with Moses, David and the kingdom of Israel, and ultimately Jesus and the Church.[4] From beginning to end, salvation history flows in covenantal continuity.

In Christian understanding, then, the Old Testament story of Israel's sacred covenantal line culminates in Jesus, the ideal Israelite, who founds a Church to continue the line. Redemption is thus divided into three scenes, Israel, Jesus, and the Church. The Church looks forward to the end (Judgment Day, the Second Coming), which is Glory. The Bible, then, presumes and presents this drama: The Christian Old Testament presents Creation, Fall, and the first scene of Redemption, Israel. The New Testament tells of Jesus and the Church, the second and third

---

thousand years cannot properly be compared to inert shreds [*sic*] which have lain in the ground for centuries."

3 See St. Augustine, *Catech.* [Catechizing the Uninstructed], 5, 10–11, 29–49 *et alibi.*

4 On the covenantal structure of Scripture and the familial nature of the covenants therein, see Scott Hahn, *A Father Who Keeps His Promises: God's Covenant Love in Scripture* (Cincinnati, OH: Servant Books, 1998), and Scott Hahn, *Kinship by Covenant: A Canonical Approach to the Fulfillment of God's Saving Promises*, Anchor Yale Bible Reference Library (New Haven, CT: Yale University Press, 2009).

scenes of Redemption, and the Church in all times and places looks forward to that Glory of which the prophets and Jesus himself spoke.

The Christian drama assumes continuity. Jesus and the Church do not make doctrine and practice up out of whole cloth. Even those elements that may seem new have Old Testament antecedents. Christian convictions concerning continuity explain the shape of the Christian Old Testament and New Testament and their relationship to each other.

We see the Church's concern for continuity in the order of its Old Testament (which is not the "Hebrew Bible" of modern terminology, which properly belongs to Judaism). The Hebrew Bible is structured according to the acronym TaNaK, for Torah (Law), Nevi'im (Prophets), and Ketuvim (Writings). The Law takes priority, while the Prophets call people back to fidelity to the Law, and the Writings give guidance for life before the Messiah's coming.

But Christians believe the Messiah has indeed already come in Jesus. And based on the conviction that the prophets prophesied the coming of Jesus, the Christian Old Testament places the prophets last so that they come immediately before the Gospels, which tell of Jesus, their fulfillment.

The New Testament, then, follows a fourfold structure. The Gospels come first because they tell directly of Jesus, the fulfillment of the Old Testament, and the Gospel of Matthew comes first among them because (among other things) it is a Gospel of fulfillment. Acts then tells the story of the earliest Church, founded by Jesus, as it expands into the ancient Roman world to embrace the nations. The letters come next, being written by those who have their stories told in the Gospels and Acts. Revelation forms a fitting conclusion, as the Church founded by Jesus whose story is told in Acts without end anticipates the return of the Lord and the consummation of creation.[5]

This story of continuity—from creation and fall to redemption through Israel, Jesus and the Church, culminating in glory—forms the basis for perceiving unity in the Christian canon. This means that unity is not a matter of systematizing the superficial meanings of the various versified parts. Rather, the unity of the canon is found in this narrative structure. Indeed, this is not a novel concept: the patristic rule of faith has a similar story structure which issues forth in the historic creeds of the Church, especially the Nicene Creed and Apostles' Creed. And so St. Irenaeus and other early Fathers provided a rule of faith in story form that would provide the "hypothesis," the narrative key for organizing the mosaic of the Scriptures.[6]

---

5 On the rhetorical structure of the New Testament canon, see George A. Kennedy, *New Testament Interpretation through Rhetorical Criticism*, Studies in Religion (Chapel Hill, NC: The University of North Carolina Press, 1984), 97–98, at 97: "First come the Gospels, which proclaim the message; then the narrative of Acts, which describes its reception; then the epistles, which may be viewed as arguing out an interpretation of the message; and finally the Apocalypse, as a dramatic epilogue."

6 See Irenaeus, *Adv. Haer.* [Against Heresies], 1.9–10.

And it is precisely the conviction that the same God superintends the salvific story from creation to consummation that guaranteed the continuity of the Christian story of salvation history. That conviction in turn required the appropriation of allegory (which in the West looked much like what today is called typology, although the word was not in use until the mid-nineteenth century) as the tool for understanding the Old Testament rightly. Thus certain words of St. Augustine become the celebrated phrase, *Novum Testamentum* in *Vetere latet, Vetus in Novo patet* (The New Testament is latent in the Old, the Old is made patent in the New).[7]

But the story of salvation is not only ideal but also historical. Whatever genres the sacred authors employed and however they and tradents before them shaped their material, the story of salvation continues in the real history of the Church, even today. Allegory culminates in mystagogy in a threefold movement, as the events foreshadowed in the Old Testament are fulfilled in the New Testament and then made real in the present in the Church's sacramental mysteries. For instance, the Passover becomes a type of Christ's sacrifice and supper which are in turn celebrated in the Church's celebration of the Eucharist.[8]

Biblical interpretation, then, is ultimately not academic but liturgical. For the Catholic, the Bible is realized in the Mass,[9] where elements of creation become the agents of our redemption necessitated by the fall while with them we anticipate the consummation. Creation, fall, redemption, and glory are all found there.

II. Matthew and the Fourfold Gospel Canon

The Gospels are central to the Liturgy of the Word: Catholics (and other liturgical Christians) sit for the Old Testament reading, the Psalm, and the Epistle, but stand for the reading of the Gospel. The Gospels are central to the Liturgy of the Word because they are central to Scripture, and they are central to Scripture because they tell directly of the coming of Jesus Christ, the Son of God, who by the incarnation is the immediate and ultimate revelation of God himself to humanity, in the very flesh.

If the Gospels are the theological center of the Canon, then the Gospel of Matthew stands at the forefront of the fourfold Gospel canon as the most im-

---

7 See St. Augustine, *Quaest. Hept.* [Questions on the Heptateuch], 73. Augustine actually says, *Loquere tu nobis, et non loquatur ad nos Deus, ne quando moriamur* [Exod. 20:19]. *Multum et solide significatur, ad Vetus Testamentum timorem potius pertinere, sicut ad Novum dilectionem: quamquam et in Vetere Novum lateat, et in Novo Vetus pateat* ("You speak to us, and do not let God speak to us, that we might not die" [Exod. 20:19]. It is noted very firmly that fear pertains to the Old Testament, just as joy to the New, even though the New lies hidden in the Old, and the Old in the New).

8 On allegory, mystagogy, and liturgy, see Leroy A. Huizenga, "The Tradition of Christian Allegory Yesterday and Today," *Letter & Spirit* 8 (2013): 77–99.

9 See Scott Hahn, *Letter and Spirit: From Written Text to Living Word in the Liturgy* (New York: Image, 2005).

portant Gospel. Calling the Gospel of Matthew the "First Gospel" need not be merely a clever way to duck questions of authorship but a way of recognizing its preeminence, for it has been regarded not only as first among equals but even more as that Gospel which regulates readings of the others.

To distinguish among the contents of the canon of Scripture in this way is not to affirm some sort of "canon within a canon" determined by a priori confessional commitments with the effect of tossing wide swaths of sacred Scripture overboard, but rather to recognize Scripture as a coherent story in which every word plays its role, a mosaic in which every tessera matters and contributes to the picture of the whole. And for the historic Church, all roads lead to the Gospel of Matthew.[10]

Why has the Gospel of Matthew achieved such preeminence in Christian history, not only among Catholics but also among Christians of the radical Reformation?[11]

First, the Gospel of Matthew has proven itself in liturgy and life. It has been found practical and relatively easy to preach. The reason for this concerns in turn the breadth, depth, and clarity of its comprehensive content. Stories teaching what became fundamental Christian doctrine are found therein, such as the Virgin Birth, the sacrificial crucifixion and Eucharist, and the resurrection and ascension, while Jesus issues plenty of direct and applicable teaching in his five great discourses (especially the beloved Sermon on the Mount) and teaches by example in the narrative sections.

Second, until relatively recently in Christian and academic history, the Gospel of Matthew was thought to be not only the first written but also an eyewit-

---

10 And thus not to Romans. Here we find a major difference concerning construals of sacred Scripture between the Catholic perspective, which, reflecting historic Christian tradition, has regarded the Gospels as preeminent among the Scriptures and Matthew as preeminent among the Gospels, and the magisterial Protestant perspective (that is, Lutherans and the Reformed tradition), which has privileged Romans above all else. In his *Preface* to Romans, Martin Luther wrote, "This epistle is in truth the most important document in the New Testament, the gospel in its purest expression...in essence, it is a brilliant light, almost enough to illumine the whole Bible." Similarly, in the dedication of his commentary on Romans, John Calvin wrote, "For when anyone understands this Epistle, he has a passage opened to him to the understanding of the whole Scripture." In our own day, the Anglican Evangelical J.I. Packer has written, "All roads in the Bible lead to Romans, and all views afforded by the Bible are seen most clearly from Romans, and when the message of Romans gets into a person's heart there is no telling what may happen" (*Knowing God* [Downers Grove, IL: InterVarsity Press, 1973], 230). Whatever its merits and however well Protestant interpreters read Paul, the claim that Romans is central to the canon of Scripture is a *novum* of the sixteenth century departing from longstanding liturgical, theological, and hermeneutical tradition. Christians of the radical Reformation (for example, Mennonites and Hutterites), however, maintain the Gospel of Matthew in pride of place thanks largely to the Sermon on the Mount.

11 As regards the Gospels, the magisterial Reformation has preferred the Gospel of John, given its emphasis on faith, while the Gospel of Mark began to receive renewed and deserved attention among Lutheran exegetes and theologians in the nineteenth and twentieth centuries, given its radical focus on the cross.

ness account.[12] The Gospel of Mark was thought to be a summary of the Gospel of Matthew, the Lukan prologue admits its account is derivative,[13] and John was thought to have written a spiritual, theological Gospel complementing the three prior Gospels.[14] And thus the fourfold Gospel canon received its canonical order for deep theological and historical reasons. In the canonical order, one also sees movement from the particularity of the Gospel of Matthew, situated as it is within the orbit of conservative normative and Pharisaic Judaism, to the universality of the Gospels of Luke and John, in which Gentile inclusion in the people of God is clear throughout.

A third, if subtle, reason for the Gospel of Matthew's preeminence and position in the canon and Christian history as the first Gospel concerns that very particular nature. Salvation history culminates in Jesus the Jew, as salvation is from the Jews;[15] the gospel is for the Jew first, then the Gentile.[16] The Gospel of Matthew is concerned with fulfillment. All is fulfilled in the Matthean Jesus—the Scriptures, righteousness, obedience, the various Old Testament types Jesus completes. And so the Gospel of Matthew shows most clearly the culmination of salvation history in Jesus the Jew sent to Israel[17] and then commands his disciples to take him and his teaching to the nations.[18]

The story of salvation history begins with the parents of the universal human race, but narrows as it goes on, running through the southern tribes of Judah and Benjamin, the Jews. But with the coming of Jesus Christ it begins to open up again, as it were, as the promises to Abraham concerning not just Israel or the Jews but indeed the whole human race are fulfilled. Part of God's original promises to Abraham was that in him "all the families of the earth shall be blessed,"[19] a promise with universal import that the prophets reaffirmed in their own oracles.[20]

Now the Gospel of Matthew is sometimes colloquially called a "Jewish" Gospel. This is misleading because all the New Testament documents are funda-

12 While most scholars nowadays hold that the Gospel of Matthew is a derivative account dependent on the Gospel of Mark, Q, and perhaps "special M" whose empirical author is lost to us, good reasons remain for affirming Matthean priority and possibly Matthean authorship. One wonders if the freshets of academic skepticism that have called the Q hypothesis into serious question will one day soon be leveled at Markan priority, given that both the hypothesis of Q and the hypothesis of Markan priority trade on similar formal assumptions and methodologies.

13 See Luke 1:1–4.

14 See St. Augustine, *De cons. ev.* [On the Harmony of the Gospels], 1.4; St. Clement of Alexandria, *Quis div.* [Salvation of the Rich], 42.1; and Origen, *Comm. Jo.* [Commentary on John], 10.4.6.

15 John 4:22.

16 Rom. 1:16.

17 Matt. 10:5–6, 15:24.

18 Matt. 28:16–20.

19 Gen. 12:3b (RSVCE alt.).

20 See, for instance, Isa. 56:6–8.

mentally Jewish, since early Christianity was a Jewish phenomenon, firmly rooted in the practice and belief of normative common Judaism even as it expanded beyond the bounds of the holy land and incorporated Gentiles.[21] Basic Christian beliefs like monotheism, election, God as lawgiver, and the eschaton are Jewish and in no way pagan. The pagan gods neither choose a people nor give them a way to live out of love nor judge the world at the end of time. But the misnomer is meant to convey a truth. The Gospel of Matthew is concerned with the concerns of conservative common Judaism: how to interpret the law, what makes for righteousness, what does it mean to be a child of Abraham, how Scripture is fulfilled. The Matthean Jesus looks very much like his Pharisaic opponents (a conservative Jew of the holy land concerned for the right interpretation of the law while affirming the law's enduring relevance[22]) and a large part of the reason for their mutual hostility[23] lies in their common convictions. In any event one observes that the Matthean genealogy begins not with Adam (as in the Gospel of Luke, which does so to signal the universal relevance of the gospel message) but Abraham (thus signaling concern for intramural Jewish issues), and the Matthean Jesus himself evinces little interest in Gentiles until his resurrection,[24] going so far as to declare his mission restricted to Israel on two occasions.[25]

Given this ethos, it makes canonical sense for the Gospel of Matthew to be situated at the beginning of the fourfold Gospel canon, for salvation history has not yet widened out again, as it were, to the universal embrace of the nations, something which happens at the very end of the Gospel of Matthew. The Gospel of Matthew marks the shift from particular to universal in its own narrative, as the Gospel most concerned with fulfillment shows in the unfolding of its story that God's purposes and prophecies are being fulfilled not only for Jews but also for Gentiles.

III. The Matthean Story

The Gospel of Matthew understands itself as a universal, authoritative document persisting for all time and its community as the universal Church perduring to the end of time. It understands itself and the Church in this way because it believes Jesus Christ the Jew, the divine Son of God in whom resides all authority, to be the final fulfillment of God's promises not only for Jews but also Gentiles, inaugurating the final period of God's plan, until the end of the age should come, and that

21 Christianity remains so today, which is why the novelist, essayist, and Catholic convert Walker Percy spoke of "that Jewish sect, the Catholic Church," and why Pius XI said in the face of the rise of Nazi power, "Spiritually, we are Semites."

22 See Matt. 5:17–18 and 23:23.

23 See Matt. 23.

24 See Matt. 28:16–20.

25 Matt. 10:5–6 and 15:24.

Jesus Christ has commanded that which the Gospel of Matthew records to be taught to disciples in the age of the Church until the end.

Reading the Gospel of Matthew

The Gospel of Matthew presents itself as such through its narrative, through the form of a story. Reading the Gospel of Matthew, then, requires significant attention to its narrative dynamics. Redaction criticism fails to take account of narrative dynamics and ironically goes beyond and behind an evangelist's intention. The evangelists did not intend their Gospels to be read in the way redaction critics read, with such scrupulous attention to presumed prior sources (in the case of the Gospel of Mark) and utterly hypothetical, non-extant sources (in the case of Q). The Gospels draw attention to the Old Testament through the rhetorical devices of allusion and quotation but they do not quote material from other Gospels directly. Above all, the Gospels read well as stories, as narratives, for that is what they are, as the evangelists composed wholes and intended them to be read as such. Moreover, when one reads the Gospels using redaction criticism, they become surreptitious stories about crises in hypothetical communities when they in fact present themselves openly as stories about Jesus. Finally, in canonical perspective, the Gospel of Matthew's primary position in the fourfold Gospel canon suggests it is to be read before the other Gospels.

For these reasons, I will read the Gospel of Matthew as the narrative it purports to be and speak of the "Model Reader," a concept developed by the Italian theorist Umberto Eco,[26] much like the more familiar "ideal reader," a regulative concept used to determine what sense should be made of the text itself apart from any consideration of the empirical author or real readers. Speaking of the Model Reader instead of what the empirical author may have intended permits the entirety of the text of the Gospel of Matthew to be taken into account (unlike redaction criticism, which focuses on that small percentage of a Gospel's text that constitutes additions, omissions, and changes) and its narrative dynamics.

When one examines the narrative of the Gospel of Matthew, one finds the Gospel pushing not backward but forward. Its final words are oriented not to its own original community in some sort of self-referential way but to the future. True, it draws deeply on the past; it is a Gospel of radical continuity with the tradition of the Scriptures of Israel and their community of Israel. Yet that continuity is neither repristination nor nostalgia. It draws on that tradition as a resource for mission in the perpetual present, as the tips of leaves draw on roots.

The Gospel of Matthew tells an ironic story of reversal that is one of both tragedy and triumph. Ironic, because the initial expectations the Gospel raises for

26 See Umberto Eco, *The Role of the Reader: Explorations in the Semiotics of Texts*, Advances in Semiotics (Bloomington, IN: Indiana University Press, 1979). For Eco's applicability to biblical studies, see Leroy Huizenga, *The New Isaac: Tradition and Intertextuality in the Gospel of Matthew*, Supplements to Novum Testamentum 131 (Leiden: Brill, 2009; repr. 2012), 21–74.

the Model Reader are ultimately reversed, and tragic, for Israel qua Israel loses its status as the privileged community of mission, but triumphal in that God's purposes for the world are not thwarted in spite of the human race's rejection of the Christ. Indeed, as the Matthean Jesus is the embodiment of Israel and the fulfillment of its promises and mission, in Jesus' vindication and exaltation Israel is vindicated and exalted and Israel's mission to be a "light to the nations"[27] commences anew.

Initial Expectations: How Will He Save His People, and Who Are They?

The first chapter of the Gospel sets the Model Reader deeply in the world of traditional, conservative first-century Palestinian Judaism. The first verse suggests that Jesus Christ is to be understood in terms of two fundamental Christological categories, Messiah (=son of David) and sacrifice like Isaac (=son of Abraham).[28] The genealogy begins with Abraham, the Father of faith.[29] And then the Model Reader confronts the story of the Virgin Birth, identifying Jesus Christ with God[30] and thus investing him with divine personhood and authority. Most interesting is the explanation of Jesus' name: "You shall call his name Jesus, for he will save his people from their sins."[31] The explanation raises two implicit questions for the Model Reader: Who are his people, and how will he save them from their sins?[32]

In reading, the human mind confronts and answers questions raised by such nodes (Eco's term) of the text automatically again and again in a subconscious fashion. But here it is helpful to engage in some conscious hypothesizing: the intratextual constitution of the text here raises these questions for the Model Reader, and drawing on encyclopedic, intertextual knowledge, the Model Reader first hazards that "his people" are the Jews and he will save them from their sins by killing for them. For while there were indeed diverse messianic understandings in antiquity, that is what the Davidic Messiah was generally expected to do. The people are under the oppression of Roman rule (however indirectly, it is true that there was not an Italian centurion on every street corner in Jerusalem) because of their sins, and forgiveness of sins means violent liberation from oppression so that the Jews once more might have something even more than what the Hasmoneans achieved. They might have a new, eschatological United Monarchy ruled by a new David.[33]

---

27 See Isa. 49:6.

28 See Huizenga, *New Isaac*, 139–143.

29 See Matt. 1:2–17.

30 Matt. 1:23.

31 Matt. 1:21.

32 See Mark Allan Powell, "The Plot and Subplots of Matthew's Gospel," *New Testament Studies* 38 (1992): 196.

33 See Warren Carter, "Evoking Isaiah: Matthean Soteriology and an Intertextual Reading of Isaiah 7–9 and Matthew 1:23 and 4:15–16," *Journal of Biblical Literature* 119 (2000): 503–520;

So far, then, the Model Reader expects a story of violent conquest in which Israel's liberation will be achieved in the time of the eschaton. But for the Model Reader those initial assumptions are almost immediately thrown into question with the story of the Magi in Matthew chapter two. The Magi, pagan astrologers from the East, arrive searching for the "King of the Jews," a title already bequeathed to Herod the Great by the Roman Senate roughly forty years prior, a fact known to the Model Reader by virtue of encyclopedic knowledge. Herod is "troubled" and "all Jerusalem with him,"[34] not pleased, not overjoyed, by news that some are seeking a new king. Unless one is in Narnia, there can be only one king (or queen). And so Herod tries to kill baby Jesus. Herod wants to destroy him.[35] Being warned about this in a dream, Joseph takes mother and child and flees to Egypt. Then follows the formula citation of Hosea 11:1b in Matthew 2:15: "Out of Egypt have I called my son," which functions to present Jesus as the embodiment of Israel, as Israel/Jacob is the son of Hosea 11. Further, the formula quotation occurs immediately after the Holy Family travels to Egypt and they do not return from Egypt to Galilee until Matthew 2:19–21. The Gospel of Matthew thus subtly describes the infant Jesus' contemporary Israel as Egypt, and therefore inverts Egypt and Israel. Moreover, it is Herod, the king of Israel, who seeks to destroy Jesus, whereas the Magi, Gentile foreigners, are paying Jesus the homage he deserves. Finally, Hosea provides no heroic recollection of the Exodus. Rather, God's love for Israel is contrasted with Israel's abject failure, detailed in Hosea 11:2: "The more I called them, the more they went from me; they kept sacrificing to the Baals, and burning incense to idols." The episode is thus an early instance of the significant Matthean theme of Jesus' conflict with Jewish leadership leading to Gentile inclusion.

Jesus' Perspective and God's Perspective on the Extent of Jesus' Mission

The Matthean Jesus, however, does not know that his mission extends to the Gentiles. He sends his disciples only to the lost sheep of the house of Israel[36] and refuses, at first, to aid a Canaanite woman's daughter because he believes himself to have been sent only to the lost sheep of the house of Israel.[37] In the instance of the healing of the centurion's servant the Matthean Jesus does voice the conviction that "many will come from east and west and sit at table with Abraham, Isaac, and Jacob in the kingdom of heaven, while the sons of the kingdom will be thrown into the outer darkness,"[38] but otherwise seeks out no Gentiles and says nothing

---

and Warren Carter, "Matthew and the Gentiles: Individual Conversion and/or Systemic Transformation?" *Journal for the Study of the New Testament* 26 (2004): 259–282.

34 Matt. 2:3.

35 Matt. 2:13; see 12:14 and 27:20.

36 Matt. 10:5–6.

37 Matt. 15:21–28.

38 Matt. 8:11–12.

positive about them until the after the resurrection.[39] Given that the healing of the centurion's servant appears before Jesus' declaration of the restriction of his mission to the house of Israel, it is likely that the Matthean Jesus is thinking not of a mission to the Gentiles in history, in the time of Israel or the Church, but the eschatological coming of the Gentiles to Zion.[40] The centurion comes to him; Jesus does not go to the centurion.

The divine perspective is different, however. The narrator shows in the story of the Magi and tells through explicit prophecy that God's promises to the Gentiles will be realized in Jesus through the quotation of Isaiah 9 in Matthew 4 and above all of Isaiah 42 in Matthew 12: "He shall proclaim justice to the Gentiles...and in his name will the Gentiles hope."[41] The transformation of Jesus' perspective that his mission is restricted to Israel is achieved only after the resurrection and only then reconciled with the Model Reader's knowledge that God intends Jesus' mission to extend to Gentiles.

But if the God of Israel who prophesied through Isaiah knew all along that Gentiles would receive their promised blessings through Jesus, their inclusion requires Jewish rejection of Jesus on a human level, a pattern seen throughout the New Testament.[42] Herod, the King of the Jews, had tried to kill little baby Jesus, and John the Baptist excoriates those who will become Jesus' foremost opponents even before his baptism of the latter. Indeed, in an oft-overlooked instance of Matthean parallelism, the Gospel presents both John and Jesus facing mortal threats that lead to Jesus' withdrawal and then a quotation from Isaiah promising Gentile inclusion. In Matthew 4:12 Jesus hears that John is arrested and withdraws (*ἀνεχώρησεν*) from there to Capernaum, near Zebulun and Naphtali, occasioning a quote from Isaiah 9:1–2 promising good things to pagans:

> The land of Zebulun and the land of Naphtali, toward the sea, across the Jordan, Galilee of the Gentiles—the people who sat in darkness have seen a great light, and for those who sat in the region and shadow of death light has dawned (Matt. 4:15–16).

In Matthew 12:14–21, Jesus encounters the threat of the Pharisees' murderous conspiracy and aware of it "withdrew" (*ἀνεχώρησεν*) from there, upon which the narrator supplies another quote from Isaiah promising good things to pagans, this time from Isaiah 42: "He shall proclaim justice to the Gentiles...and in his name will the Gentiles hope."[43]

---

39 Matt. 28:16–20.

40 See Isa. 2:2, 5:26, 49:6b.

41 Matt. 12:18, 21.

42 See Acts 28:28; Rom. 9–11.

43 Matt. 12:18, 21.

The Eucharistic Mission of the Matthean Church

In Matthew 16, then, after rising opposition, Jesus founds a Church, a remnant community formed to continue Israel's mission of redemption of the world as Israel's leadership refuses to let Jesus lead.[44] But here Gentiles are not yet in view. In the prior chapter Jesus had ignored the Canaanite woman[45] and refused her request for a remote exorcism of her daughter, claiming again that he was sent only to the lost sheep of the house of Israel.[46] Too often popular piety protects Jesus in this passage, claiming that Jesus is trying to tease faith out of the woman but really wants to help her all along. A better reading, more faithful to the cultural and literary context of the passage, sees the Matthean Jesus here as a conservative male Jew who has little time for either women or pagans.

So the Church in Matthew 16 should not yet be envisioned to include Gentiles. The Church appears implicitly in the Parable of the Wicked Tenants.[47] Jesus tells the parable against "the chief priests and the elders of the people,"[48] telling them fatefully, "The kingdom of God will be taken away from you and given to a nation (*ἔθνει*) producing the fruits of it."[49] "Nation" here is singular, not plural; we do not have here—nor do we find elsewhere in the Gospel of Matthew—ethnic Israel replaced by a Gentile Church. Rather, given the flow of the narrative, at this point the singular "nation" is likely the Church, but the Church is as of yet regarded as exclusively Jewish, a remnant body from within Israel continuing Israel's redeeming work in the world.

But it will continue that redeeming work apart from the mainstream body of Israel's institutions, such as rabbinate ("rabbi" is never a positive word in the Gospel of Matthew[50]) and Temple (as Jesus predicts its destruction[51]). By this point in the narrative, the Model Reader is considering a different answer to the question, "Who are his people?" The initial and justified assumption is that his people are Israel, the Jews. But now the Model Reader is starting to see that "his people" is the Church. And as that body breaks from the parent body, the Model Reader finds Jesus erecting himself and his sacrifice as replacements for the rabbinate and the Temple. Jesus says, "But you are not to be called rabbi, for you have one teacher"—

---

44 Crucial reading on this difficult point is Matthias Konradt, *Israel, Church, and the Gentiles in the Gospel of Matthew*, trans. Kathleen Ess, Baylor-Mohr Siebeck Studies in Early Christianity (Waco, TX: Baylor University Press, 2014), who, against readings of the Gospel of Matthew that present a Gentile Church replacing a forfeit, forsaken Israel, argues that Jesus' mission fulfills God's promises to Israel while opening up salvation to all in the Church.

45 Matt. 15:21–28.

46 Matt. 15:24.

47 Matt. 21:33–46.

48 Matt. 21:23.

49 Matt. 21:43.

50 See Matt. 23:7, 26:25, and 26:49.

51 Matt. 24:2.

presumably Jesus himself—"and you are all brethren."[52] Jesus "cleanses" the temple and not so subtly prophesies its destruction not only by turning over tables but also by alluding to Jeremiah 7 in Matthew 21:13b, an allusion to Jeremiah's prophecy of the destruction of the first Temple which then functions as Jesus' prophecy of the destruction of the second Temple, a prophecy made explicit to his disciples and the Model Reader in Matthew 24:2. And most notably in Matthew 26:26–29 Jesus institutes the Eucharist in the context of the Passover meal. Here Jesus sets himself up as a new Passover, something well understood in early Christianity.[53] He takes the Passover ritual but transforms it into his own rite. In particular, Jesus claims the chalice is "my blood of the [new] covenant, which is poured out for many for the forgiveness of sins." His blood is "poured out," or "shed," *ἐκχυννόμενον*, from *ἐκχύννω*, a technical word with sacrificial denotations and connotations in the LXX.[54] The answer to the second question, "How will he save his people from their sins?" is thus unexpected: He will save his people not by killing for them but by dying for them, offering himself as a sacrifice in crucifixion and chalice.

Jesus' Mission to the Gentiles

By this point in the narrative, then, the Messiah has fulfilled the promises to Israel and ushered in the inbreaking of the Kingdom. But having encountered opposition, he founds the Church as a remnant community to carry forth Israel's work of redemption in the world, a community with its teacher in Jesus, its leaders in the Twelve, and its sacrifice in the Eucharist.

When, then, do Gentiles enter Jesus' plans? After the Israel contemporary with Jesus rejects him utterly. Jesus Christ is before Pilate, along with Jesus Barabbas.[55] Pilate attempts to release Jesus Christ, whom the Model Reader knows is the true Son of the Father,[56] but the crowd demands his crucifixion and the release of the imposter son of the Father, Barabbas. The craven Pilate washes his hands of the matter and declares he is innocent of Jesus' blood.[57] And then "all the people" cry out some of the most horrifying and consequential words in human history: "His blood be on us and on our children!"[58] The phrase "All the people"

52 Matt. 23:8.

53 See 1 Cor. 5:7.

54 See, for instance, Exod. 29:12 and Lev. 4:7, 12, 25, 30, 8:15, 9:9.

55 Craig Evans contends that one should read "Jesus Barabbas" (*Ἰησοῦν Βαραββᾶν*) in Matt. 27:16–17, finding it more likely that a scribe would eliminate "Jesus" for reasons of reverence rather than add it for reasons of parallelism. See Evans, *Matthew*, New Cambridge Bible Commentary (Cambridge, UK: Cambridge University Press, 2012), 453.

56 See here the "Johannine thunderbolt" of Matt. 11:27, "All things have been delivered to me by my Father; and no one knows the Son except the Father, and no one knows the Father except the Son and any one to whom the Son chooses to reveal him."

57 Matt. 27:24.

58 Matt. 27:25.

recalls for the Model Reader "all Jerusalem" being troubled along with Herod at the rumors of the birth of a new King of the Jews,[59] and here what is adumbrated in the story of the Magi is fulfilled: the ultimate rejection of Jesus not just by Jewish leadership, parties, and sects, but indeed "all the people."

It is crucial at this point to understand several things: First, Gentiles are not yet in Jesus' picture; ethnic Israel is not being replaced by a Church of Gentiles. Second, Jesus remains Jewish, and his original disciples remain Jewish, and remain so past the time of the Gospel into the period of the Church and indeed the eschaton. Third, "His blood be on us and on our children" need not imply a perpetual curse upon ethnic Jews. Rather, in the world of the Matthean story, any "curse" here lasts two generations: upon the generation calling for Jesus' crucifixion, and then their children, the generation which endures the horrors of the siege and destruction of Jerusalem and its temple predicted by Jesus himself.

But again, on a human level, this Jewish rejection of Jesus precipitates Gentile inclusion. Only after—but soon after—"all the people" utter these terrifying words does Jesus utter a definitive positive mention of a Gentile mission: "Go therefore and make disciples of all nations, baptizing them in the name of the Father, and of the Son, and of the Holy Spirit, teaching them to observe all that I have commanded you."[60] Here, now, for the first time, Jesus clearly and directly encourages mission to Gentiles. The direction is important: Jesus sends the Church to them. In the story of the Gospel itself, Jesus never goes to Gentiles; they come to him, whether the Magi,[61] the centurion in Capernaum[62] (though Jesus is willing to go with him, the centurion comes first to him, and Jesus ultimately does not go with him), or the Canaanite woman.[63] Here, then, at the end of the Gospel, is something new: deliberate mission to the Gentiles.

Rereading the Gospel of Matthew as Christian Scripture

Now many interpreters of Scripture operate with a hermeneutics of the gap, thinking that the idea is to bridge a chasm between the Bible in the ancient world and their situation in the modern world. But reading with a sense of continuity in which we stand in the time of the Church, anticipating the eschaton, helps us to read the Gospel of Matthew as Christian Scripture. For the Gospel of Matthew, it is the time of the Church from resurrection to eschaton.

A particular phrase from Jesus' Great Commission, "teaching them to observe all that I have commanded you,"[64] functions to make the Gospel of Matthew

59 Matt. 2:3.

60 Matt. 28:19–20a.

61 Matt. 2:1–12.

62 Matt. 8:5–13.

63 Matt. 15:21–28.

64 Matt. 28:20a.

more than a mere Jewish document from antiquity, a textual artifact bearing witness to a long-dead apocalyptic sect within Judaism. Rather, it is a Christian document of perpetual relevance, sacred Scripture. For as many Matthean scholars have recognized, the phrase invites rereading of the Gospel of Matthew with the knowledge that the Model Reader has acquired along the way, as all that Jesus has commanded them and now commands them to teach others among the nations is contained in the prior material of the Gospel itself.[65]

This enables a reading of Matthew that is allegorical (as St. Augustine and St. Thomas Aquinas, as representatives of the West, would understand it, in a limited sense, rooted in the letter). For instance, in light of Jesus' institution of the Eucharist, references to the altar throughout the Gospel of Matthew may now be understood to refer to the Christian altar of the Eucharist[66] and not only the altar of the temple, as in Matthew 5:23–24: "So if you are offering your gift at the altar, and there remember that your brother has something against you, leave your gift there before the altar and go." In this way does material that Jesus' predictions of the destruction of the temple would seem to render more or less pointless after the fact find perpetual relevance. Put simply, why would the Jesus of the Gospel of Matthew spend so much time on the concerns of Judaism in the shadow of the temple when he knows it will not long endure? If on a first reading the Gospel of Matthew presents a Jesus who would lead Israel into and in the new age as her Messiah and savior, on a second reading the Gospel of Matthew presents a Jesus who would lead the Church into and in the new age as her Messiah and savior.

One might say that there are thus two Gospels of Matthew the Model Reader encounters, as "teaching them to observe all that I have commanded you" puts the Model Reader on a cyclical loop into that future "to the close of the age,"[67] making the Gospel of Matthew a document of perpetual relevance for the Church. And in either of these Gospels—the one the Model Reader encounters on a first reading, or the one the Model Reader encounters on a second reading—it is a time of fulfillment.

---

65 See, for example, Dale C. Allison, "Foreshadowing the Passion," in *Studies in Matthew* (Grand Rapids, MI: Baker Academic, 2005), 218–219; R. W. L. Moberly, *The Bible, Theology, and Faith A Study of Abraham and Jesus*, Cambridge Studies in Christian Doctrine (Cambridge, UK: Cambridge University Press, 2000), 189–191; Ulrich Luz, *The Theology of the Gospel of Matthew*, New Testament Theology (Cambridge, UK: Cambridge University Press, 1995), 5–6; Ulrich Luz, "Matthean Christology Outlined in Theses," in *Studies in Matthew* (Grand Rapids, MI: Eerdmans, 2005), 83.

66 Early Christians were indeed speaking in terms of an altar, as Hebrews, another document from the orbit of early Jewish Christianity, and perhaps roughly the time of the production of the Gospel of Matthew, makes plain: "We have an altar from which those who serve the tent have no right to eat" (Heb. 13:10). See also 1 Cor. 10, which presents significant parallels between the Jewish altar and the Christian Eucharist.

67 Matt. 28:20.

The theme of "fulfillment" in the Gospel of Matthew has occasioned much discussion, particularly in light of the "lure" of the formula quotations, which have drawn attention away from other ways in which the Gospel of Matthew appropriates Scripture (for example, allusion) by their formal prominence.[68] Perhaps one of the best but neglected pieces on the issue belongs to J. R. Daniel Kirk, "Conceptualizing Fulfillment in Matthew."[69] Avoiding the "lure," Kirk proposes a "narratival typology" that avoids collecting isolated typological resonances and instead "see[s] that [Jesus'] life takes the shape of Israel's story."[70] Kirk's approach makes sense of the structure of the Christian Scriptures, which situates the Gospel of Matthew in the canonical center as the First Gospel, and it makes sense of the Gospel of Matthew itself. The Gospel of Matthew comes first precisely because it is a Gospel of fulfillment, the canon suggesting to Christians that Jesus is indeed the fulfillment of the prophets' words, which come last in the Christian Old Testament. Further, in and of itself, the Gospel of Matthew presents Jesus as a new Israel, as the embodiment of Israel. The formula citation of Hosea 11:1b in Matthew 2:15 ("out of Egypt I called my son") functions to present Jesus as the embodiment of Israel.[71] So too does the Testing narrative[72] concern the testing of Jesus as the embodiment of Israel.

There is some question, however, as to whether Jesus will be faithful, for Israel's history contains instances of gross failure and disobedience by corporate Israel and otherwise heroic individuals therein.[73] Hosea 11 itself recounts the disobedience of Israel. The Testing narrative answers this question affirmatively and definitively.[74] Jesus is tested; Israel was tested in the wilderness.[75] Jesus is in

68 Donald Senior's phrase, from his piece "The Lure of the Formula Quotations: Re-Assessing Matthew as A Test Case," in *The Scriptures in the Gospels*, ed. C. M. Tuckett, Bibliotheca ephemeridum theologicarum lovansiensium 131 (Leuven: Leuven University Press, 1997), 89–115.

69 See J. R. Daniel Kirk, "Conceptualizing Fulfillment in Matthew," *Tyndale Bulletin* 59 (2008): 77–98.

70 Kirk, "Conceptualizing Fulfillment," 77.

71 See also Exod. 4:22–23: "And you shall say to Pharaoh, 'Thus says the LORD, Israel is my first-born son, and I say to you, "Let my son go that he may serve me."'"

72 Matt. 4:1–11.

73 It is often noted that the genealogy itself indicates this. See Stefan Alkier, "Zeichen der Erinnerung: Die Genealogie in Mt 1 als intertextuelle Disposition" [Signs of Memory: The Genealogy in Matthew 1 as Intertextual Disposition], in *Bekenntnis und Erinnerung* [Confession and Memory], eds. K.–M. Bull and Eckart Reinmuth, Rostocker Theologische Studien 16 (Münster: Lit Verlag, 2004), 108–128 for an insightful treatment of its intertextual dynamics.

74 On this, see Birger Gerhardsson, *The Testing of God's Son (Matt 4:1–11 & Par): An Analysis of an Early Christian Midrash* (Lund: Gleerup, 1966), who argues that this episode is similar to rabbinic exposition of the Shema. The pertinent rabbinic texts are *m. Ber.* 9:5 and *Sipre Deut.* 6:5.

75 Matt. 4:1; Deut. 8:2.

the desert forty days and nights; Israel was in the wilderness forty years.[76] Jesus is hungry; Israel was hungry.[77] In this brief story there are three quotations from Deuteronomy.[78] Indeed, in this section of Deuteronomy Israel is adjured repeatedly to be faithful to the Lord in light of the Exodus and the giving of the Commandments.[79] As such, Matthew 4:1–11 presents Jesus recapitulating Israel's experience in the desert as detailed in Deuteronomy 6–8.[80] Jesus obeys perfectly, unlike Israel in the wilderness. On an incarnational reading of "Emmanuel,"[81] then, God himself (who is not the God of the philosophers, but the God of Abraham, Isaac, and Jacob, the God of Israel) in Jesus fulfills Israel's story. All other christological typologies and titles ought to be subordinated to this one. Jesus fulfills not only particular biblical personalities in a typological way but indeed the entirety of the "law and the prophets."[82]

If the God of Israel fulfills Israel's story in Jesus, then the Model Reader sees more clearly the Matthean emphasis on continuity. It is easy to emphasize discontinuity in the Gospel of Matthew, given the history of Christian anti-Judaism, the Gospel's own historical role in generating that history as it suffers misreading, and the radical claims of newness in the Gospel rooted in the uniqueness of the divine authority of Jesus' person ("for he taught them as one who had authority, and not as their scribes"[83]), the one who is so bold as to issue his own commandments.[84] Jesus fulfills the line of Israel as son of Abraham (a new Isaac, and thus a sacrifice) and son of David (Messiah)[85] as God himself come to earth[86] who is with us always.[87]

Jesus is and remains Jewish. Jesus assumes a Jewish worldview, whatever his particular mindset within Judaism. Jesus does not start from scratch, as docetic and moralistic Enlightenment theology would have it. And the Model Reader perceives that continuity. The story of Israel culminates in Jesus the Jew, but—as

76 Matt. 4:1; Deut. 8:2.

77 Matt. 4:1; Deut. 8:3.

78 Deut. 8:3 in Matt. 4:4; Deut. 6:16 in Matt. 4:7; Deut. 6:13 in Matt. 4:10.

79 Deut. 5.

80 See W. D. Davies and Dale C. Allison, *A Critical and Exegetical Commentary on the Gospel According to Saint Matthew*, 3 vols. (Edinburgh: T. & T. Clark, 1988–1997), 1:352.

81 Matt. 1:23.

82 Matt. 5:17.

83 Matt. 7:29.

84 See Matt. 5:19–20, in which the proximal demonstrative pronoun "these" qualifies "commandments," as well as the repeated references to the Kingdom of God which Jesus inaugurates beginning in Matthew 4:17 seem to indicate not that the Law and Prophets *per se* are in view, but Jesus' own commandments which follow in the Sermon on the Mount and in the Gospel as a whole.

85 Matt. 1:1 and 2–17.

86 Matt. 1:18–25.

87 Matt. 1:23; 28:20.

a result both of the divine plan as indicated in the story of the Magi and the quotations of Isaiah 9 and 12 and also human hostility—Jesus founds the Church not to replace Israel in a brute substitution but to continue her work to be the servant proclaiming "justice to the Gentiles." Jesus himself will lead those Jews (and post-resurrection, Gentiles) who would join him as his disciples as he, God with them,[88] present in their midst when gathered,[89] promises to be with them to the end of the age.[90] The time of the Gospel of Matthew, then, is now: the time of the Eucharistic mission of the Church to all the nations, as the Church is to do what Jesus commands, which chief among many other things is to celebrate the Eucharist.[91] The Gospel of Matthew makes clear that Jesus Christ stands at the center of salvation history and that his presence in the Eucharist stands at the center of our salvation today.

IV. Hermeneutical Implications of Reading Scripture as Story

I would offer, then, some hermeneutical reflections on reading the Scripture in terms of salvation history with the Gospel of Matthew at its center. First, and above all, this interpretive stance helps us see that Jesus Christ remains Jewish and thus that the Faith remains Jewish in character, since the Matthean Christ is situated deeply in the world of conservative first-century common Judaism. Too often the noble desire for enculturation results in the creation of a Christ in one's own image abstracted from the Gospels and removed from the very real salvation history he as the incarnation of the second person of the Trinity superintends. One winds up with an ideal and thus unreal Christ, not the real resurrected and ascended Christ who sits *ad dexteram patris*. Enculturation risks making particular cultures normative and thus determinative of the gospel.[92] But Christ is more than a teacher and Christianity more than a doctrinal system. Even as it permeates particular human cultures, it is its own culture rooted in the cultus of the Eucharistic liturgy. The Church is its own nation[93] with its own practices and beliefs, its own culture.

Second, recognizing continuity in salvation history means we read Scripture from within the story itself as part of that ecclesial culture Scripture itself has generated and nurtured. We do not stand outside and above Scripture's story, as if the Bible were a discrete object and its constituent verses crash upon us at once, requiring us to sift and sort them with some interpretive principle as if there is a

88 Matt. 1:23.

89 Matt. 18:20.

90 Matt. 28:20.

91 Matt. 26:26–29.

92 The extreme negative example of this is Nazi theology. See Robert P. Ericksen, *Theologians Under Hitler* (New Haven, CT: Yale University Press, 1985); and more recently Susanna Heschel, *The Aryan Jesus: Christian Theologians and the Bible in Nazi Germany* (Princeton, NJ: Princeton University Press, 2010).

93 Matt. 21:43.

hermeneutical gap. Rather, we stand in the time of the Church, like the Matthean community itself, and hear Jesus' words directly as did they as part of the same Church he founded.

Letter & Spirit 9 (2014): 31-50

Jesus as the "Fulfillment" of the Law and His Teaching on Divorce in Matthew

~: **Michael Patrick Barber** :~

John Paul the Great Catholic University

In the Sermon on the Mount we find Matthew's most explicit account of Jesus' teaching regarding his "fulfillment" (*plēroō*) of the law. However, as is well known, the logical progression of the Sermon is difficult to follow.[1] On the one hand, Jesus insists he has come not to "abolish" (*katalysai*) the law and the prophets (5:17). He even emphatically states, "till heaven and earth pass away, not an iota, not a dot, will pass from the law until all is accomplished" (Matt. 5:18), adding that whoever relaxes "one of the least of these commandments ... shall be called least in the kingdom of heaven" (Matt. 5:19).[2] Yet, in the teachings that immediately follow these statements, the so-called "antitheses" (5:21–48), Jesus appears to do just that, that is, nullify the law.[3]

While it is true that some of the "antitheses" may be understood in terms of an "intensification" of the law's demands (for example, lust as adultery in 5:27–30), others are difficult to describe in such terms. One especially difficult element in this regard is Jesus' equation of divorce and remarriage with adultery

---

1 For a survey of different approaches see W. D. Davies and Dale Allison, *Matthew*, International Critical Commentary, 3 vols. (Edinburgh: T & T Clark, 1988), 505–509; Hans Dieter Betz, *The Sermon on the Mount* (Minneapolis: Augsburg, 1995), 200–214.

2 Unless otherwise noted, quotations from the Bible are taken from the Revised Standard Version Catholic Edition. Commentators typically acknowledge Jesus' insistence on the validity and ongoing value of the law in these verses. See, for example, David L. Turner, *Matthew*, Black's New Testament Commentaries (Grand Rapids: Baker Academic, 2008), 163: "It would be hard to make a stronger statement about the ongoing authority of the Torah than that made in 5:18." Likewise, Pinchas Lapide (*The Sermon on the Mount* [Maryknoll: Orbis Books 1986], 14) writes: "... in all rabbinic literature I know of no more unequivocal, fiery acknowledgement of Israel's holy scripture than this opening to the Instruction on the Mount. Jesus is here more radical even than Rabbi Hiyya bar Abba and Rabbi Johanan, both of whom were prepared to renounce a letter—that is a written character of the Torah—if doing so would publicly sanctify the name of God ..." In addition, David Seeley (*Deconstructing the New Testament* [Leiden: Brill, 1994], 25) states: "In Mt. 5:17–20, Jesus links himself to 'the law and the prophets' more stridently than anywhere else in the New Testament."

3 That this constituted a problem for the earliest Christians is clear. The Pseudo-Clementine homilies insist, "And in saying: '*I am not come to destroy the law*' [Matt. 5:17] and yet destroying something [that is, in the antitheses], he indicated that what he destroyed had not originally belonged to the law" (*Ps.-Clem. Hom.* 3.51.2–3 and 52.1), cited from Wilhelm Schneemelcher, ed., *New Testament Apocrypha, Volume 2: Writings Relating to the Apostles; Apocalypses and Related Subjects*, rev. ed., trans. R. McL. Wilson (Louisville: Westminster John Knox, 1992), 534.

in Matthew 5:31–32.[4] Of course, the law itself provided specific provisions for divorce and remarriage (see especially Deut. 24:1–4). In light of this, scholars such as E.P. Sanders and John P. Meier explain that it is therefore difficult to see Jesus' teaching on this matter as merely an "intensification" of the law's requirements. To put it baldly, Jesus appears to be *explicitly* prohibiting something the law expressly permits.[5] How is this not "abolishing" the law? Is there any way to explain this apparent problem?

This paper proposes a solution. In short, as many now recognize, at certain points the Mosaic law itself seems to conflict with its own standards. As Old Testament scholars have observed, Deuteronomy in particular seems to codify practices at odds with the teaching of the preceding books of the Torah. Scholars such as Goldingay have recognized that Deuteronomy seems to, in some sense, "lower the bar" by accommodating certain practices that appear to be at odds and even in some cases expressly forbidden in the laws of Exodus, Leviticus and Numbers (for example, profane slaughter: compare Deut. 12:15–25 with Lev. 17:1–4). In fact, as Hahn and Bergsma have shown, it is likely Ezekiel had precisely these types of concessions in view when he declared that God had given Israel "statutes that were not good" (Ezek. 20:25).

In this article we will argue that Ezekiel's recognition of certain "tensions" within the Torah itself offers a helpful backdrop for understanding Jesus' teaching on divorce and remarriage in Matthew. As we shall see, like Ezekiel, Jesus explains that certain aspects of the Old Testament were only imposed upon Israel as a response to their sin. In other words, the laws themselves pointed to Israel's failure to achieve God's standard of righteousness. However, the prophetic literature suggests that the eschatological age will involve a new order of righteousness that will transcend that required by the law. In Matthew, Jesus proclaims that he has come to usher in this era. In this, he brings true fulfillment to the law. Even though certain elements of it are now "surpassed," he does not "abolish" it. Regulations such as those regarding divorce and remarriage—given because of Israel's "hardness of heart"—point to Israel's need for a deeper righteousness that is only made possible with the coming of the Messiah.

---

4 See W. D. Davies, *Christian Origins and Judaism* (Philadelphia: The Westminster Press, 1962), 39: "There are items in the Antitheses where the old Law's demands are radically deepened … [T]here are others where the Law itself is cited and particular provisions abrogated (Matt. 5:31, 38)." In addition, see also, for example, Davies and Allison, *Matthew*, 508; Klyne Snodgrass, "Matthew and the Law," in *Treasures Old and New: Recent Contributions to Matthean Studies, Society of Biblical Literature Seminar Papers* 1, eds. D. Bauer and M. A. Powell (Atlanta: Scholars Press, 1996), 121; Daniel J. Harrington, *The Gospel of Matthew*, Sacra Pagina 1 (Collegeville: The Liturgical Press, 1991), 91.

5 See John P. Meier, *A Marginal Jew: Rethinking the Historical Jesus, vol. 4: Law and Love*, Anchor Yale Bible Reference Library (New Haven: Yale University Press, 2009), 95: "When one stops to think what this involves, Jesus' prohibition of divorce is nothing short of astounding. Jesus presumes to teach that what the Law permits and regulates is actually the sin of adultery."

The Concept of Deuteronomic Concessions

As scholars familiar with the book know, Deuteronomy contains many unique laws that appear nowhere else in the Pentateuch. In fact, Deuteronomy even seems to offer legislation that explicitly contradicts regulations found in the earlier books of the Torah:[6]

1. *Worship at one sanctuary.* In Deuteronomy, acceptable cultic worship is restricted to one sanctuary (Deut. 12:5–18), an idea never articulated in the laws of Exodus–Numbers.[7]

2. *Profane slaughter.* Whereas Leviticus 17:1–4 prohibits the killing of animals outside of the sanctuary, Deuteronomy 12:15–24 explicitly allows for the practice.[8]

3. *Laws for a king.* While God is described as Israel's king in the Exodus narrative, legal provisions are made for a human king in Deuteronomy 17:14–20—an office nowhere mentioned in the previous books of the Torah.[9]

4. *War of total destruction.* Israelites are given the horrific commandment to engage in *ḥērem* warfare in Deuteronomy 20:16–17[10], a decree nowhere found in the previous books of the Torah.[11]

---

6 For the following list and secondary literature on each item, see Scott W. Hahn, *Kinship by Covenant: A Canonical Approach to the Fulfillment of God's Saving Promises*, Anchor Yale Bible Reference Library (New Haven / London: Yale University Press, 2009), 73–77.

7 Contra Walter Kaiser, Jr., *A Biblical Theology of the Old and New Covenants* (Grand Rapids: Zondervan, 2008), 98–99, who overlooks the way Deut. 12:15–24 presupposes a single sacrificial site and the possibility that the one sacred place could be transferred (for example, from Mt. Ebal at one time to Shiloh or Jerusalem later).

8 While some attempts have been made to harmonize the two laws such attempts have been unconvincing. See, for example, Christophe Nihan, *From Priestly Torah to Pentateuch: A Study in the Composition of the Book of Leviticus*, Forchungen zum Alten Testament 2/25 (Tübingen: Mohr-Siebeck, 2007), 411.

9 Although acknowledging that the idea of kingship was not entirely new to Israel since the Patriarchs were told that kings will come forth from them (see Gen. 17:6, 16; 35:11), Daniel I. Block (*How I Love Your Torah, O Lord!: Studies in the Book of Deuteronomy* [Eugene, Oregon: Wipf & Stock, 2011], 121) explains that Deuteronomy, "... catches the reader by surprise. Neither in the previous chapters of Deuteronomy nor in the narratives of Exodus and Numbers has anyone in Israel imagined the nation being constituted as a monarchy with a king other than YHWH their God."

10 The Israelites are told not to spare the lives of any living thing, including women, children, and other noncombatants. See also Deut. 7:1–5.

11 See, for example, Jacob Milgrom, "Profane Slaughter and a Formulaic Key to the Composition of Deuteronomy," *Hebrew Union College Annual* 47 (1976): 6.

5. *Usury.* Deuteronomy allows Israelites to charge interest from non-Israelites (Deut. 15:3; 23:20), a concession not made in the previous books of the Torah.

6. *Divorce and remarriage.* Deuteronomy makes provisions for divorce and remarriage, regulations that are nowhere present in the other books of the Torah (24:1–4). In fact, Leviticus 21 prohibits a priest from marrying two specific kinds of women: prostitutes and *divorced* women, both said to be "defiled" (Lev. 21:7, 14).[12]

Although diachronic approaches have attempted to address such tensions in the Torah, these explanations are of little help in looking at Deuteronomy in light of the New Testament since its authors would not have been familiar with such solutions.

Nonetheless, contemporary Old Testament scholarship has offered some relevant insights into the possible rationale of Deuteronomy's approach. Many scholars have noted that God appears to accommodate certain sinful practices in Deuteronomy that, though perhaps at odds with the law's ideals, could not be realistically eradicated. Thus Goldingay identifies what he calls a "Pastoral Strategy" in the book. He explains that certain laws

> … presuppose various realities of a sinful world, such as slavery through impoverishment (15:12–18), the desire to have a king, as other nations do (17:14–20), legal disputes (19:15–21; 25:1–3), war (20:1–20), marital and other family problems (21:10–21; 22:13–29; 24:1–4); they do not forbid slavery, monarchy, war, polygamy, or divorce. … indeed, each of them fits ill with Deuteronomy's ideals … Yet in the light of Israel's sinfulness, simply to ban them would be unrealistic. Deuteronomy's policy is to circumscribe them by, and to harness them to, the values and theology it propounds.[13]

In this vein, scholars such as Dale Allison have spoken of the way the Torah contains "divine concessions to human sin or compromises for it" which promoted "less than the ideal human behavior."[14]

---

12 It is also perhaps significant to note the reason Lev. 21 gives for such restrictions: they are called to be "holy"—notably, a vocation elsewhere given to all of Israel (see, for example, Exod. 19:22; 19:2; Num. 15:40; Deut. 7:6).

13 John Goldingay, *Theological Diversity and the Authority of the Old Testament* (Grand Rapids: Eerdmans, 1987), 155–56.

14 See Dale C. Allison, *Resurrecting Jesus: The Earliest Christian Tradition and Its Interpreters* (London: T & T Clark, 2005), 185. Here Allison draws upon David Daube, "Concessions to Sinfulness in Jewish Law," *Journal of Jewish Studies* 10 (1959): 1–13.

Ezekiel and the "Laws That Were Not Good"

Given their intimate knowledge of the biblical texts, it is hard to believe that ancient readers failed to recognize such discrepancies within the law. The book of Ezekiel offers strong evidence that they were, in fact, aware of them. Ezekiel 20:25–26 reads:

> Moreover I gave them statutes that were not good and ordinances by which they could not have life; and I defiled them through their very gifts in making them offer[15] all their first-born, that I might horrify them; I did it that they might know that I am the Lord.

While some have interpreted this passage as a description of human sacrifice sanctioned by the God of Israel,[16] Scott Hahn and John Bergsma offer another proposal[17] that has since been endorsed by other exegetes.[18] Analyzing the structure of the chapter and the language employed, they show that the "statutes that were not good" should most likely be identified with the Deuteronomic legislation. Let us briefly summarize their treatment.

As many have observed, Ezekiel 20 appears to summarize the account of Israel's Exodus and wilderness experience recounted in the Torah.[19] In the opening section the prophet relates Israel's captivity in Egypt. Going on, he relates how the Lord led the Israelites out of Egypt into the wilderness, recalling how he gave them his law. This latter element recalls the Sinai experience of Exodus 20–23 (see Ezek. 20:11–12). Next, in Ezekiel 20:13–15 we find an account of the people's revolt against the Lord, relating the divine threat triggered by their sin. This sin is best understood as a reference to the worship of the golden calf and God's

---

15 Some translations add "by fire" though no such language is found in the Hebrew text.

16 See, for example, Moshe Greenberg, *Ezekiel 1–20* (Garden City: Doubleday, 1983), 369–370.

17 See Scott Hahn and John Sietze Bergsma, "What Laws Were 'Not Good'? A Canonical Approach to the Theological Problem of Ezekiel 20:25–26," *Journal of Biblical Literature* 123/2 (2004): 201–218.

18 See, for example, John W. Olley, *Ezekiel: A Commentary based on Iezekiēl in Codex Vaticanus*, Septuagint Commentary Series (Leiden: Brill, 2009), 367; Brian Neil Peterson, *Ezekiel in Context: Ezekiel's Message Understood in Its Historical Setting of Covenant Curses and Ancient Near Eastern Mythological Motifs*, Princeton Theological Monograph Series 182 (Eugene: Pickwick Publications, 2012), 187.

19 Hahn and Bergsma ("What Laws Were 'Not Good'?," 203 n. 10) cite Corrine Patton, "'I Myself Gave Them Laws That Were Not Good': Ezekiel 20 and the Exodus Traditions," *Journal for the Study of the Old Testament* 69 [1996]: 74–75: "The clearest references to the exodus in the book of Ezekiel occur in ch. 20. The text shows clear familiarity with the exodus tradition: sojourn in Egypt (5–8), deliverance by the LORD (9–10), two generations in the wilderness (10–25), the giving of the law in the wilderness (11–13 and 25–26) and entry into the land (28).… The scheme certainly matches historical reviews present and presumed in Deuteronomic texts, including the historical review in Deuteronomy 1–11, the speech of Solomon in 1 Kings 8, and the speech of Joshua in Joshua 24."

response to it in Exodus 32–33 (see Ezek. 20:13–15). Finally, in Ezekiel 20:21 we read about the rebellion of the children of the Exodus generation, which is most likely a description of the disobedience of the second generation recounted at the end of the book of Numbers.[20] In light of this, the laws Ezekiel mentions next in 20:25—the "statutes that were not good"—should likely be linked with those given in Deuteronomy.

This reading is supported by a close examination of the language employed. God's sworn oath in Ezekiel 20:23 to scatter Israel among the nations uses the exact same terminology employed in Deuteronomy.[21] Further, the word used in Ezekiel 20:25 for the "statutes" that were "not good" is the masculine plural, *huqqîm*. Up until this point in the chapter a different form of the word, the feminine plural, had been used to refer to the divine legislation (see, for example, Ezek. 20:24, *ḥuqqôtay*). Yet it is the masculine plural—the form that appears in Ezekiel 20:25 for the "*statutes* that were not good"—that is more commonly associated with the laws of Deuteronomy. Indeed, the masculine plural form (*huqqîm*) introduces the Deuteronomic legislation in Deuteronomy 12:1. Significantly, while the masculine plural form dominates Deuteronomy, it appears only two times in all of Leviticus (10:11; 26:46). In addition, Ezekiel 20:25 also pairs *huqqîm* with *ûmišpātîm*, which is noteworthy since the expression *huqqîm ûmišpātîm* occurs exclusively in Deuteronomy.[22]

Making the distinction between the previous Torah legislation and that associated with Deuteronomy is thus key to understanding the reference to these "statutes that were not good" and the difficult statement in Ezekiel 20:26, "I defiled them through their very gifts, in their offering up all their *firstborn*, in order that I might horrify them ..."

Because the terminology *bĕha ăbîr* ("offering up") used in 20:26 is elsewhere associated with the Molech cult (see Ezek. 20:31) some have argued that such worship is in view here. The term, however, is also frequently used in Ezekiel for offerings that have no association at all with Molech (see Ezek. 5:1; 14:15; 20:37; 37:2; 46:21; 47:3–4; 48:14). Moreover, Molech worship was never linked to the offering of *firstborn* children.[23]

---

20 For a fuller argument for this identification see Hahn and Bergsma "What Laws Were 'Not Good'?," 204.

21 While some might argue that the language is intended to evoke the curses of Leviticus 26, Hahn and Bergsma demonstrate that Deuteronomy is a much better fit: (1) in Lev. 26 the dispersion of Israel is only mentioned as a possibility, however, in Deuteronomy it is assured by a divine oath; (2) the terminology employed by Ezek. 20:23 mirrors that found in the Deuteronomic legislation (not that found in the Holiness Code). See Hahn and Bergsma, "What Laws Were 'Not Good'?," 205–206.

22 Hahn and Bergsma, "What Laws Were 'Not Good'?," 207 citing Risa Levitt Kohn, *A New Heart and New Soul: Ezekiel, the Exile, and the Torah*, Journal for the Study of the Old Testament Supplement 358 (Sheffield: Sheffield Academic Press, 2002), 85.

23 Hahn and Bergsma, "What Laws Were 'Not Good'?," 211–213.

According to Hahn and Bergsma, the description of the sacrifices as "defiling" arises instead from a careful understanding of the nuances of the Deuteronomic law and their lack of conformity to the earlier Torah legislation. The Deuteronomic laws permitted something that was expressly condemned by the Levitical legislation: the killing of animals and the spilling of blood outside of the sanctuary. As we have mentioned, while Leviticus requires one to sacrifice all animals at the central sanctuary (see Lev. 17:1–8), Deuteronomy only requires an annual sacrifice of the firstborn animals (see Deut. 12:6, 17; 15:19, 20). Given this, it is easy to see why Ezekiel would describe the offering of the firstborn as defiling. From the perspective of Leviticus, *all* animals should be killed at the temple, not simply the firstborn. In fact, Ezekiel 20:26 uses the precise form of the verb "to offer" (hiphil of *'ābăr*) that the pre-Deuteronomic legislation uses to describe the offering of the firstborn animals (see Exod. 13:12). In sum, it seems that this accommodation in Deuteronomy—a "defiling" concession from the standpoint of Leviticus—is what the author has in mind when he speaks of "statutes that were not good."[24]

Objections to Hahn and Bergsma's Approach

Before moving on it is important to respond to criticisms of Hahn and Bergsma's reading. While affirming that Hahn and Bergsma have demonstrated persuasively that Ezekiel 20:25 refers to Deuteronomic legislation, Gile believes that their reading is unconvincing.[25] First, Gile holds that while Hahn and Bergsma are correct that the offering of the firstborn in Exodus 13 excludes human offspring, such an exemption is not clear in Ezekiel 20:26 and should therefore not be understood as operative there. Second, he takes Hahn and Bergsma to task for failing to consider the possibility that non-Molech human sacrificial rites are in view in Ezekiel 20:26. Third, Gile argues that a close reading of Deuteronomy suggests that the book itself provides the rationale for licit profane sacrifice. He insists that the entire land is sacralized in Deuteronomy thus constituting the entire region as an extension of the sanctuary. Moreover, he insists that Deuteronomy recognizes that Israel's new circumstances of living in the land will necessitate accommodations to cultic norms, specifically profane slaughter, since many will now have to travel a great distance to the sanctuary (see Deut. 12:20–21; 14:24–26). Fourth, given that Ezekiel elsewhere accepts the validity of the Deuteronomic legislation, Gile insists that it seems unlikely that the book views its laws as "not good."[26]

---

24 Hahn and Bergsma, citing Moshe Weinfeld and Risa Levitt Kohn, write: "If, as Weinfeld and others argue, much of P represents an older theology than that of D, adherents of Priestly thought may have found the 'secularization' of the Deuteronomic legislation both threatening and deficient" ("What Laws Were 'Not Good'?," 209).

25 See Jason Gile, "Deuteronomy and Ezekiel's Theology of Exile," in *For Our Good Always: Studies on the Message and Influence of Deuteronomy in Honor of Daniel I. Block* (Winona Lake, Ind.: Eisenbrauns, 2013), 297.

26 See Jason Gile, "Deuteronomic Influence in the Book of Ezekiel" (Ph.D. diss., Wheaton College,

Drawing on Friebel,[27] Gile argues for another view of Ezekiel 20:25. In his view, rather than referring to divine legislation ("statutes" and "ordinances"), *huqqîm* and *mišpātîm* should be linked to God's "decrees" and "judgments" in Ezekiel 20:23 announcing the punishment of exile. Thus, according to Gile, in 20:25 the idea is not that God gave Israel "laws" that were not good, but instead that Israel had triggered the dreadful curses of Deuteronomy 4:25–28.[28] Yet Gile's objections are far from insurmountable and the solution drawn from Friebel's work is problematic.

First, while it is not explicitly stated that the exemption of human offspring from the offering of the "firstborn" found in Exodus 13 is in place in Ezekiel 20:26, nothing in the text demands that "firstborn" refer to human sacrifices. That firstborn terminology is used elsewhere in the Torah to refer to animal victims alone (see, for example, Lev. 27:26; Num. 18:17; Deut. 15:19; 33:17) should be enough to call into question the view that human sacrifices are *necessarily* implied. Further, legislation prohibiting human sacrifice is found elsewhere in the Torah besides Exodus 13 (see Exod. 34:20; Num. 3:40–51; 18:14–15). Given the Torah's multiple prohibitions, it is unlikely that ancient readers would have understood the sacrifices in Ezekiel 20:26 as human beings. What decisively tips the scales against such a reading is that Ezekiel 20 describes the laws as having been given by God himself. Given that we have evidence of laws that fit the language of Ezekiel 20:26 in the Torah—that is, the offering of the firstborn *animals*—it seems like special pleading to insist that something else is in view.

Second, Gile's objection that Hahn and Bergsma overlook the possibility of non-Molech rites in Ezekiel 20:26 has one major flaw: Molech sacrifices are mentioned in the immediate context (see 20:31). Thus, if Ezekiel 20:26 is referring to human sacrifice it would be hard to believe that Molech rites were not somehow being suggested. Again, however, such a reading is unlikely.

Third, while Deuteronomy does explain that its cultic laws accommodate the new circumstances of the people in the land it does not specifically explain why pouring out blood on the land would not defile it. The suggestion that the land was seen as an extension of the sanctuary is inadequate. If the land is simply to be equated with the sanctuary, why must sacrificial offerings of the firstborn be offered and eaten *at the sanctuary?*

Fourth, it is not at all surprising, on Hahn and Bergsma's reading, that Ezekiel accepts elements of Deuteronomy in their interpretation, since Ezekiel believes that the Deuteronomic laws were given *by God*. What Hahn and Bergsma offer is simply a nuanced view of Ezekiel's reception of Deuteronomy. That Ezekiel

2013), 130–134.

27 Kelvin G. Friebel, "The Decrees of Yahweh that Are 'Not Good': Ezekiel 20:25–26," in *Seeking Out the Wisdom of the Ancients: Essays Offered to Honor Michael V. Fox on the Occasion of His Sixty-Fifth Birthday*, eds. R. L. Troxel, K. G. Friebel, and D. R. Magary (Winona Lake, Ind.: Eisenbrauns, 2005), 21–36.

28 Gile, "Deuteronomic Influence in the Book of Ezekiel," 190–196.

did indeed have such a sophisticated reading is suggested by the subtle shift from the feminine plural *ḥuqqôtay* (Ezek. 20:24) to the masculine plural *huqqîm* (Ezek. 20:25) as described above. Ezekiel was a careful reader of the Torah and took seriously *all* of the Pentateuchal legislation. Unwilling to simply gloss over an apparent conflict in the law—a conflict never actually resolved in the Torah—Ezekiel was willing to accept the idea that God had apparently given laws to Israel that "were not good." Leviticus explains that pouring out blood on the land will defile it. Ezekiel takes this warning seriously and concludes that the Deuteronomic laws themselves were thus "not good," given in response to the climactic rebellion of the second generation described at the end of Numbers.

Finally, Friebel's solution has linguistic and contextual problems. Linguistically, it overlooks how the pairing of *huqqîm* and *mišpātîm* used elsewhere refers to Torah legislation (see, for example, Neh. 9:13; 10:29).[29] In terms of context, as others such as Choi have observed, the suggestion by Freibel that what is in view are "judgments" and not "laws" "does violence to the plain sense of the text. Admittedly, it is theologically troubling to assert that Yahweh would give bad laws, but this is what the text says in unambiguous fashion."[30] In short, the reading offered by Friebel and Gile fails to explain why 20:25–26 links what God gave to the Israelites to their defilement ("*I gave them* statutes that were not good ... and *I defiled them* through their very gifts."). Hahn and Bergsma's view, however, does just that. In sum, the reading they advance simply has greater explanatory power in addressing the various facets of Ezekiel 20 and should therefore be preferred.

Deuteronomic Allusions in Jesus' Teaching on Marriage in Matthew 19

Turning to the Gospel of Matthew we can note that Jesus specifically identifies divorce and remarriage—one of the provisions unique to the Deuteronomic legislation—as a concessionary regulation given to Israel because of its sinfulness. Asked by the Pharisees why Moses gave Israel provisions for divorce and remarriage, Jesus explains, "*For your hardness of heart* Moses allowed you to divorce your wives, *but from the beginning it was not so*" (Matt. 19:8). Our discussion in the previous section supports Jesus' affirmation: the allowance of divorce and remarriage was not "from the beginning" (that is, found in Genesis–Numbers) but appears for the first time in Deuteronomy.

---

29 The language in Neh. 9:13, that the laws given at Sinai were "right ordinances [*mišpātîm*] and true laws, good statutes [*huqqîm*] and commandments," so closely parallels Ezek. 20:26 that one wonders about a possible relationship between the two texts.

30 See the discussion in John H. Choi, *Traditions at Odds: The Reception of the Pentateuch in Biblical and Second Temple Period Literature* (London: T & T Clark, 2010), 203–204. Choi's own solution, however, is no more convincing. In his view there is no clear referent to the laws that were not good. Yet this clearly ignores the Deuteronomic echoes and connections suggested by the text of Ezek. 20. He also goes too far in describing them as bad when they are merely "not good" (i.e. imperfect).

In fact, in Matthew, Jesus not only rejects Deuteronomy's allowance of divorce and remarriage, he understands it as a kind of "defiling" concession—at least in a moral sense. In Matthew 19, Jesus explains, "whoever divorces his wife, except for unchastity, and marries another, commits adultery; and he who marries a divorced woman, commits adultery" (Matt 19:9). Likewise, earlier, in Matthew 5, we find him teaching in a similar vein: "every one who divorces his wife, except on the ground of unchastity, makes her an adulteress; and whoever marries a divorced woman commits adultery" (Matt. 5:32). In other words, as Meier has pointed out, however one reads the controversial exception clause in these passages, according to Matthew's account of Jesus' teaching the legal provision for divorce and remarriage in Deuteronomy sanctioned nothing less than adultery.[31]

Indeed, language used by Matthew suggests that the idea of *Deuteronomic* concessions is specifically intended. The scene in Matthew 19 opens with a description of Jesus' movements, connecting the episode of Jesus' teaching on divorce to a specific location: "the region of Judea *beyond the Jordan* [*peran tou Iordanou*]" (Matt. 19:1). It seems hard to believe it is just a coincidence that this is the precise place the laws of Deuteronomy were said to be delivered to Israel in Deuteronomy 1:1 and 1:5 (LXX: *peran tou Iordanou*). Moreover, without insisting that Jesus' teaching directly evokes Ezekiel 20, we can note a similarity between the two passages. Like Ezekiel, Jesus suggests that the Deuteronomic law involved the institution of a kind of defiling concession: divorce and remarriage—that is, a statute that "was not good."

Jesus' "Fulfillment" of the Law

With all of this in mind, we can now turn to the question of Jesus' teaching in Matthew 5 and the apparent tension in the flow of thought there. The solemn affirmation of the law's value in 5:17–20 is immediately followed by a series of sayings in which Jesus compares the law's requirements to his teachings.[32] This section is conventionally referred to as the "six antitheses" (see Matt. 5:21–48).[33]

---

31 See Meier, *Law and History in Matthew's Gospel*, 140–150.

32 See Dale Allison, "The Structure of the Sermon on the Mount," in *Journal of Biblical Literature* 106/3 (1987): 424 n. 8 [423–445] who briefly lays out the various approaches advanced by other scholars. In addition, see the more recent discussions in Glen H. Stassen, "The Fourteen Triads of the Sermon of the Mount (Matthew 5:21–7:12)," *Journal of Biblical Literature* 122/2 (2003): 267–308; John W. Welch, *The Sermon on the Mount in the Light of the Temple* (Farnham: Ashgate, 2009), 1–14.

33 Scholars widely recognize that this section forms a discreet literary unit in the Sermon. Each of these sayings contain the formula (or something very close to it) "you have heard that it was said ... but I say" (see Matt. 5:21–22, 27–28, 5:31–32, 33–34, 38–39, 43–44). Observing that Matthew is fond of triadic structures, Davies and Allison argue that the six antitheses should be understood as two sets of three teachings (5:21–32 and 5:33–48). See Davies and Allison, *Matthew*, 1:504; see also Allison, "Structure of the Sermon on the Mount," 433. This view is supported by the following: (1) the appearance of "again" (*palin*) in v. 33 seems to serve as an indicator that a new triad is beginning; (2) the full phrase, "You have heard that it was said to

Here Jesus cites a passage from the Torah[34] and then offers a saying that begins with the formula "but I say to you" (*egō de legō hymin*—see 5:22, 28, 32, 34, 39, 44).

There is, of course, tremendous controversy surrounding the meaning of this latter phrase. Does the language "but I say to you" signal a rejection of the Torah? Many scholars observe that Jesus' insistence on the enduring value of the law in 5:17–20 in the immediately preceding verses militates against such a reading.[35] In addition, Jesus' use of the word *de* (mildly contrastive) and not *alla*

---

the men of old" (*Ēkousate hoti errethē tois archaiois*) occurs only in 5:21 and 5:33 (after "Again" [*Palin*]); (3) while the word "that" (*hoti*) appears after Jesus' words "but I say to you" (*egō de legō hymin*) in 5:22, 28, and 32, it is absent from 5:34, 39, and 44; (4) though Jesus' words "but I say to you" (*egō de legō hymin*) preface a legal ordinance which begins with the word "that" (*hoti*) in 22, 28 and 32, in 34, 39 and 44 the saying leads into a "straightforward imperative"; and (5) all three of Jesus' quotations in 5:21, 27, and 31 are found in Deuteronomy (though admittedly not exclusively there; see respectively Deut. 5:17, 18, 24:1–4) and all three of the quotations in 5:33, 38, and 43 can be located in Leviticus (though, again, not exclusively there; see respectively Lev. 19:12; 24:20; 19:18).

34 That the written "law" is in view is clear not only from the citations to it that follow in the antitheses but also from the language of "iota" and "dot." See Betz, *Sermon on the Mount*, 182. That the five books attributed to Moses, known as the Torah (see *4 Macc.* 1:34; 2:5–6, 9; 9:2; Matt. 12:5; Josephus, *A.J.* 17:15), were recognized as having authoritative status in the Second Temple period is evidenced by the following: (1) Sir. 24:43, which speaks of "the book of the covenant of the Most High God, the law which Moses commanded us as an inheritance for the congregations of Jacob"; (2) Josephus, who distinguishes the Pharisees from the Sadducees by, in part, noting that the Pharisees "have delivered to the people a great many observances by succession from their fathers, which are not written in the law of Moses" (*A.J.* 13.297); (3) the existence of the Samaritan Pentateuch (see, for example, the discussion in Emmanuel Tov, *Textual Criticism of the Hebrew Bible*, 2d rev. ed. (Minneapolis: Fortress Press, 2001), 80–99; (4) in the Dead Sea Scrolls we read, "You must understand the book of Moses [and] the book[s of the pr]ophets and Davi[d...]" (4Q397 14–21,10; 4Q398 14–17; 4QMMT C 9–16); and (5) the New Testament, for example, the Gospel of Luke has Jesus referring to "the law of Moses and the prophets and the psalms" (Luke 24:44; see also, for example, Matt. 15:2, 3, 6). For further discussion see the collection of essays in Lee Martin McDonald and James A. Sanders, eds., *The Canon Debate* (Peabody: Hendricksen, 2002), in particular, Julio C. Trebolle Barrera, "Origins of a Tripartite Old Testament Canon," 128–145; Jack P. Lews, "Jamnia Revisited," 146–162; Jack N. Lightstone, "The Rabbis' Bible: The Canon of the Hebrew Bible in the Early Rabbinic Guild," 163–184; Craig A. Evans, "The Scriptures of Jesus and His Earliest Followers," 185–195.

35 The language of "antitheses" (that is, teachings "antithetical" to the Law) is thus not exactly accurate and survives only as a vestige of a previous era of scholarship. Of course, scholars such as Rudolf Bultmann (*Die Geschichte der synoptischen Tradition* [*The History of the Synoptic Tradition*][5th ed.; Göttingen: Vandenhoeck & Ruprecht, 1961 (1921)], 142–144) and those associated with the New Quest (for example, Ernst Käsemann, "Probleme neutestamentlicher Arbeit in Deutschland" ["Problems of New Testament Research in Germany"], in *Die Freiheit des Evangeliums und die Ordnung der Gesellschaft* [*The Freedom of the Gospel and the Social Order*] [Munich: Chr. Kaiser Verlag, 1952], 144) especially pointed to these sayings in support of their approaches which defined Jesus *against* the Judaism of his day. See, for example, Geza Vermes, *The Religion of Jesus the Jew* (Minneapolis: Augsburg Fortress Press, 1993), 33–37; Daniel J. Harrington, *The Gospel of Matthew*, Sacra Pagina 1 (Collegeville: The Liturgical Press, 1991), 90; Roland Deines, "Not the Law but the Messiah," in *Built Upon the Rock: Studies in the Gospel of Matthew*, eds. D. M. Gurtner and J. Nolland (Grand Rapids: Eerdmans, 2008), 64 [53–84];

(strongly contrastive) suggests that something other than outright rejection is in view.[36] Moreover, the hinge between the two sections seems to be Jesus' call for a "better righteousness" (*dikaiosynē pleion*) in 5:20. Here scholars have recognized the stated rationale for the antitheses that follow in 5:21–48.[37] Yet what this "better righteousness" exactly entails is debated.

Some have argued that rather than contrasting his teaching to the law *itself*, Jesus is simply intensifying its demands.[38] Highlighting the presence of language used by the rabbis,[39] some have argued that Jesus is simply contrasting

---

M. Eugene Boring, "The Gospel of Matthew," in *The New Interpreter's Bible*, 12 vols., eds. L. E. Keck et al (Nashville: Abingdon, 1995), 8:188 [89–505]. Interestingly, it appears that the first to use such language was Marcion. See Betz, *Sermon on the Mount*, 200–201.

36 See the discussion in Davies and Allison, *Matthew*, 1:507; Craig Keener, *A Commentary on the Gospel of Matthew* (Grand Rapids: Eerdmans, 1999), 181; Anthony J. Saldarini, "Matthew," in *Eerdmans Commentary on the Bible*, eds. J. D. G. Dunn and J. W. Rogerson (Grand Rapids: Eerdmans, 2003), 1015–1016.

37 See Meier, *Law and History in Matthew's Gospel*, 41–42: "Mt 5:17–20 also has an important place within the Sermon on the Mount ... This programmatic statement on the Law is ... illustrated by six antitheses (5:21–48), which are introduced by 5:20 (and, in a broader sense, by the whole of 5:17–20). Mt. 5:20 thus serves as a type of 'bridge' or transition between the statement of the principle (5:17–19) and the applications or illustrations (5:21–48). Vs. 5:20 both sums up what has preceded and inaugurates what follows." Likewise, see John Nolland, *The Gospel of Matthew*, New International Greek Testament Commentary (Grand Rapids: Eerdmans, 2005), 228: "The six antitheses are prepared for in 5:17–20 by the report both of Jesus' insistence that he came not to abolish the Law but to see it fulfilled more effectively, and of his stern words on the need for an abundant righteousness."

38 See, for example, Richard A. Burridge (*Imitating Jesus: An Inclusive Approach to New Testament Ethics* [Grand Rapids: Eerdmans, 2007], 209–210): "... the 'exceeding' righteousness is shown by the following antitheses not to be a nit-picking or legalistic interpretation of the law; rather, his hearers are to go beyond merely avoiding murder or adultery to living a life without hatred or lust, speaking truth instead and loving enemies. This is what Jesus means when he says he has come to 'fulfill' the law (5.17)." Likewise, see, for example, Kyle D. Fedler, *Exploring Christian Ethics: Biblical Foundations for Morality* (Louisville: Westminster John Knox Press, 2006), 169; Louise Joy Lawrence, *An Ethnography of the Gospel of Matthew*, Wissenschaftliche Untersuchungen zum Neuen Testament 165/2 (Tübingen: Mohr-Siebeck, 2003), 152: "Jesus' stipulations are only intensifying the original covenant requisites."

39 See David Daube, *The New Testament and Rabbinic Interpretation: Jordan Lectures in Comparative Religion* (London: The Athlone Press, 1956), 55–62, who argues that the expression "you have heard that it was said" seems to parallel the language used by the rabbis to contrast teachings of different rabbis (for example, see Matt. 5:28 and *Pesiq. Rab.* 24.2). This rabbinic context is often seen as the background for Matthew's account of Jesus' condemnation of divorce (Matt. 5:32). Some have understood Jesus' teaching in terms of the rabbinic debate about divorce (see *m. Git.* 9.10; *b. Git.* 90a–b; *Sipre* on Deut. 24.; see also Phillip Sigal, *The Halakhah of Jesus of Nazareth according to the Gospel of Matthew* [Atlanta: Society of Biblical Literature, 2007], 105–144). Meier (*A Marginal Jew*, 4:95) dismisses this reading as anachronistic. Moreover, see Donald Hagner, *Matthew*, 2 vols., Word Biblical Commentary 33a–b (Dallas: Word, 1993–1995), 1:125, who argues that the view that Jesus is inserting a rabbinic exception clause to his prohibition of divorce conflicts with the absolute nature of the second half of the statement in Matt. 5:32 and renders the stunned reaction of the apostles to Jesus' reiteration of the teaching in 19:10–11 inexplicable. See also Robert A. Guelich, "The Antitheses of Matthew V. 21–48: Traditional and/or Redactional?," *New Testament Studies* 22/4 (1976): 455–457 [444–457].

his teaching—not with the Torah itself—but with simplistic literal interpretations advanced by other teachers of his day.[40] Yet the problem with such a view is that in almost every instance Jesus cites the law *itself*, not simply other interpretations of it.[41] Further, as we have already mentioned, while some of the antitheses can be explained as an intensification of the demands of the Torah (for example, the association of lust with adultery in 5:27–30), others are harder to explain along these lines. In particular, as noted above, Jesus' equation of divorce and remarriage with adultery is very hard to explain as merely an intensification of the Torah's requirements since he explicitly prohibits something the law permits.[42]

It appears, then, that Jesus is doing something more than simply increasing the law's requirements. Jesus' words "but I say to you" (*egō de legō hymin*) underscore the focus on his *own* authority.[43] The antitheses are thus likely related to the important christological assertion in 5:17: Jesus has come not to *abolish* (*katalysai*) the law and the prophets but so that they may be "fulfilled" (*plērōsai*).[44]

---

40 See, for example, Leon Morris, *The Gospel According to Matthew*, PNTC (Grand Rapids: Eerdmans, InterVarsity Press, 1992), 112: "Jesus is protesting against a strictly literal interpretation of the commands, an interpretation that indicates an apparent willingness to obey what God has said, but which imposes a strict limit on obedience and leaves scope for a good deal of ungodly behavior."

41 See, for example, Davies and Allison, *Matthew*, 506; Ulrich Luz, *Das Evangelium nach Matthäus* [*The Gospel according to Matthew*], Evangelisch-katholischer Kommentar zum Neuen Testament I-IV, 4 vols. (Zürich: Benziger, 1985), 1:328–331; David L. Turner, *Matthew*, Baker Commentary on the New Testament (Grand Rapids: Baker Academic, 2008), 166–167.

42 See n. 5 above.

43 See Morna D. Hooker, "Creative Conflict: The Torah and Christology," in *Christology, Controversy, & Community: New Testament Essays in Honour of David R. Catchpole*, eds. D. G. Horrell and C. M. Tuckett (Leiden: Brill, 2000), 125–126 [137–156]: "Is Jesus, like a Jewish rabbi, simply contrasting previous interpretation of the torah with his own? The emphatic ['but I say to you'] suggests that what Jesus is presenting is more than mere 'interpretation' of the torah. ... Although Matthew's Jesus does not challenge the teaching of Moses, he does far more here than simply interpret its meaning, since his words stand in contrast to those of Moses." In addition, see Byrskog, *Jesus the Only Teacher: Didactic Authority and Transmission in Ancient Israel, Ancient Judaism, and the Matthean Community*, Coniectanea biblica, New Testament 24 (Stockholm: Almqvist & Wiksell, 1994), 294–296, who understands Jesus' use of "I" in the antitheses as referring to "divine categories." Likewise, see, for example, Guelich, "The Antitheses of Matthew V. 21-48," 455–457; Robert Guelich, *The Sermon on the Mount: A Foundation for Understanding* (Waco: Word Books, 1982), 185; Keener, *Matthew*, 182.

44 This saying is one of six recorded in Matthew's Gospel in which Jesus explains why "I came" (*ēlthon*), all of which have important Christological implications (see Matt. 5:17; 9:13; 10:34; 11:19; 18:11; 20:28). See Robert Banks, "Matthew's Understanding of the Law: Authenticity and Interpretation in Matthew 5:17–20," *Journal of Biblical Literature* 93/2 (1974): 226–242; James D. G. Dunn, *Jesus Remembered*, vol. 1 in *Christianity in the Making* (Grand Rapids: Eerdmans, 2003), 526; Aquila H. I. Lee, *From Messiah to Preexistent Son: Jesus' Self-Consciousness and Early Christian Exegesis of Messianic Psalms*, Wissenschaftliche Untersuchungen zum Neuen Testament 2/192 (Tübingen: Mohr-Siebeck, 2005), 182–196. Such a focus on the person of Christ is further suggested by the identification of the Gospels as *bioi*. See Richard Burridge, *What Are the Gospels?: A Comparison with Graeco-Roman Biography*, 2d ed. (Cambridge: Cambridge University Press, 1995), 325–326.

It seems, therefore, that the interpretive crux resides in the meaning of the word "fulfilled" (*plēroō*). The key question is: what sort of "fulfillment" is in view?[45] Of course, taken by itself, the term *plēroō* can be translated in various ways.[46] However, since the word is contrasted with *katalysai* ("abolish"), which carries the meaning of "destroying"[47] or "annulling,"[48] the most likely reading would appear to involve an antithetical meaning, namely, "to uphold" or "to maintain."[49] Moreover, we should also not neglect the other element Jesus says he has come to "fulfill" (*plēroō*) in verse 17: "the prophets."[50] The fulfillment of the prophets is a recurring theme in Matthew.[51] In passages relating this motif, the word for "fulfill" (*plēroō*) is,

---

45 See Davies and Allison, *Matthew*, 1:485: "The crux of this clause—and of all of v. 17—is the meaning of *plēroō*."

46 Davies and Allison, *Matthew*, 1:484–486, offer a helpful catalogue of options. Likewise, see John Yueh-Han Yieh, *One Teacher: Jesus' Teaching Role in Matthew's Gospel Report*, Beihefte zur ZNW 124 (Berlin: Walter de Gruyter, 2004), 76–79; Henrik Ljungman, *Das Gesetz Erfüllen* (Lund: Gleerup, 1954), 19–36; Davies, *Christian Origins and Judaism*, 32–33.

47 This is clearly the meaning of the word elsewhere in Matthew's Gospel (see Matt. 24:2; 26:61; 27:40).

48 The term *katalysai* means "to annul" when used in reference to an authoritative text or law. See, for example, 2 Macc. 2:22, which describes how, after their successful revolt against the Greeks, the Maccabees "restored the laws that were about to be *abolished* [*katalyō*]" (see also 2 Macc. 4:11). Josephus uses the term in relating how Nicolas of Damascus defended the Jews who lived in Ionia, explaining that "they would rather suffer all manner of things than *violate* [*katalyō*] any of their country's customs" (*A.J.* 16:35 [Marcus, LCL]; see also *A.J.* 20.81). Philo also uses the word to describe efforts to "destroy" [*katalyō*] the Jewish observance of the Sabbath (see Philo, *Som.* 2.123). 4 Maccabees also has Eleazar speaking of how he pitied his old age less than "breaking" [*katalyō*] the Law (see 4 Macc. 5:33). See the discussion in Nolland, *Matthew*, 217–218; Davies and Allison, *Matthew*, 1:484; Paul Foster, *Community, Law and Mission in Matthew's Gospel*, Wissenschaftliche Untersuchungen zum Neuen Testament 177/2 (Tübingen: Mohr-Siebeck, 2004), 184–185; R. T. France, *The Gospel of Matthew*, New International Commentary on the New Testament; Grand Rapids: Eerdmans, 2007), 182.

49 See, for example, Nolland, *Matthew*, 218: "'Fulfill' must be taken in a manner that allows it to be an appropriate counterpart to 'annul'." See also the discussions in Daube, *New Testament and Rabbinic Judaism*, 60–62; David Flusser, *Judaism and the Origins of Christianity* (Jerusalem: Magnes Press, 1988), 495.

50 Along these lines, it is significant to note that Meier (*Law and History in Matthew's Gospel*, 75) points out that *plēroō* is not linked with the Law in the LXX, though it is linked with the prophets.

51 See Matt. 1:22; 2:15, 17, 23; 4:14; 8:17; 12:17; 13:14, 35; 21:4; 26:54, 56; 27:9. In addition, see 7:12 and 22:40 where the Law and Prophets are likewise linked together. In fact, the other Synoptic Gospels also report that Jesus taught that he was bringing *fulfillment* to the Scriptures (see Mark 14:49; Luke 4:21; 21:22; 22:37; 24:44). It should also be pointed out that the Synoptic Gospels frequently have Jesus linking the "law" and the "prophets" (see Matt. 7:12; 11:13; Luke 16:16; 24:44 ["the law of Moses and the prophets"]; see Luke 16:29, 31 ["Moses and the prophets"] and Luke 24:27 ["Moses and all the prophets"]). See also William Carter, "Jesus' 'I have come' Statements in Matthew's Gospel," *Catholic Biblical Quarterly* 60 (1988): 44–62, who argues that these statements are all ultimately meant to be read as a fulfillment of Matt. 1:21–23, in which Jesus' mission is first announced. Furthermore see R. T. France, *Matthew: Evangelist and Teacher* (Exeter: Paternoster Press, 1989; repr., Eugene: Wipf & Stock, 2004), 166–205.

in some sense, used to describe the arrival of that which the prophets announced, which, in most cases, is understood as Jesus himself.

An especially important parallel is found in Matthew 11:13–14. There Jesus states: "For all the prophets and the law prophesied [*eprophēteusan*] until John; and if you are willing to accept it, he is Elijah who is to come." Without entering into an extended exegesis of this passage, we can make three important observations about it. First, in addition to the prophets, the law is understood as having *prophetic* value; *both* the law *and* the prophets are said to have "prophesied."[52] Second, the law and the prophets are described as being in some sense *provisional*; John the Baptist's arrival seems to mark the appearance of what they were anticipating.[53] Third, this fulfillment is *eschatological* since John's ministry is linked to future hopes for the coming of Elijah, a figure associated with eschatological hopes.[54]

It is very difficult to imagine that Jesus' reference to *fulfilling* the law and the prophets in Matthew 5:17 should be taken in an entirely different sense than elsewhere in Matthew. Therefore, we should likely conclude that in Matthew 5

---

52 In connection with this, it should be kept in mind that Moses—to whom the Torah was principally attributed—was seen as the prophet *par excellence* in Second Temple Judaism. Thus, instead of reading the first five books in terms of hypothetical pre-canonical sources, ancient Jews viewed these books as the writings of the greatest prophet of all. In fact, many passages in the Pentateuch were viewed as having *prophetic* value. For example, Gen. 49, which relates Jacob's final words to his sons came to be understood as an eschatological prophecy (see 2Q252 V, 1–2; *Tg. Onq.* on Gen. 49:10; *Tg. Neof.* on Gen. 49:10; *Jub.* 45:14). Likewise, Balaam's prophecy in Num. 24:17–19 was taken by some ancient writers as a prophecy relating eschatological figures (see CD-A 7:18–21 [=4Q266 3 iii 18–22]; 1Q28b 5:27; *T. Levi* 18:3; *T. Judah* 24:1). See Robert Banks, *Jesus and the Law in the Synoptic Tradition*, Society for New Testament Studies 28 (Cambridge: Cambridge University Press, 1975), 210, who discusses how the *prophetic* dimension of the Law has been neglected by scholars: "What I would argue then, and it is this possibility that seems to have been constantly overlooked, is that precisely the same meaning should be given to the term *plēroun* when it is used of the Law as that which it has when it is used of the Prophets."

53 See France, *Gospel of Matthew*, 183, who, commenting on Matt. 11:13, writes, "The law is thus linked with the prophets as looking forward to a time of fulfillment which has now arrived. The Torah, then, is not God's last word to his people, but is in a sense provisional, looking forward to a time of fulfillment through the Messiah."

54 Malachi ends with the Lord promising to send the prophet Elijah (Mal. 4:5–6). In fact, Jesus links John with the eschatological messenger of Mal. 3:1, whom many scholars think is to be identified with Elijah since the latter is clearly in view in 4:5–6. Eschatological hopes for Elijah's coming are also present in Sir. 48:10–11, where his coming is also linked with the restoration of Israel: "you [Elijah] who are ready at the appointed time, it is written, to calm the wrath of God before it breaks out in fury, to turn the heart of the father to the son, and to restore the tribes of Jacob." Elijah was thus linked with eschatological expectations in other texts (see 4Q521 2 iii 1; 4Q558 1 ii 4; *4 Ezra* 6:24–28; *m.'Ed.* 8.7; *b. Soṭah* 9:15). For an especially insightful treatment, see Brant Pitre, *Jesus, the Tribulation, and the End of the Exile: Restoration Eschatology and the Origin of the Atonement*, Wissenschaftliche Untersuchungen zum Neuen Testament 2/104 (Tubingen: Mohr Siebeck, 2005), 177–198, who demonstrates that it was believed that Elijah's appearance would coincide with the eschatological tribulation. Going on, Pitre convincingly argues that Jesus believed that with the death of John—the eschatological Elijah—that period had arrived.

Jesus is explaining that he brings fulfillment to the law and the prophets because *he* is the one to whom they pointed. In the "antitheses," then, Jesus does not merely intensify the Torah's demands but brings about what these precepts ultimately anticipated: a "better" righteousness, an eschatological holiness.

Still, we must ask: how did the law point to a better holiness? A good explanation would involve the recognition that the law itself made concessions to sin that in some way sanctioned a "less than ideal" standard of righteousness. Accordingly, Jesus has come to usher in the age of eschatological holiness—a radically new kind of righteousness that the law itself, with its many concessions to sinfulness, could not presume. Indeed, such a reading would fit well within first-century Judaism.

Eschatological Righteousness and Deuteronomic Concessions

That the eschatological age would involve a radically new kind of righteousness and the total eradication of impurity is attested in numerous prophetic texts. Here we can mention the famous "new covenant" prophecy in Jeremiah 31, a chapter cited from in Matthew 2 and also likely alluded to in Matthew's institution narrative of the Last Supper:[55]

> "But this is the covenant which I will make with the house of Israel after those days, says the LORD: I will put my law within them, and I will write it upon their hearts; and I will be their God, and they shall be my people. [34] And no longer shall each man teach his neighbor and each his brother, saying, 'Know the LORD,' for they shall all know me, from the least of them to the greatest, says the LORD; for I will forgive their iniquity, and I will remember their sin no more" (Jer. 31:33–34).

Ezekiel has a similar vision, announcing that God will cleanse his people from uncleanness through the sprinkling of water, giving his people "a new heart" and "a new spirit," describing how he will cause them "to walk in my statutes and be careful to observe my ordinances" (Ezek. 36:26–27).

---

55 Matthew clearly draws from this chapter in 2:17–18 (citing Jer. 31:15). Many scholars also think an allusion to the "new covenant" announced in Jer. 31:31 is present in Matthew's account of the Last Supper where Jesus speaks of the "blood of the covenant." See, for example, Hagner, *Matthew*, 2:773: "The blood here is not the blood that was necessary to the first covenant (cf. Heb 9:18) but that which inaugurates the new covenant; thus although the word *kainē*, 'new,' does not occur here ... it is to be presupposed ..." That Matthew has Jesus make the additional mention of his blood being poured out for the forgiveness of sins seems to cement the allusion to Jer. 31: "Now it is important to note that in Jer. 31.31–34 the promise of a new covenant is paralleled by the promise of forgiveness for the sins under the old covenant. This combination of new covenant and forgiveness of sins is present whenever this passage of Jeremiah is referred to in the New Testament (Heb. 8:8; 9:14f.; 10.16f.; cf. also Rom 11.27" (Seyoon Kim, *The Son of Man as the Son of God*, Wissenschaftliche Untersuchungen zum Neuen Testament 30 [Tübingen: Mohr-Siebeck, 1983], 62).

Some texts even envision Gentiles seeking righteousness and learning the law of God in the future.[56] A number of texts also link the eschatological age with purification and the cleansing of uncleanness.[57] Zechariah explains that *all* the pots in Jerusalem—not simply those used in the Temple—will be sacred to the Lord (see Zech. 14:21). Such hopes are also attested in other Second Temple sources,[58] and later Jewish works.[59] Clearly such ideas would imply a transcending of clean/unclean categories presumed by the law.

Moreover—and this is crucial—*in many cases eschatological holiness seems to entail certain realities that conflict with the norms of the Torah.* Such is the case with the scenario envisioned in Isaiah 19:19, where the eschatological age is linked with the offering of sacrifices on an *altar in Egypt*—something which conflicts with the law's regulations for a central sanctuary in Deuteronomy 12:13–14.[60] Likewise,

---

56 See, for example, Isa. 2:3; 42:4; 51:4; Mic. 4:2.

57 See, for example, Isa. 4:4; 30:22; 35:8; 52:1, 11; Jer. 33:8; 43:12 Ezek. 36:25, 29, 33; 37:23; 39:12, 14, 16, 24; 43:20, 22–23; 44:23; 45:18; Dan. 11:35; 12:8; Zech. 13:1, 2; 14:21; Mal. 3:3.

58 This expectation is especially seen in the Dead Sea Community whose eschatological outlook was inextricably linked with strict Torah observance and purity concerns. Numerous texts could be mentioned here. 4Q394–399 explains that the community separated themselves from the people because of the need to escape the impurity that had resulted from disobedience to the law. 1Q28 5:7–12 explains that all enrolled in the community—which was apparently understood in terms of the eschatological remnant (for example, CD 6:19; 8:21; 15:5–8; 19:33–34; 20:10–12)—were required to swear an oath to keep the law of Moses (CD 15:7–10). 1Q28 3:4–6 explains that he who is not a part of the community is defiled. Furthermore, the Temple Scroll looks forward to the coming of the eschatological age in which purity will be restored (see 11Q19 47:3–17). For a fuller discussion, see Hannah K. Harrington, "Purity" in *Encyclopedia of the Dead Sea Scrolls*, eds. L. H. Schiffman and J. C. VanderKam, 2 vols. (Oxford: Oxford University Press, 2000), 724–729; Karen J. Wenell, *Jesus and Land: Sacred and Social Space in Second Temple Judaism*, Library of New Testament Studies 334 (London: T & T Clark, 2007), 85–91. The eradication of impurity and the establishment of righteousness is also a major theme in *Psalms of Solomon* 17 (see 17:22, 26–27, 30, 32). In addition, see *Jubilees* 50:5: "And jubilees will pass until Israel is purified from all the sin of fornication, and defilement, and uncleanness, and sin and error. And then it will not have any Satan or evil (one). And the land will be purified from that time and forever" (*OTP* 2:142).

59 Certain passages even indicate the coming of a new Torah. The Targum on Isa. 12:3 reads: "*And* you will accept *a new teaching* with joy from *the chosen ones of righteousness*" (Chilton, *Isaiah Targum*, 29). Likewise, see *Midrash Ecclesiastes* 2:1: "All the Torah which you learn in this world is 'vanity' in comparison with Torah [which will be learnt] in the World to Come" (cited from M. Simon, ed., *Midrash Rabbah, VIII: Ruth, Ecclesiastes* [London/New York: Soncino Press, 1983], 51). The new law is even specifically linked with the Messiah: "God will sit and expound a new Torah which he will give, on days, by the hand of the Messiah" (*Yal.* on Isa. 26:2). See W. D. Davies, *The Setting of the Sermon on the Mount*, repr. (Cambridge: Cambridge University Press, 1966 [1963]), 183–190 (446–447); W. D. Davies, *Torah in the Messianic Age and/or the Age to Come*, Society of Biblical Literature Monograph Series 7 (Philadelphia: Society of Biblical Literature, 1952). Of course, these texts are difficult to date and do appear somewhat obscure. See Peter Schäfer, "Die Torah der messianischen Zeit," *Zeitschrift für die neutestamentliche Wissenschaft* 65 (1974): 27–42.

60 See John D. Watts, *Isaiah 1–33*, Word Biblical Commentary 24, rev. ed. (Dallas: Thomas Nelson, 2005), 315: "This is the most positive interpretation of the outward flow of population

Isaiah indicates that the eunuchs and foreigners will worship with Israel at the Temple (see Isa. 56:3–8)—something which obviously stands in tension with the law's exclusion of such people from the cultic assembly in Deuteronomy 23:1–6.[61] In other words, Israel's prophetic texts and other Jewish works seem to imply that the righteousness of the eschatological age will transcend the regulations of the law.

Later Jewish interpretation would therefore recognize that some aspects of the Torah would not remain binding after the coming of the Messiah. For example, it was believed that, with the exception of the thank offering, sacrifices would cease (see *Pesiq. Rab.* 12; *Lev. Rab.* 9.7). Likewise, *Yalqut* on Proverbs 9:2 explains that all the festivals will cease except Purim and the Day of Atonement. The Midrash on Psalm 146:7 suggests that the kosher laws will also pass away.[62] While these rabbinic teachings are clearly taken from much later sources, they highlight the notion that an eschatological transcending of the law, clearly suggested in the scriptures of Israel, is consistent with a Jewish context.

In light of such expectations we can perhaps better understand Jesus' teaching in Matthew. In teaching that he has come to fulfill the law and the prophets in Matthew 5:17, Jesus explains that the law pointed forward to him and to the eschatological age that he heralds.[63] The fulfillment he has brought in no way an-

---

from Israel in the OT (comparable only to the NT's commissions in Matt. 28:19–20; Acts 1:8) … An altar implies sacrifice and a priesthood (perhaps, though not necessarily, even a temple)." The passage goes on to describe how the Assyrians will join with the Egyptians in worshipping the Lord (see Isa. 19:23).

61 The inconsistency is recognized by many scholars. See Allison, *Resurrecting Jesus*, 192: "Isa 56:1–8 which in Jesus' day would have been understood as eschatological, plainly depicts the undoing of Deuteronomy's exclusion of eunuchs from the temple." See, for example, the discussion in Grace J. Emmerson, *Isaiah 56–66* (Sheffield: Sheffield Academic Press, 1992), 15: "Deut 23:1–3 is replaced by a new prophetic *torah* by which both foreigners and eunuchs … are welcomed into the worshipping community." Others have also made this point. See, for example, Amy L. Grant-Henderson, *Inclusive Voices in Post-Exilic Judah* (Collegeville: The Liturgical Press, 2002), 2–3; William F. Herzog, *Jesus, Justice and the Reign of God: A Ministry of Liberation* (Louisville: Westminster John Knox Press, 2000), 140–141; John Oswalt, *Writing and Reading the Scroll of Isaiah: Studies of an Interpretive Tradition*, 2 vols., eds. C. C. Broyles and C. A. Evans (Leiden: Brill, 1997), 1:426; John Oswalt, *The Book of Isaiah: Chapters 40–66*, New International Commentary on the Old Testament (Grand Rapids: Eerdmans, 1998), 458.

62 See the further discussion in Davies, *Torah in the Messianic Age*, 50–83; Davies, *Setting of the Sermon on the Mount*, 161–172.

63 This view has been gaining adherents in recent research. See, for example, France, *Gospel of Matthew*, 183–184; France, *Matthew*, 113–114; Banks, *Jesus and the Law in the Synoptic Tradition*, 203–235; Banks, "Matthew's Understanding of the Law: Authenticity and Interpretation in Matthew 5:17–20," *Journal of Biblical Literature* 93 (1974): 226–242; John P. Meier, *Law and History in Matthew's Gospel*, 41–124, especially 160–161; Douglas J. Moo, "Jesus and the Authority of the Mosaic Law," *Journal for the Study of the New Testament* 20 (1984): 3–49; Yong-Eui Yang, *Jesus and the Sabbath in Matthew's Gospel*, Journal for the Study of the New Testament Supplement Series 139 (Sheffield: Sheffield Academic Press, 1997), 106–120, 128–129; Davies and Allison, *Matthew*, 1:486–487; Keener, *Matthew*, 177–178; M. Eugene Boring, "The Gospel of Matthew," 189; Turner, *Matthew*, 162.

nuls the law and the prophets. On the contrary, it offers their definitive validation since what they pointed to has now arrived.[64] Jesus' teaching in 5:21–22, "you have heard that it was said ... but I say to you," and the teaching which follows must therefore be understood against this backdrop.[65]

Moreover, according to Matthew, for Jesus the fulfillment of the law does not necessarily involve recognizing each and every one of the commandments as upholding the perfect standard of righteousness. As the prophets and later Jewish writers hoped, Jesus indicates that the dawning of the eschatological age involves a transcending of the Torah. This is especially clear in Jesus' teaching on divorce and remarriage in Matthew 5 and 19. Certain aspects of the law were in fact concessions to Israel's "hardness of heart." Some laws effectively sanctioned behavior that involved material evil (for example, divorce and remarriage are equated with adultery). The fulfillment that Jesus makes a reality does not involve rejecting the value of these laws. Yet their value must be carefully understood—ultimately they pointed beyond themselves. By accommodating Israel's sinfulness, such concessionary precepts actually revealed the penultimate nature of the law. That certain regulations were given because of Israel's "hardness of heart" highlighted the law's insufficiency and pointed beyond itself. Jesus' fulfillment of the law thus involves his announcement of the age of eschatological holiness that restores in some sense what was "from the beginning." He has come not to "relax" the law's standards but to bring about a better holiness, one that does not require these concessions.

Conclusion

Matthew 5 is a complex text. In 5:17–20, Jesus insists that he has come not to abolish the law and the prophets. However, in the so-called "antitheses" that follow

64 See Davies and Allison, *Matthew*, 1:487: "... if the law is fulfilled, it cannot on that account be set aside. Fulfillment can only confirm the Torah's truth, not cast doubt upon it." Helpful also is the conclusion offered by France (*Gospel of Matthew*, 186), who sums up the meaning of v. 18 as follows: "The jots and tittles are there to be fulfilled, not discarded, and that is what Jesus has come to do. They are not lost, but taken up into the eschatological events to which they pointed forward ... [W]e might paraphrase the whole saying as follows: 'The law, down to its smallest details, is as permanent as heaven and earth, and will never lose its significance; on the contrary, all that it points forward to will in fact become a reality.' Now that that reality has arrived in Jesus, the jots and tittles will be seen in a new light, but they still cannot be discarded."

65 See Andrew Chester, *Messiah and Exaltation: Jewish Messianic and Visionary Traditions and New Testament Christology*, Wissenschaftliche Untersuchungen zum Neuen Testament 207 (Tubingen: Brill, 2007), 505: "[W]hat we have in these Antitheses is an *eschatological transcending* of the provision of the Torah. That does not mean that the Torah is abandoned, or simply contradicted. But in this altogether new age, Torah is now taken to an utterly new level. It is both taken up and transformed. Thus it is now fulfilled in the truest sense. ... What [Jesus' teaching] involves, in fact, is potentially a whole way of life that takes on a radically new dimension, and transcends what has been countenanced hitherto." See also Harrington, *Matthew*, 90: "Since the antitheses follow Matt 5:17–20 which affirms that Jesus came not to abolish but to 'fulfill' the Law and the Prophets, it would seem that the antitheses are intended to illustrate in what that fulfillment consists."

in vv. 21–46, he seems to contrast his teaching with the standards of the law itself. In particular, Jesus' teaching on divorce and remarriage seems to involve doing precisely what he had said he had *not* come to do: nullify the law.

In this article we have argued that Jesus recognized what many Old Testament scholars have noted: at points the law itself seems to sanction practices that are contrary to its own principles. In particular, Deuteronomy seems to make concessions to behavior not only absent in the preceding books of the Torah but that even contradict the law's own stated standards. Indeed, as we have argued above, Ezekiel's recognition that God gave Israel "statutes that were not good" reveals that ancient readers caught such inconsistencies in the law.

Jesus' teaching on divorce and remarriage in Matthew 19 seems to echo a view similar to Ezekiel's. There he explains that divorce and remarriage was only tolerated by Moses because of Israel's "hardness of heart," stating that "from the beginning it was not so." This, as we have seen, summarizes the canonical record: there is no provision for divorce and remarriage until the book of Deuteronomy. For Jesus in Matthew, the regulations for this practice entailed nothing less than the sanctioning of adultery. Moreover, that the specific idea of Deuteronomic concessions is in view seems to be suggested from the geography of the passage—Jesus offers his teaching on divorce and remarriage in the very place where Moses delivered the laws of Deuteronomy to Israel ("the region beyond the Jordan").

In Matthew 5, then, Jesus maintains that he has brought fulfillment to the law and the prophets because he has ushered in what they anticipated. The concessionary ordinances of the law are not rejected as evil but as evidence of the penultimate nature of the law itself. The prophetic hope for an age marked by a radically new kind of holiness has arrived. With the dawning of the new covenant age, Jesus calls his disciples to be "perfect as your heavenly father is perfect" (Matt. 5:48), a standard of righteousness impossible to achieve on one's own but now made possible by God (see Matt. 19:26). Because of this the concessionary laws have now been transcended. Jesus has ushered in the age of a "better holiness" in which such precepts are no longer necessary.[66]

66 The author would like to thank John Bergsma, Brant Pitre, and Curtis Mitch for making helpful comments on this paper, which strengthened the argument. However, any shortcomings in this paper should be attributed to the author and not to them.

Letter & Spirit 9 (2014): 51-75

"These Least Brothers of Mine"
A Reappraisal of the Great Judgment Scene as Apocalyptic Retribution in Matthew 25:31–46

William A. Bales

Mount St. Mary's Seminary

I. Introduction

"And the King will answer them, 'Truly, I say to you, as you did it to one of these least brothers of mine, you did it to me.'" So reads the verse at the very heart of one of the most misunderstood passages in the Gospel of Matthew. The general contours of the dramatic scene in Matthew 25:31–46 are well known. Jesus comes with the angelic hosts in great power and glory to a vast multitude of people, identified as "all the nations." From his glorious throne he sits as judge to separate this multitude into two groups, one signified "sheep," the other, "goats." The criteria for this separation are revealed as six specific charitable works performed on yet another group, identified as "these least brothers of mine." The seriousness of the drama reaches shocking proportions as the group signified as "goats" are sent away to everlasting punishment, while the "sheep" inherit the heavenly kingdom, everlasting life.

The interpreter is confronted with a raft of puzzling questions[1]: (1) identifying "these least brothers of mine"; (2) finding the significance, if any, of the six specific "works of mercy" Jesus lists; (3) classifying the genre of the passage; (4) finding the significance and contribution of the passage at this juncture in Matthew's gospel narrative, and, more specifically, its significance at this point (the conclusion) in the so-called "Olivet" discourse (Matt. 24–25); (5) correlating themes and ideas from the passage with texts elsewhere in Matthew; (6) situating this scene in the overall eschatology of Matthew's gospel; (7) identifying the "nations" in 25:32; (8) how people could have served Jesus without, apparently, having ever met him; (9) understanding how the time frame of the scene (AD 70? The end of the world?).

The almost ubiquitous understanding of the text today—especially at the popular level—is that an individual's eternal destiny hinges upon whether or not, in the course of one's life, one has performed the six works of mercy listed in verses 35–36 (and, perhaps, similar works) to persons in need (understood as "these least brothers" of Jesus).[2] Helping the poor, the "disenfranchised," the "unfortunates" of

---

1 I list here the primary interpretive problems; there are others. Here I list them in order of priority or seriousness, at least as I see it. Not all of these will be addressed in this article.

2 The text of Matt. 25:35–36 (RSV) reads, "For I was (1) hungry and you gave me food, I was (2) thirsty and you gave me drink, I was (3) a stranger and you welcomed me, I was (4) ill-clad and you clothed me, I was (5) sick and you visited me, I was (6) in prison and you came

the world becomes therefore the primary focus of the Christian life, inasmuch as attaining unending life in the heavenly kingdom would (rationally) be a person's highest aspiration. "As you did it to these least ..."—interpreted as helping the "unfortunates" among us—has become the motto of many parishes and charitable organizations and is a common rhetorical prod in fundraising efforts. Indeed, Matthew 25:31–46 has been employed by countless groups, both religious and otherwise, in their efforts to raise money to help people with various needs.

Taken to its logical conclusion, one which I have encountered from various pulpits over the last 25 years many times, the "unfortunates" interpretation calls into question the necessity of God even sending his son into the world as savior. If our primary obligation in life is to take care of the unfortunates among us, then what's the point of believing in Christ? The world had access to this sort of ethic long before Christ came (for example, in the OT, as well as in many other religions and philosophies). What's the point of a church if attaining the heavenly kingdom is possible by simply taking care of "the least of these"? And why, on Sunday morning, are we not down the street serving at a soup kitchen or helping out at Habitat

---

to me" [works enumerated]. Scholars who hold to the more common interpretation—what I will call the "unfortunates" interpretation in this article—include, for example, Rudolph Schnackenburg, *The Gospel of Matthew*, trans. Robert R. Barr (Grand Rapids: Eerdmans, 2002), 258–259; Douglas Hare, *Matthew* (Louisville: John Knox, 1993), 290; John P. Meier, *Matthew* (Collegeville, MN: The Liturgical Press, 1980), 304; Frederick D. Bruner, *Matthew, A Commentary: The Churchbook, Matthew 13–28* (Grand Rapids: Eerdmans, 2004), 563–577; W. D. Davies and Dales C. Allison, *The Gospel According to Saint Mathew*, 3 vols., International Critical Commentary (Edinburgh: T & T Clark, 1997), 429–430.

A minority of scholars hold that "the least" should be restricted to needy Christians, for example, Donald A. Hagner, *Matthew 14–28*, Word Biblical Commentary, vol. 33b (Nashville: Thomas Nelson, 1995), 744–745; Graham Stanton, *A Gospel for a New People: Studies in Matthew* (Edinburgh: T & T Clark, 1992), 207–231; Daniel J. Harrington, *The Gospel of Matthew*, Sacra Pagina vol. 1 (Collegeville, MN: Liturgical Press, 1991, 2007), 358–359 (Harrington thinks "the least" could include missionaries); R. T. France, *The Gospel According to Matthew: An Introduction and Commentary* (Grand Rapids: Eerdmans, 1985), 357–358; D. A. Carson, *Matthew*, The Expositor's Bible Commentary, vol. 8 (Grand Rapids: Zondervan, 1984), 518–521.

Another minority holds that by "the least," Jesus means missionary Christians, and perhaps the apostles (this is the view defended in this article). See, for example, Donald Senior, *Matthew*, Abingdon New Testament Commentaries (Nashville: Abingdon Press, 1998), 282–284; Craig S. Keener, *A Commentary on the Gospel of Matthew* (Grand Rapids: Eerdmans, 1999), 604–606; Robert H. Gundry, *Matthew: A Commentary on His Literary and Theological Art* (Grand Rapids: Eerdmans, 1982), 514; Richard B. Gardner, *Matthew* (Scottdale, PA: Herald Press, 1991), 358–360; David E. Garland, *Reading Matthew: A Literary and Theological Commentary on the First Gospel* (New York: Crossroad, 1993), 243–254; David L. Turner, *Matthew*, Baker Exegetical Commentary on the New Testament (Grand Rapids: Baker Academic, 2008), 604–611; George E. Ladd, *A Theology of the New Testament* (Grand Rapids: Eerdmans, 1974), 118–119; Lamar Cope, "Matthew XXV: 31–46, 'The Sheep and the Goats' Reinterpreted," *Novum Testamentum* 11 (1969): 32–44 at 39–40; J. Ramsey Michaels, "Apostolic Hardships and Righteous Gentiles," *Journal of Biblical Literature* 84 (1965): 27–37 at 28–31; T. W. Manson, *The Sayings of Jesus As Recorded in the Gospels According to St. Matthew and St. Luke* (Grand Rapids: Eerdmans, 1979), 248–252.

for Humanity instead of going to church? Not surprisingly, certain commentators who embrace today's standard approach to the passage have said as much. Arland Hultgren, in his well-known commentary on the parables of Jesus, concludes his treatment of Matthew 25:31–46 as follows:

> If Christ is seen clearly in the disfigured faces of the unfortunates, one may indeed be moved to serve him. But, in fact, according to this passage, Christ is actually hidden in those faces; his face is obscured by the faces of the unfortunates. People therefore do not know that it is Christ whom they serve—or fail to serve. Gone is the view here that the only way one can serve Christ (or God) is a prior commitment to him. The old argument that one must be religious in order to be moral—and so religious faith becomes only instrumental to ethics—goes by the board. The down-to-earth service of the person in need—without any sense of religious obligation or motivation—*that* is service to Christ! Christ's true servants, then, know nothing about him, but seek only to serve the neighbor.[3] [his emphasis]

Francis Watson states the matter a little more baldly:

> The parable of the sheep and the goats asserts both the secret solidarity of the Son of man with the oppressed and the possibility that his true servants are those who know nothing of him but only seek to serve their oppressed neighbor. *The heathen* may act not so much as "anonymous Christians" but as servants of the anonymous Christ. ... Naturally the church should perform works of mercy to the oppressed inside and outside its own communal boundaries, and in so far as it does so its members will be found among the sheep rather than the goats. But if the works of justice and mercy are regarded as the sole criterion, then *the communal and confessional context out of which they proceed is irrelevant*. Even *the worshippers of idols*, who constitute the overwhelming majority in the group designated as *panta ta ethnē* ["all the nations"] (25.32), may feed the hungry and visit the prisoners; and in so far as they do so *they are the true servants of the anonymous Christ.*[4] [my emphasis]

3 Arland J. Hultgren, *The Parables of Jesus: A Commentary* (Grand Rapids, MI: Eerdmans, 2000), 326–327.

4 Francis Watson, "Liberating the Reader: A Theological-Exegetical Study of the Parable of the Sheep and the Goats (Matt. 25.31–46)," in *The Open Text: New Directions for Biblical Studies?* (London: SCM Press, 1993), 71–72. Examples of this sort of interpretation could be multiplied. See, for example, Bruner, *Matthew*, 563–577.

The purpose of this study is to present a more satisfactory understanding of Matthew 25:31–46. First I will point out some of the serious problems with the "unfortunates" interpretation, then move to an analysis of the genre and text of the passage with the aim of ascertaining Matthew's primary intention and meaning.

II. Problems with the "Unfortunates" Interpretation

Soteriology[5]

Inasmuch as Matthew 25:31–46 has an acute concern about how a person will or will not attain everlasting life, an important question to ask is whether or not the "unfortunates" interpretation of how a person attains this wonderful end is found elsewhere in Matthew. The answer is an unambiguous "no."

In Matthew, the basis of individual salvation is exercising faith in the only one who can save, Jesus. That, after all, was the reason behind his naming, for "he will save his people from their sins" (Matt. 1:21). In Matthew, humans are in a catastrophic situation as a result of sin. Utterly lost and without hope, salvation is, humanly speaking, "impossible" (Matt. 19:26). In Matthew, the program of salvation is illustrated by the many maladies Jesus miraculously heals. He alone is portrayed as the source of healing, restoration, and wholeness. What Matthew conveys via the narration of Jesus' marvelous physical restorations is the notion of a metaphysical restoration involving the forgiveness of sins, a transformed human nature, and restored fellowship with God (hence one of Jesus' other titles in Matthew, "Emmanuel"—God with us).

Thus, in Matthew, Jesus' primary concerns are to forgive sin (Matt. 9:2, 6), restore a disfigured and fatally flawed humanity, and reconcile people to God. Jesus' statement about coming to "serve" by giving his life as a "ransom for many" (Matt. 20:28) is pointedly connected with his passion and death by which a remedy to these problems would become available:

> [Jesus] will consummate this service [20:28] by the death of the suffering servant, an atoning sacrifice for the sake of and in the place of "many". ... His death above all is a sacrifice "for the remission of sins" (cf. 26:28), a "ransom" (*lytron*) which buys back, redeems, frees captive mankind from the grip of evil. ... Thus does the messianic king "save his people (the church) from their sins" (1:21).[6]

In Matthew, Jesus comes to save a humanity sunk in the mire of sin and guilt, incapable of extrication or transformation. He comes to offer a renewed spiritual

---

5 Or, "the study of salvation."

6 Meier, *Matthew*, 229.

life and hope for a life beyond this life. For Matthew, there is no other possible solution to humanity's dire and bleak situation than faith in Jesus.

Matthew's soteriology is rooted in his christology. It is because of Jesus' unique (divine) person, power, and authority that he, and he alone, can solve and rectify humanity's condition. Various titles and rhetoric are used by Matthew to convey this christology. Jesus is the Son of David and Son of Abraham (1:1)[7]. He is Emmanuel (1:23), the Savior (1:21), the King of the Jews (2:2; 27:11, 29, 37), the Christ (1:1; 2:4; 16:16 and others), and Son of God (3:17; 8:29; 16:16 and others). More Matthean christological titles could be added, but these suffice to show Matthew's portrayal of Jesus as the fulfillment of all the great promises of the Old Testament—promises having to do with a coming ruler, savior, judge, restorer, and deliverer who would set all things right.

Besides titles, many events in Matthew's narrative advance a christology which shows that faith in Jesus is indispensable for personal salvation. Jesus receives the adoring worship of the Magi, something Matthew's Jewish audience would have known was reserved only for divinity ("... and falling down, they [the Magi] worshipped him." [Matt. 2:11]). The great prophet, John the Baptist, by his own self-testimony is just a house-slave—if even that—compared to Jesus and compared to what Jesus was about to bring to the world (the Holy Spirit—Matt. 3:11). Jesus' miracles show him as the bringer-of-new-life, both physical and spiritual (see chapters 8–9, 12, 14–15, 20:29–33, 21:14). Especially important in this regard are the miracles that symbolically reconcile a person with God by removing uncleanness—for example, the leper, stopping a blood flow, and performing exorcisms.[8] Jesus is the rest-giver (11:28). He is the "ransom" for humanity (20:26–28; 26:28). Unique among the gospels, Matthew depicts certain events at Jesus' death as *life-giving*,[9] indicating, among other things, that only Jesus' death on the cross can bring *the dead to life* (27:51–54).[10]

More than the other gospels, Matthew portrays Jesus as a new and greater Moses, bringing a new and greater salvation (and law) that is patterned after the life of Moses and events connected with the Exodus, Passover, escape from Egypt, giving of the Law, and journey to the promised land.[11] Matthew's careful and

---

7 "Son" titles indicate that Jesus, as the "son" of these men will fulfill the covenant promises that God gave them. For a detailed study of these covenants and their promises, see Scott W. Hahn, *Kinship By Covenant: A Canonical Approach to the Fulfillment of God's Saving Promises*, Anchor Yale Bible Reference Library (New Haven, CT: Yale University Press, 2009), 101–135, 176–237. The covenantal promises are staggering in scope, emphasizing Matthew's high christology.

8 On this, see John Paul Heil, "Significant Aspects of the Healing Miracles in Matthew," *Catholic Biblical Quarterly* 41 (1979): 274–287.

9 Rocks were split, "the tombs also were opened, and many bodies of the saints who had fallen asleep were raised ... coming out of the tombs after his resurrection ..." (Matt. 27:51–53).

10 See Meier, *Matthew*, 352–353.

11 On this, see especially Dale C. Allison, *The New Moses: A Matthean Typology* (Minneapolis, MN: Fortress Press, 1993). Just one obvious and early example: Herod's attack on the

deliberate construction of Jesus as the new and perfect Moses builds a christology that sees Jesus' career as analogous to what Moses was and did. At the time of the Exodus, faith in and obedience to Moses were essential if one was to be "saved" from slavery in Egypt. One had to *follow him* (literally). So in Matthew: faith in and obedience to the New Moses, Jesus, is clearly necessary. Jesus alone can rescue a person from the "slavery" of sin and death (and from the tyrannical dominion of Pharaoh / Satan), bring his people through the sea (baptism), through the wilderness, provide sustaining manna and an abiding presence (in the Eucharist), give the law (the Sermon on the Mount), and (as Jesus / Joshua) bring them into the promised land.

The notion that Matthew would introduce a kind of "short cut" in 25:31–46—that having worked in one's life to meet the needs of the "unfortunates" will result in being ushered into the heavenly kingdom—irrespective of one's faith or even knowledge of Christ—would be, soteriologically speaking, astonishing. It would render as completely irrelevant the rich soteriological tapestry that Matthew has so carefully woven throughout his gospel narrative.

Further, in Matthew, being connected to the church is, soteriologically, a very important thing. Keeping in mind the new exodus theme, the church is the new Israel that goes out with the new Moses to get the new law, and, provided with the sustaining powers of the new sacraments, finally enters the new promised land. Matthew is clear about presenting the church as the channel or vehicle through which saving "graces" would be made available to the nations.

In Matthew 16:18 Jesus speaks of building his church, through which he will engage and conquer the "powers of death."[12] In Matthew 10 the pattern appears to be set (repeated in Matt. 24–25 and 28) that Jesus will authorize certain chosen ones to evangelize the nations. The feeding miracles in both 14:13–21 (the feeding of the 5000) and 15:32–39 (the feeding of the 4000)—both anticipating the eucharistic banquet (26:26–29)—portray life-giving food as being mediated by the disciples (probably meaning the twelve). These feeding actions anticipate a church with leadership that mediates God's saving gifts. In 18:15–20, it is *the church* that functions organizationally and juridically. In 28:16–20 the nations will be baptized into the church via the missionary efforts of Jesus' chosen and appointed emissaries. The "unfortunates" view of Matthew 25:31–46, if correct, would constitute a glaring aberration from a Matthean soteriology so closely connected with ecclesiology.

(angelically extricated) Christ-child (Matt. 2:13–18) is certainly intended by Matthew to recall Pharaoh's attack on Israelite male-children and Moses' providential extrication from that attack (Exod. 1:15–2:10). Jesus is a new Moses / Savior preserved from the murderous aspirations of a new Pharaoh / King via God's providential protection.

12 A useful (RSV) translation of the Greek *pulai hadou*, literally, "gates of Hades."

"Brethren" in Matthew

Another problem for the "unfortunates" interpretation of Matthew 25:31–46 is that when the word for "brother" (Greek = *adelphos*) is used in Matthew (often on the lips of Jesus), it is not used to refer to "any and all human beings." Matthew uses the term to indicate a more focused and specific group—usually those who have become his disciples—those who appear to have repented (to one degree or another), put their faith in him, and are following him.

It is true that the Greek word (*adelphos*) behind translations such as "brethren" or "brother(s)" is used in Matthew to indicate relations other than disciples. For example, the use of *adelphos* meaning "brother" as we understand it in our modern western culture (that is, as offspring of the same mother and/or father) is the clear meaning in Matthew 1:2, 11; 4:18, 21; 10:2, 21; 14:3; 17:1; 19:29; 20:24; and 22:24, 25. The meaning of *adelphos* is disputed at 12:46–48 and 13:55. Some hold it to mean "blood brother," that is, offspring of the same mother or father, as just previous. The other uses of the word *adelphos* in Matthew indicate a quasi-familial relation based on adherence to a common religious tradition. In some cases it refers to those who share the common tradition of Judaism with Jesus (5:22, 23, 24, 47; 7:3, 4, 5),[13] in others it refers to persons who are showing, at some level at least, faith in him (12:49, 50; 18:15, 21, 35; 23:8; 28:10).[14]

When Jesus speaks of "these least *brothers*" in Matthew 25:40, the meaning, especially in the context of Matthew 24–25 (where he is clearly addressing his *disciples*) is likely restricted to those who have put their faith in him. It is likely to be further restricted as meaning simply the twelve. As chapter 24 and 25 flow into chapter 26, the same group designated "disciples" in 24 and 25—and in the beginning of 26—becomes seamlessly "the twelve" at the Passover supper (see 26:19–20).

Taking Care of the Poor Not a Matthean Emphasis

Another problem for the standard "unfortunates" interpretation of Matthew 25:31–46 is the modest observation that *care for the poor is simply not an emphasis in the Gospel of Matthew.*[15] The word for "poor" (Greek = *ptochos*) is used only

---

13 The view of Benedict T. Viviano ("The Gospel According to Matthew," in *The New Jerome Biblical Commentary* [Englewood Cliffs, NJ: Prentice Hall, 1990], 669) and others who understand the "brethren" references in the Sermon on the Mount as being somewhat universal, that is, as meaning "all of humanity" is unlikely. In the Sermon on the Mount Jesus is addressing his *disciples* and others from a decidedly *Jewish* society, a "closed" religious group, the analog of those who would later constitute his church.

14 Some occurrences are, admittedly, ambiguous. See, for example, Matt. 23:8 where Jesus proclaims a group identified as "the crowds and his disciples" as brethren.

15 In this respect Matthew is very different from the Gospel of Luke, whose narrative is strewn with various material and references that show a keen concern for the poor and economically less fortunate. Luke also gives strong warnings about the danger of seeking riches. Some scholars point to Matt. 5:7; 9:13; 12:7; and 23:23 as "evidence" that Matthew does have a

five times in the entire gospel. In Matthew 11:5 and 19:21 it is used in contexts where helping the poor is not the issue.[16] In Matthew 5:3 "poor" is mentioned, but it is used in the phrase "poor in spirit," a phrase that certainly means something more than simply economic want. The word "poor" is also used in 26:9 and 26:11 in connection with Jesus having his head anointed with expensive ointment. In Matthew 6:2–4 the giving of alms appears, yet the issue at hand is not helping those in need so much as warning against hypocrisy. Besides this lexical data, the *theme* of helping the poor and needy is simply not in Matthew.

How astounding then, when the reader arrives at Matthew 25:31–46 and learns that his eternal destiny hinges *solely* on whether or not he has helped the poor! As we will see below, being astounded should serve as a hint that the reader has missed Matthew's (and Jesus') point.

One should also note that the Old Testament *sine qua non* of works done for the less fortunate—that of *taking care of widows and orphans*—is missing from Jesus' catalogue of works in Matthew 25:35–36 (repeated in 25:42–43). Numerous Old Testament texts implore the care of widows and orphans.[17] The "sojourner" is often grouped with the widow and orphan as persons singled out for special concern and attention, especially in Deuteronomy.[18] It is possible that this grouping, "sojourners, widows, and orphans" functioned in the OT as a metonym for any needy person or persons. It is surprising, therefore, for Jesus to make no mention of widows and orphans in the list of works in Matthew 25, if his purpose was to enjoin care for the unfortunates of the world.

A related problem for the "unfortunates" interpretation of Matthew 25:31–46 is that the idea of Jesus so closely identifying himself with the poor—again, *any* poor—would be unique in the gospel of Matthew. The two other places in Matthew where Jesus uses similar "identity" language are in 10:40 and 18:5. In 10:40 Jesus states: "He who receives you receives me, and he who receives me receives him who sent me." Here Jesus identifies himself not with the poor but with the twelve disciples being sent out on mission. Jesus tells the twelve that whenever people "receive" them (which would entail accepting their message [see 10:14])

---

thematic concern for the poor (see, for example, Schnackenburg, *Matthew*, 258). In response: Matt. 5:7 ("Blessed are the merciful" & etc.) certainly has more in view than just the materially needy. Matt. 9:13 and 12:7 reference Hos. 6:6, where the underlying Hebrew is *hesed* ("covenant fidelity"). Translated by the LXX and carried over into the NT as *eleos*, the meaning at 9:13 and 12:7 is better understood as it is in Hosea, "covenant fidelity." Matt. 23:23 (also *eleos*) may also have *hesed* underlying it. That one must scrape the barrel in this manner in order to find such scanty evidence of "helping the unfortunates" in Matthew only succeeds in proving my point.

16 The issue in 11:5 is that of compiling a list of deeds being done by Jesus as a message for the imprisoned John the Baptist. In 19:21 the context is that of challenging a wealthy man to overcome his love for riches.

17 To list but a few of the several dozen possible examples, see Deut. 24:17, 19–21; 26:12; Job 22:9; Pss. 94:6; 146:9; Jer. 22:3.

18 See throughout Deut. (11x); Pss. 94:6; 146:9; Ezek. 22:7; Zech. 7:10.

their "receptors" are actually receiving Him. "Identity" language is also found in Matthew 18:5: "Whoever receives one such child in my name receives me." Here, however, Jesus is teaching on humility and on turning from the natural tendency to want to be considered important, not on caring for the less fortunate.

The "unfortunates" interpretation has a further problem: none of the six works *necessarily* suggest that the recipients of the works are poor. They could just as easily suggest someone who is simply in need of one or more of the works at a specific time and place.

Another problem is that some commentators push the rhetorical severity of the six works so that the "least" are viewed as, for example, the downtrodden, the marginalized, the disenfranchised, the disfigured, and / or the oppressed.[19] None of the six works mentioned in Matthew 25:31–46 necessarily suggest any of these severe conditions. This sort of hyperbolic "shove" may be at home in the rhetoric of incautious homilies, but it is not the fruit of careful exegesis.

The "Unfortunates" View a Novelty in the History of Interpretation

Strangely, what seems like such an obvious interpretation of Matthew 25:31–46 to modern interpreters has not seemed so obvious to prominent interpreters and commentators down through the centuries. In his extensive treatment of the history of the interpretation of Matthew 25:31–46, Sherman Gray has shown that it wasn't until the *twentieth century* that the "unfortunates" view became the majority interpretation (65% of commentators investigated).[20] The nineteenth century was somewhat mixed (60% of commentators investigated interpreted the "least" as Christians or missionaries).[21] Prior to 1800, however, in every quarter and age, the more restricted view of the "least"—interpreted as either Christians or missionaries—was dominant.[22] The "unfortunates" interpretation was held by only a small minority of Church Fathers, for the most part as a secondary or tertiary interpretation.[23]

Gray's study does not prove the view that will be set forth in this article. It does, however, demonstrate that the dominant view at present is a relative newcomer, and is not firmly rooted in the interpretive tradition of the Church.

---

19 See, for example, Hultgren, *Parables*, 326; Watson, "Liberating the Reader," 69.

20 Sherman W. Gray, *The Least of My Brothers: Matthew 25:31–46; A History of Interpretation*, Society of Biblical Literature Dissertation Series 114 (Atlanta: Scholars Press, 1989), 347. All who wrestle with Matt. 25:31–46 are deeply indebted to Gray for this magisterial work.

21 Gray, *The Least of My Brothers*, 346.

22 Gray, *The Least of My Brothers*, 331–346.

23 Gray, *The Least of My Brothers*, 11–126, 331–342.

III. Toward a More Satisfying Interpretation of Matthew 25:31–46

The Genre of Matthew 24–25

In moving from an analysis of the many problems stemming from the common interpretation of Matthew 25:31–46, an important question to ask of the passage is that of genre. While virtually all commentators acknowledge that Matthew 24 is apocalyptic in genre, most do not see—or at least leave unstated—that the genre extends into chapter 25. By the time 25:31–46 is finally analyzed, a sustained awareness of the apocalyptic genre as *the* crucial interpretive backdrop has disappeared. The discussion of genre moves myopically to that of parable, pronouncement story, or whatever.[24] This is one of the most serious errors in the interpretive process for Matthew 25:31–46.

The genre categorized as "apocalyptic" is distinctive and is found in ancient sources like Daniel, Isaiah, 1 Enoch, and quintessentially, in the Book of Revelation.[25] The following elements are characteristic of the genre:

1. The life-setting is that the people of God are in, or, more commonly, *will be in*, some sort of serious distress, brought about by evil powers (human and/or angelic).

2. A messenger from heaven conveys a message, often to some important prophetic figure, to reveal (*apokaluptō*) what is about to take place—usually in a dream or trance-like setting. If the suffering is future, both the suffering and the subsequent vindication of God's people will be disclosed by the heavenly messenger. If the suffering is taking place at the time of the revelation, then what will primarily be in view is future vindication.

3. The people of God are either explicitly or implicitly exhorted and warned to remain faithful and loyal to God, his ways, and his mission during this upcoming time of suffering and distress (see Rev. 2–3; Dan. 7:25; 11:31–35; 12:10).

---

24 Notable exceptions to this critique are the studies by Graham N. Stanton, "The Gospel of Matthew and Judaism," *Bulletin of the John Rylands University Library of Manchester* 66 (1984): 264–284 at 280–281; and David C. Sim, *Apocalyptic Eschatology in the Gospel of Matthew* (Cambridge: Cambridge University Press, 1996), 227–235.

25 On this genre, see espec. Sim, *Apocalyptic Eschatology*, 31–69; also John J. Collins and Adela Y. Collins, "Apocalypses and Apocalypticism," *The Anchor Bible Dictionary*, 6 vols. (New York: Doubleday, 1992), 1.279–292; Alexander A. Di Lella, *The Book of Daniel: A New Translation with Introduction and Commentary*, Anchor Bible vol. 23 (Garden City, N.Y.: Doubleday, 1977), 62–77; Richard Bauckham, *The Theology of the Book of Revelation* (Cambridge: Cambridge University Press, 1993), 5–12.

4. A very important part of this genre concerns the announcement that a savior figure will eventually arrive in a glorious and spectacular fashion, usually with an angelic host, who will set things right by destroying the forces of evil and rewarding and thereby vindicating God's people who have remained faithful through the time of distress. The ultimate fate of both the righteous and the wicked is disclosed, and this fate is intimately connected to the coming or arrival of the savior figure.

5. In general, the arrival of the savior figure will be soon (relative to the "revelation").

6. In general, his arrival will be connected with what is understood as the "end" of time or at least the end of an epoch, ushering in some sort of new and revived world situation.

7. Before his arrival at the "end," various catastrophic "woes" will be unleashed or allowed by God on the world (for example, earthquakes, famines, lawlessness, the proliferation of evil in general, an unleashing of the forces of evil on God's people—both of a deceptive nature and perhaps physical persecution). These "woes" serve as signs of the impending end and function to alert God's people and perhaps others that the end is near.

8. These "woes" may affect all peoples, both the righteous and the wicked, but sometimes only the wicked are targeted.

9. Two qualities permeate apocalyptic: (1) dualism (both in the angelic and in the human sphere)—the radical disjunction and enmity between the forces of good and evil—and (2) an emphasis on a kind of "determinism" or divine sovereignty. In the midst of all the chaos and suffering, God is still in total control. Though it may not appear to be so, everything is going according to the divine plan and thus God will work everything out in his own time for the good of his people and for his own glory.

Apocalypses—be they brief (Matt. 10:16-42) or extensive (The Book of Revelation)—serve several purposes: (1) They encourage the people of God in and through their present trials and in anticipation of the coming woes via a heavenly disclosure that all will ultimately be set right. The labor, mission, and endurance of God's people will not be in vain. The righteous will be vindicated and receive salvation and various rewards; the wicked, especially those who persecute God's people and oppose his purposes, will be condemned and punished severely. (2) While the current (or soon-to-be) unhappy circumstances are not exactly explained in the apocalypse proper, the people of God are informed that God's good purposes are being realized even in the midst of their distress. All is taking place according to his plan—thus mitigating their anxiety and helping them to maintain their confidence in God. (3) The people of God are able to deduce that they are, in fact, God's chosen ones. They and they alone are "legitimized" in their own minds, bringing strength, encouragement, and comfort in the face of impending trial. (4) Importantly, and beyond *encouragement*, the people of God are *warned* in various ways to maintain their fidelity and trust in him during the present and upcoming distress.[26]

All of these elements are present in Matthew 24–25, marking the entire discourse, and not just Matthew 24, as a unified apocalypse:

1. The people of God (in this case, the twelve) are about to suffer distress in various ways. The general environment will be dangerous and fearful; deceivers will be about (24:4–5) and the twelve will be surrounded by unstable political conditions that will lead to wars and rumors of wars (24:6–7). Because of their missionary activity (24:14) they will suffer tribulation (undefined), hatred, betrayal, and death (24:9–12). Because of the delay of Jesus' parousia, the disciples will be tempted to stray from the path of righteousness (this is the basic hazard presented in the parables of the wicked household servant [24:45–51], the ten virgins [25:1–13], and the talent-entrusted servants [25:14–30]).

2. Here in Matthew 24–25, as in the "mini-apocalypse" of Matthew 10:16–42, the heavenly messenger (Jesus) is already present on the scene, so there is no need for a messenger to be sent from heaven, appearing in some dream or trance.

3. The apostles are exhorted / warned to fidelity (and to specific precautionary measures) during the upcoming time of distress, the interim period between Jesus' death / resurrection and his parousia. These exhortations / warnings occur throughout chapter 24. At the end of chapter 24, and continuing through 25:30, the warnings become longer, more descriptive, and parabolic. These warnings are primarily focused on being productive, diligent, and faithful during the time of mission, the interim time before the return of the

26 For more on the function of the genre, see Sim, *Apocalyptic Eschatology*, 220–241.

king. The warnings (exhortations) are logically connected to the (previously mentioned—24:14) upcoming mission of proclaiming the Kingdom. The Noahic simile (24:37–41), indicating that the exact day of Christ's parousia is unknown, leads to the warning (24:42) of constant readiness—meaning productive, faithful kingdom service, and, pointedly for the twelve, the mission to the nations mentioned in 24:14. The keynote theme of 24:42 (readiness for Christ's parousia) serves as an introduction that is developed first in the short analogy of the thief and householder (24:43–44), and then in three longer parables: the wicked household servant (24:45–51), the ten virgins (25:1–13), and the talent-entrusted servants (25:14–30).

4. Various eschatological "woes" and other signs (some spectacular) occur before Jesus' parousia. See (1) 24:6–8; (2) 24:11–12; (3) 24:15; (4) 24:24; (5) 24:29; (6) 24:37–39.

5. The savior figure, with his angels, arrives in a glorious and spectacular fashion, setting all things right by condemning the forces of evil and rewarding and vindicating God's faithful people: (1) 24:27; (2) 24:30–31; (3) 24:39–41; and, most importantly, (4) 25:31–46. Final judgment, salvation, and vindication are portrayed in 25:31–46 with a striking twist vis-a-vis comparable apocalypses. It's not just that the apostles will be saved and those who reject them and / or persecute them be condemned (as would be expected in normal apocalypses). Rather, the success and vindication of their *mission* is also in view.[27] Their *mission* of proclaiming the kingdom to the world (Matt. 24:14; see 10:5–7; 28:16–20) is vindicated—a group has responded to them and to their message (really two inseparable matters) and so are saved; those who reject them and their message are condemned.

Of note is that Jesus' discussion of his actual parousia as savior / judge before he arrives at 25:31–46 is rather sparse. Only in 25:31–46 do we find the kind of resolution one expects in apocalypses. Matthew 25:31–46 resumes and completes the parousia scene that was stated tersely in 24:27 and then again quite briefly and incompletely in two short verses just follow-

27 This assertion will be argued at length below; I make it here to give the reader a complete picture of the apocalypse that is present in Matt. 24–25.

> ing, 24:30–31. Matthew 25:31–46 presents the same scene, the same players, only now expanded and, fittingly, concluded.

Matthew 10:16–42: Relevance and Genre

Relevance

The missionary discourse in Matthew 10:16–42, while given to the twelve by Jesus before their proto-mission (explained in 10:1–15), clearly has more relevance to the post-resurrection mission given to them in chapter 28 than to the limited mission narrated in chapter 10. Matthew narrates nothing about the actual results or activities of this (evidently small and short) mission. When the twelve rejoin Jesus in 12:1 (plucking grain on the Sabbath), it's as if nothing had even taken place. There is no narration of any of the remarkable and severe events that Jesus foretells and warns of in 10:16–42. Though one could suppose that during this "proto-mission" the twelve experienced some opposition and some need for the kind of exhortative encouragement found in the discourse, they were manifestly not delivered up to councils, flogged in synagogues, dragged before governors and kings, or delivered up to death. Jesus didn't "come" before they had gone through all the towns of Israel (10:23).

All of this would happen post-resurrection, after the "great commission" in 28:16–20. Jesus uses the occasion of this first, limited mission—using elements of the apocalyptic genre—to convey the kind of information to the twelve that apocalypses generally convey and for reasons that apocalypses are generally used. When Jesus later speaks of the twelve's mission to the nations in 24:9, 14 and in 28:16-20, this information will not be repeated.[28] It is here instead.

Genre

Matthew 10:16–42 contains many elements of the apocalyptic genre, and therefore can fairly be categorized as a "mini-apocalypse." Of the nine elements listed above[29]—all of which are found in Matthew 24–25—the following are present in 10:16–42:

1. A heavenly messenger (Jesus) reveals what is about to take place (suffering, persecution, etc.).

2. The life-setting of the message is the proto-mission, but also (see just above) the mission post-resurrection, where the twelve will experience serious distress brought about by evil human beings, precipitated by the mission (10:16–25).

---

28 Matt. 24:9 very briefly mentions that the mission will end in death for some, but gives none of the extensive details that we find in chapter 10.

29 See above in the section just prior, *The Genre of Matthew 24–25*.

3. The twelve are explicitly exhorted and warned to remain faithful and loyal to God, His ways, and His mission during this upcoming time of difficult labor, hardship, and distress (10:24–39).

4. Jesus reveals that he (the savior figure) will arrive, it will be soon (10:23), and he will set things right by destroying the forces of evil and rewarding and vindicating the twelve, as well as vindicating the divine origins of their mission and message (10:40–42). The notice of Jesus' "coming" in 10:23, while not presented with the rich symbolism usually associated with apocalyptic, nonetheless permeates the rest of the discourse, intimating that all will be, in the end, set right.

5. Though not overtly concerned with notions of the "end" of time, ushering in some sort of new and revived world situation, 10:16–42 nevertheless gives certain information that presupposes that an eschaton will arrive with the coming of Jesus (10:26, 28, 32–33, 39, 40–42).

6. While 10:16–42 does not catalogue the kind of catastrophic "woes" typical of some apocalyptic, the interim time of the mission will nonetheless be punctuated by a general cold-heartedness that will lead to betrayal and murder—a kind of moral chaos (compare 10:34–36 with Matt. 24:10, 12).

7. Matthew 10:16–42 manifests both a dualism and an overlaying divine sovereignty that are typical of apocalypses. Evident is the dualistic language of us against them, light contrasted with dark, being acknowledged or denied, a sharp division among peoples, being worthy or not, and being rewarded or losing one's reward. God is, as well, sovereign over coming events. Jesus is not speaking of possibilities but certainties. In the midst of upcoming suffering, God is in control—everything works inexorably toward the time of judgment and retribution (10:26, 40–42).

Identifying Matthew 10:16–42 as apocalyptic, along with seeing the obvious parallel in concern (the mission to the nations) with chapters 24–25, help inform our interpretation of 24–25, which are concerned with the same mission. This is particularly the case when we come to interpret the *end* or conclusion of each respective apocalypse (that is, comparing 10:40–42 with 25:31-46). Both apocalypses end, as one would expect, with a glimpse of final retribution and vindication, which brings encouragement and hope to the twelve.[30] Both end, though using different rhetoric, with the notice that those who have (or, have not) *received the twelve* (and their message), have (or have not) actually *received Jesus*, and will be repaid accordingly.[31]

Analysis of Matthew 25:31–46

The context of Matthew 25:31–46 within Matthew 24–25

Jesus' lengthy response in 24:4–25:31 is to the disciples' question in 24:3, where they ask him concerning the timetable of the temple's destruction, the end of the age, and Jesus' parousia (his "coming"):[32] "Tell us, when will this be, and what will be the sign of your coming (*parousia*) and of the close of the age?" Much of the ensuing discourse, however, is taken up with matters pertaining to the upcoming apostolic mission to the nations,[33] directed as exhortations and warnings to the disciples.

Indeed, exhortations / warnings regarding the disciples upcoming *mission* begin in 24:37 and continue uninterrupted until 25:31. Matthew 25:31 once

30 I interpret the four groups mentioned in 10:40–42 as different ways of designating the *same* group—the group Jesus is talking to, the twelve. They are the ones being sent, they are the prophets, they are the righteous ones, they are the "little ones"—an appellation that anticipates "these least" in chapter 25. The reason I take these four to be the same group is that Jesus is speaking to *one group* (the disciples) who, given their new status as "sent ones," could have readily identified with the designations "prophet," "righteous man," and "little one." As such (meaning, "as all three"), they were about to be sent to whoever would receive them.

31 I realize that with respect to Matt. 25:31–46 this appears to beg the question; that "the least brethren" are the *twelve* who were (or were not) received on their gospel-proclaiming mission will be developed below.

32 I understand these three things as happening concurrently, at one and the same event. The temple's destruction will bring about the end of the age, and this only at Jesus' parousia. A detailed defense of this view is beyond the scope of this study. See, however, how earlier in Matt. 16:27–28 Jesus predicts that his parousia will take place before the death of some of the twelve present there at Caesarea Philippi—to me, at least, an obvious reference to AD 70, the time when the temple was destroyed (compare 24:34: "Truly, I say to you, this generation will not pass away till all these things take place.") For a concurring opinion, see Scott Hahn and Curtis Mitch, *The Gospel of Matthew*, Ignatius Catholic Study Bible (Ignatius: San Francisco, 2000), 60.

33 The word translated "nations" is *ethnos* (plural = *ethnē*). The first eight occurrences of *ethnos* in Matthew clearly mean "Gentiles," that is, *non-Jewish people*. The ninth occurrence (21:43) is ambiguous. The last five occurrences (24:7 [2x], 9, 14; 25:32; 28:19) most likely mean "nations," that is, all people groups, Jew and Gentile (on this, see, for example, John Meier, "Nations or Gentiles in Matthew 28:19?," *Catholic Biblical Quarterly* 39 [1977]: 94–102).

The more interesting question, however, given the high eschatological drama taking place in Matt. 24–25, is the question of which "people groups" are intended in Matt. 25:32. One's answer to this question is intertwined with the question of the timing of the events in 25:31–46. Is this the end of the world, where all the nations of the world stand before Christ, or is this AD 70, where the many *ethnē* which constitute Palestinian Jewry are judged? I think the latter, though a full defense must wait for a later study.

again picks up the matter of the parousia and effectively resumes the drama where 24:29–31 left off.[34] The series of intervening warnings, exhortations to readiness, again, typical of apocalyptic, are over. Now, in 31–46, we are told of final vindication—the sort of thing expected of an apocalypse—for the twelve and their mission. The receptive "nations" receive salvation; the unreceptive ones, damnation. The events in 31–46 are a recapitulation and augmentation of 24:29–31, and, for that matter, of 7:21–23,[35] 10:14–15,[36] 10:40–42; 11:22–24; 12:41–42, 13:40–43, 13:49–50, 16:27, 19:28–30, and 26:64.[37]

Matthew 24–25 is Jesus' revelatory discourse to his disciples about events that will (and did) take place within a generation of his death and resurrection: the destruction of the Jerusalem temple (AD 70) and with it the end of the old covenant age and the judgment upon *that generation,* meaning all the towns and cities of what was then "Israel" (see 10:23;[38] 23:34[39]), and finally Jerusalem itself (see 23:37–39[40]). Jesus' discourse foreshadows events that will bear a similar contour at the end of the world.

Identifying "These Least Brethren of Mine"

In Matthew, the word for brethren (*adelphos*) can indicate several possible meanings.[41] Here, however, the likely meaning is *disciple,* and, more specifically, the *twelve*

---

34 Matthew 24:29–31: "Immediately after the tribulation of those days the sun will be darkened, and the moon will not give its light, and the stars will fall from heaven, and the powers of the heavens will be shaken; [30] then will appear the sign of the Son of man in heaven, and then all the tribes of the earth will mourn, and they will see the Son of man coming on the clouds of heaven with power and great glory; [31] and he will send out his angels with a loud trumpet call, and they will gather his elect from the four winds, from one end of heaven to the other."

35 Matthew 7:21–23: [21] "Not every one who says to me, 'Lord, Lord,' shall enter the kingdom of heaven, but he who does the will of my Father who is in heaven. [22] On that day many will say to me, 'Lord, Lord, did we not prophesy in your name, and cast out demons in your name, and do many mighty works in your name?' [23] And then will I declare to them, 'I never knew you; depart from me, you evildoers.'"

36 Matthew 10:14–15: "And if any one will not receive you or listen to your words, shake off the dust from your feet as you leave that house or town. Truly, I say to you, it shall be more tolerable on the day of judgment for the land of Sodom and Gomorrah than for that town."

37 Matthew 26:64: "Jesus said to him, 'You have said so. But I tell you, *hereafter you will see the Son of man seated at the right hand of Power, and coming on the clouds of heaven.'"*

38 Matthew 10:23: "When they persecute you in one town, flee to the next; for truly, I say to you, you will not have gone through all the towns of Israel, before the Son of man comes."

39 Matthew 23:34: "Therefore I send you prophets and wise men and scribes, some of whom you will kill and crucify, and some you will scourge in your synagogues and persecute from town to town ..."

40 Matthew 23:37–39: "O Jerusalem, Jerusalem, killing the prophets and stoning those who are sent to you! How often would I have gathered your children together as a hen gathers her brood under her wings, and you would not! [38] Behold, your house is forsaken and desolate. [39] For I tell you, you will not see me again, until you say, 'Blessed is he who comes in the name of the Lord.'"

41 See above, p. 57.

disciples that Jesus has been talking to throughout chapters 24–25. Before 25:31 there has been no final resolution and vindication for the disciple / missionaries. In v. 31 Jesus shifts from warning the disciples to bringing before their minds a majestic—not to say somewhat frightening—parable-like judgment scene. Before the great throne are the sheep, the goats, and Jesus' "least brothers."

Jesus' use of the proximate demonstrative adjective "these" (*toutōn*) in the phrase "one of these least brothers of mine" (*heni toutōn tōn adelphōn mou tōn elachistōn*) suggests that at 25:31 he shifts from speaking *to* the twelve and is now speaking *about* them. "These least" are singled out, a group separate from the *sheep*—and hardly a subset of the *goats*. They are "the least" (*tōn elachistōn*) of the larger set of "brothers" (*tōn adelphōn*). They are nearby, visible, and present to both sheep and goats, and hence the use of the proximate demonstrative "these" instead of just the definite article "the" (*tōn*). Further, the "fronting" of *toutōn* in the phrase *toutōn tōn adelphōn mou tōn elachistōn* (that is, putting it before the rest of the clause), puts special emphasis on this group, suggesting that they are to be understood as a third group in the scene. The apostles are hearing about themselves in the final part of the apocalypse in this parable-like scene, even as in chapter 10 they heard about themselves at the end of the "mini-apocalypse" (10:40–42).[42]

The reference to the word "least" associates 25:40 (and 25:45) with texts from earlier in Matthew that concern Jesus' disciples. One of those places, significantly, is 10:42: "And whoever gives to one of these *little ones* even a cup of cold water—because he is a *disciple*—truly, I say to you, he shall not lose his reward." The phrase "one of these little ones ..." in 10:42 uncannily anticipates "one of these least ..." in 25:40, 45. The Greek word for "least" in chapter 25 (*elachistōn*) is used in the NT as the superlative of the word for "little ones" in 10:42 (*mikros*). Further, in Matthew 11:25 Jesus effectively refers to any and all of his disciples as "babes"; not to the wise and understanding, but to *babes* has the Father revealed the saving secrets of the kingdom. Finally, the narrative in Matthew 19:27–20:28 has an acute concern that a disciple of Jesus not seek worldly greatness, or seek to be "first" in the sense valued by the Gentiles. Rather, the disciple must seek to be a servant—and, in that sense, seek "littleness" and "lastness." With the sort of background these earlier Matthean texts provide, associating "*these least*" in 25:40, 45 with *the disciples* is not as far-fetched as might appear at first.

There is more. The nations are gathered for judgment before the exalted Christ on his "glorious throne" (*thronou doxēs*). The only other place in Matthew where the term "glorious throne" is used is when Jesus is speaking to the twelve disciples in chapter 19: "Jesus said to them, 'Truly, I say to you, in the new world, when the Son of man shall sit on his *glorious throne* (*thronou doxēs*), you who have

42 Scholars are divided on this important point—taking "these least" as a group separate from the sheep and goats. For a concurring view, see, among many others, Manson, *The Sayings of Jesus*, 248–252.

followed me will also sit on twelve thrones, judging the twelve tribes of Israel'" (Matt. 19:28). Assuming coherence in Matthew's eschatology, this reference in chapter 19 refers to the same event we are now witnessing in 25:31–46. Christ comes in glory, sitting on his glorious throne, judging the nations, of which the twelve tribes are a part. So where are the twelve disciples on their thrones? They are the "these" of 25:40, 45. Though least and of no-account in the world's eyes, they are now exalted to positions of honor before those they had been sent to evangelize. The last have become first, the first last; the least have become great, the servants now rule (Matt. 19:30; 20:16, 26–27).

Both on the level of Matthew's overall narrative and on the level of the apocalypse that is Matthew 24–25, identifying the "least" in 25:40, 45 as the disciples-now-apostles-now-judges makes good sense. Matthew's eschatology, though complicated, coheres. The apocalypse of 24–25 finds a denouement as, fittingly, all nations are judged in the presence of the "least" and on the basis of their response to the obedient proclamation of these same "least."

"These Least" and the Six Works of Mercy

Evidence from chapter 10 strengthens the understanding that the "least" in 25:40, 45 are the twelve disciples. The specific works mentioned in 25:31–46, performed for the "least," correspond remarkably to the needs that the twelve were to experience on their proto-mission in chapter 10.

The "proto-mission" in chapter 10 functions as a kind of blueprint for the post-resurrection mission to the world (seen especially in the revelatory discourse in 10:16–42). In that proto-mission, the twelve were to take no money with which to buy food or drink (10:9–10), and so they would be dependent on those who might receive them for these provisions, something we find in 25:35 ("I was hungry and you gave me food, I was thirsty and you gave me drink"). They had no money for shelter, and they were directed by Jesus to go forth with what was, effectively, insufficient clothing (10:10, "nor two tunics"). Again, they would be dependent on those who might receive them for these necessities. Correspondence is found in 25:35–36: "I was a stranger and you welcomed me, I was ill-clad[43] and you clothed me."

Before the proto-mission, Jesus tells his apostles that they would suffer bodily tortures and be dragged before governors and kings (10:17–18). The last two so-called "works of mercy" in 25:36 nicely attend to these adversities: "... ill

43 The Greek word used here, *gumnos*, can literally mean "naked" (so RSV and NABRE), but often means simply "uncovered" in the sense of being inadequately clothed or not having an outer garment. See W. Bauer, W. F. Arndt, and F. W. Gingrich, 3d ed., rev. by F. W. Danker, *Greek-English Lexicon of the NT* (Chicago: Chicago University Press, 2000), [hereafter, BDAG] s.v. γυμνος (*gumnos*). A NT example of an ill-clad missionary is the apostle Paul, who lists as one of the hardships he regularly experienced on his missions as being "in cold and exposure" (2 Cor. 11:27). See also 2 Tim. 4:13, where Paul writes to Timothy from prison, "When you come, bring the cloak that I left with Carpus at Troas. ..."

and you cared for me, in prison and you visited me." Being dragged before rulers would certainly involve some imprisonment, necessitating sustaining help from someone—in 25:36 from the "sheep."[44] The Greek word translated here as "ill," *astheneō*, denotes not only the debilitating weakness that comes as a result of disease but also the sort of weakness that comes from things like, for example, beatings, which would fit well here in Matthew 25:36, where it is coupled, as the rhetoric of the passage suggests, with imprisonment.[45]

The exalted Christ mentions these six "works of mercy" in chapter 25 because what is at issue is whether or not a particular people group received the apostles, exemplified and signified by the sorts of works he lists, works done to meet the needs of the missionary apostles. One must not miss Jesus' deeper point: the works are emblematic of having received not just the messenger but *the message* of the missionaries,[46] that is, they became disciples of Jesus through the vehicle of his emissaries. *Receiving the message* is the basis on which eternal life is granted (or not).[47] That receiving the message was the real point of the mission in chapter 10 (and thus in the post-resurrection mission that is in view in the Matthew 25 judgment scene) can be seen not only in 10:14, 40–42, but also plainly in11:20–24, where Jesus forecasts doom on the cities who had received his benefits (healings, etc.) but not his message of repentance and faith (see also 12:41–42).

Further, on the level of Matthew's story, one could posit that Jesus' words in chapter 25 to the nations about having done (or not) the six works to him would have been readily understandable and recognizable to the twelve who sat there on the Mount of Olives listening to this discourse, for during the "proto-mission" they had already lived through and experienced, at least to some limited degree, these very sorts of kindnesses or deprivations (the six works), necessitated by the terms of Jesus' commission (Matt. 10:8–11).

Works similar to those performed for the twelve in Matthew 10 and 25, signifying being on mission or signifying the reception of the Gospel message, are found in Paul: (1)"To the present hour we hunger and thirst, we are ill-clad and buffeted and homeless ..." (1 Cor. 4:11); (2) "... on frequent journeys ... in toil and

44 For a detailed and illuminating treatment of prisons and imprisonment in the ancient Roman world, see Craig S. Wansink, *Chained in Christ: The Experience and Rhetoric of Paul's Imprisonments*, Journal for the Study of the New Testament Supplement Series 130 (Sheffield: Sheffield Academic Press, 1996), 27–95.

45 See BDAG s.v. ἀσθενέω (*asthenō*). The word can also simply indicate being in need of any basic material necessity (see Acts 20:34–35), though I think it more likely that the meaning of *asthenō* in 25:36 is a weakened state brought about by abusive persecution.

46 See 10:14: "And if any one will not receive you *or listen to your words*, shake off the dust from your feet as you leave that house or town."

47 And so my approach is consistent with Matthean soteriology. This explains why the list in chapter 25 omits, for example, the care of widows and orphans (something brought up earlier in this study—see p. 58). Christ's verdict here in Matthew 25 is not based on the treatment of people in general, but on how one received the missionaries and their message.

hardship, through many a sleepless night, in hunger and thirst, often without food, in cold and exposure ..." (2 Cor. 11:26–27); and (3) "you know it was because of a bodily ailment that I preached the gospel to you at first; and though my condition was a trial to you, you did not scorn or despise me, but received me as an angel of God, *as Christ Jesus*" (Gal. 4:13–14). These Pauline parallels concur with what I have been arguing above with respect to the "least".

"As you did it ... you did it to me."

Reception of the apostles is the reception of Jesus. This concept is consistent with the notion of the *shaliach* ("sent one"), someone sent with a message in the name of and on behalf of the sender, with the full authority of the sender, so that to receive or not to receive the "one sent" would be the equivalent of receiving (or not) the sender and his message. This practice can be observed in the OT (prophets, who speak with divine authority), NT (for example, Matt. 10:40; John 13:20; Acts 9:4–5, Gal. 4:13–14), and in extra-biblical sources. It is in the background both in chapter 10 (especially 10:40–42), and in the judgment scene in chapter 25.[48]

Two Objections

For some commentators, the "surprise" of the sheep and goats (25:37–39, 44) at the Great Judgment scene poses a problem for interpreting "the least" as missionaries. They argue that if the least are understood as missionaries, the sheep and goats certainly would have *known* of Jesus through the missionaries' proclamation.[49] This objection, however, misses an important rhetorical point: *only at the parousia*, when the discourse reaches its resolution and climax, do both sheep and goats *fully comprehend* just how great was the one who had been working in and through the "no-account" missionaries. Neither sheep nor goats had actually *seen* Jesus himself (and *a fortiori* had never seen the glorified Jesus as they do now at the Great Day), but they did receive or reject him when they received or rejected the lowly missionaries. The surprise manifested by both groups springs from the great contrast between the glorious, enthroned Christ and the "little ones," the apostles.

The sheep, who had become disciples, knew of course that Jesus was the one who had sent the apostles on mission to them, and that Jesus was present in and

48 For more on the *shaliach* concept and practice, see Craig S. Keener, *Matthew*, 313–315; Craig S. Keener, "The Jewish Agent as New testament Background?," in *The Gospel of John: A Commentary*, 2 vols. (Peabody, MA: Hendrickson, 2003), 1. 311–313; P. Borgen, "God's Agent in the Fourth Gospel," in *Religions in Antiquity* (Leiden: Brill, 1968), 137–148; Raymond E. Brown, *The Gospel According to John (XIII–XXI)*, Anchor Bible vol. 29A (Garden City, N.Y.: Doubleday, 1970), 632; C. K. Barrett, "Shaliah and Apostle," in *Donum Gentilicium* (Oxford: Clarendon Press, 1978), 88–102.

49 See, for example, Jan Lambrect, *Out of the Treasure: The Parables in the Gospel of Matthew*, Louvain Theological & Pastoral Monographs (Louvain: Peeters Press, 1991), 278; Hare, *Matthew*, 290; Dan O. Via, "Ethical Responsibility and Human Wholeness in Matthew 25:31–46," *Harvard Theological Review* 80/1 (1987): 92.

through them—and in the church—in some way. But the breathtaking, majestic scene they now behold of Christ enthroned in glory with all the angels makes it seem almost unbelievable that their reception of these otherwise ordinary-looking men and their message was actually the reception of this colossal figure.[50] This, then, explains the surprise of the *sheep*. With respect to the goats, there is no real problem. They rejected the missionaries as the *no-accounts* they appeared to be; now they learn the truth of things and are stunned.[51]

The "surprise" notices to the sheep and goats add a rhetorical element to this part of the apocalypse (the *encouraging* part). They add a kind of "ironic vindication" for the twelve. The twelve are let in on the "joke" that the parousia will bring marvelous surprise one day to the sheep, and terrible shock to the goats. They will be sent out, but the Lord of Glory, the Judge of all the Earth stands by them—or better—is, unawares, "through them, with them, and in them" as they go about their mission.[52]

Besides the "surprise" problem, *the feature* in 25:31–46 that is seemingly most probative *against* the view outlined in this study is that the reader or hearer simply senses that the passage is exhorting *him* to care for the "least," and is *not* focused on the comfort, encouragement, or vindication of the "*least*." The major concern seems to be with the destiny of the sheep and goats, not with the "least" (whoever *they* are). The "least" seem somewhat ancillary to the parable as a whole; they are the *means* to the more important *end* of soberly considering one's eternal destiny and acting so as to attain a good end (inheriting the kingdom). In other words, the reader senses in 31–46 that he is being exhorted by Jesus to associate himself with the sheep (not the "least," and certainly not the goats).

Here again, however, this is an objection that arises from interpreting 25:31–46 out of context (especially the context of chapters 24–25), and from missing the connections with the proto-mission in chapter 10. In chapter 10:40–42, the apostles are not being exhorted to be receptors of righteous (& etc.) men. They *are* the righteous men who will (or, will not) be received. So it is in 25:31–46: the apostles, listening to Jesus on the Mount of Olives as he comes to the end of his apocalyptic discourse are not exhorted to be like the sheep. They are the *least* who will be received by the sheep (but not by the goats). Both passages (10:40–42 and 25:31–46) serve the same rhetorical function within the context of their respective

50 In agreement with this position is, for example, John P. Meier, "Nations or Gentiles in Matthew 28:19?," *Catholic Biblical Quarterly* 39 (1977): 94–102 at 101; Blaine Charette, *The Theme of Recompense in Matthew's Gospel*, Journal for the Study of the New Testament Supplement Series 79 (Sheffield: Sheffield Academic Press, 1992), 157–158.

51 See the disdain, typical of "goats," shown by the Jewish leaders to Peter and John in Acts 4:13 "Now when they saw the boldness of Peter and John, and perceived that they were *uneducated, common men*, they wondered; and they recognized that they had been with Jesus."

52 Before the apostles are sent out on the world-wide mission, Jesus said that he would be "with them" (Matt. 28:20), and that is exactly what has happened.

apocalypses. They encourage the disciples (in manifold ways) before they are sent off on what will be, for some, a "suicidal" mission (10:21, 28—compare 24:9).

The Apostle's Message

Earlier in the discourse (24:14) Jesus says that the "gospel of the kingdom will be preached throughout the whole world, as a testimony to all nations." The *nature* of the message—the good news of the kingdom—preached by the apostles and received by the sheep, is worth considering briefly.

From Matthew, we have no examples of "evangelistic proclamations" like we have in Acts 2, 3, 10, 13 (to Jews), 14, 17 (to Gentiles), and 26 (to a mixed audience). From Matthew 28:16–20, we learn that the apostles will proclaim (something) so as to make disciples for Jesus, and then teach these disciples to obey all that Jesus had taught them—evidently meaning material found throughout the gospel of Matthew. While the evangelistic proclamation would likely have been in continuity with what both John the Baptist and Jesus had earlier preached (about, for example, the advent of the Kingdom of Heaven and repentance), surely Jesus' passion, death, and resurrection would also have been part of the message. Though Matthew narrates no ascension, Jesus is presented in 28:16–20 as exalted above the nations as ruler, Lord, and effectively King—this also, we expect, would have been part of the missionaries' opening proclamation.

Some, then, would accept and receive the Kingdom proclamation and begin to learn of Jesus' teaching from the apostles, others would not. What is important to note is that, for Matthew, neither the proclamation of the good news of the Kingdom nor the teaching of the gospel to newly minted disciples would have had, as a special concern, care for the unfortunates of this world.[53] The message had as its primary concerns the same concerns that John the Baptist and Jesus had in their preaching: forgiveness of sin and hope of eternal life on condition of repentance towards God (which would mean turning to follow Jesus' teaching) and faith in (the now exalted) Jesus. This was the message of the apostles in the interim; this was what was received or not received.

IV. The Meaning(s) of Matthew 25:31–46

The Primary Meaning of 31–46

After the *exhortative* material stemming from the stories and parables about Noah, two men in the field, two women at the mill, the householder, the wise servant, the 10 virgins, and the talent-entrusted servants (24:37–25:30), in 25:31–46 *the twelve are encouraged* (as in 10:40–42) that their missionary efforts, attended as they will be with trials, sufferings, and death (10:17–23, 28, 39; 24:9), will have

53 Certainly care for the needy would have been part of Christian catechesis, given under, I would guess, the larger rubric of loving one's neighbor as oneself. As pointed out earlier in the study, however, care for the needy *per se* is not a Matthean emphasis, and barely a concern.

eternal significance, success, and final vindication. Not only will their labor not be in vain, their "living out" of the previous warnings brings supremely important results: eternal consequence for the hearers (receptors) and vindication for themselves. Jesus uses this same sort of "rhetoric of encouragement" in chapter 10 (vv. 14–15, 26, 40–42), only now, in chapters 24–25, it is expanded and filled with powerful imagery. Those who receive their message, who repent and become disciples, can expect the eternal kingdom; those who reject it will suffer eternal fire and punishment (25:41, 46). The messengers themselves will be vindicated on that Great Day—the main point of 31–46, as this would be the primary concern of the apocalyptic genre—many having paid the supreme price for their missionary efforts, even as Christ himself had. On the level of the gospel story, this encouragement was for the twelve. For Matthew's first century readers, it should have encouraged any missionary endeavors at the time. For Matthew's readers down through the centuries, it should likewise encourage all missionary activity.

Christological and Soteriological Coherence with the Rest of Matthew

According to Matthew, the world's most pressing need, both in the first century and today, is not to take care of the poor. The extreme christocentricity presented in the gospel, coupled with its presentation of humanity's desperate condition, show that for Matthew the world's most pressing need is to believe in Jesus Christ and receive the forgiveness, life, and salvation that He alone offers and confers, and to become members of his church. As far as Matthew is concerned, Jesus is the only source of this forgiveness and new life, as mediated through the Church.

Further, Derivative Meanings

The alternative interpretation that understands "the least of these" as Christians (but not restricted to missionaries, as I have argued above), is somewhat legitimate, though derivative and secondary. According to Matthew, Jesus is present in his Church as well as in his missionaries and apostles (see Matt. 18:20). It would therefore be wise to treat them with the sort of kindness exemplified in the six works of mercy. This is not, however, Jesus' primary point in Matthew 25:31–46.

Further, since all human beings are made in the image of God, even though marred by the Fall, and since, according to Matthew and other Scripture texts, we are commanded to love our neighbors as ourselves (and to love even our enemies), it is certainly legitimate, in some sense, to speak accurately about doing good to Jesus when we do good to any fellow human being. This, again, is not Jesus' point in Matthew 25:31–46.

V. Conclusion

The "unfortunates" interpretation of Matthew 25:31–46 is unfortunate. It is the result of methodology that too hastily grabs at the "obvious" when, with a little more investigation, a more coherent and satisfying solution can emerge. "What's the harm?" one might ask; "The text is being employed to help people, and that's a good thing." The harm is that, theologically and pastorally speaking, this important text is being employed *horizontally* instead of how Jesus intended, that it be understood *vertically*. For Matthew, and for the rest of the New Testament, the primacy lies with embracing the missionary message that Christ is King, Savior, and Judge and responding accordingly. This is the scene we are presented with in Matthew 25:31–46; this is the message the apostles and others have taken to the nations; this is the message that, when received, results in eternal happiness—to the glory of God *and* to the glory and vindication of his holy apostles.

Letter & Spirit 9 (2014): 77-103

The Last Supper and the Quest for Jesus[1]

~: **Brant Pitre** :~

Notre Dame Seminary

Introduction

Pick up any major historical study of the life of Jesus, read it carefully from cover to cover, and you will probably find at least four key questions operative in it:

1. What is the relationship between Jesus and Judaism? This is the question of *historical context*.

2. Who did Jesus think he was? This is the question of Jesus' self-identification—or, more commonly, his *self-understanding*.

3. What did Jesus expect to happen in the future? This is the question of Jesus' *eschatology*, the discussion of which has tended to revolve around how and when he thought the kingdom of God would come.

4. What is the relationship between Jesus and the early church? This is the question of Jesus' *intentions* for those who followed him, the discussion of which has often revolved around whether or not his aims were fulfilled, abandoned, or distorted by the emerging church.[2]

At least since the eighteenth century, these four questions have dominated the historical study of Jesus and continue to play a central role in major works on his life and teaching.[3] Moreover, as a close study of competing proposals reveals, the way in which any given scholar answers these questions will to a large extent constitute some of the starkest dividing lines between their overall conclusions about who Jesus was and the meaning of what he did and said.

---

1 This article is a slightly expanded version of material that will appear in Brant Pitre, *Jesus and the Last Supper* (Grand Rapids: Eerdmans, 2015).

2 Significantly, this last question dates back to the work of Hermann Samuel Reimarus, at the very beginnings of the modern historical quest for the historical Jesus. See Hermann Samuel Reimarus, "The Aims of Jesus and His Disciples," in his *Fragments*, ed. Charles H. Talbert, trans. Ralph Fraser (Philadelphia: Fortress, 1970 [orig. 1774–78]). More recently, see Ben F. Meyer, *The Aims of Jesus* (London: SCM, 1979).

3 For similar lists, see N. T. Wright, *Jesus and the Victory of God: Christian Origins and the Question of God*, Vol. 1 (Minneapolis: Fortress, 1996), 89–116; E. P. Sanders, *Jesus and Judaism* (Philadelphia: Fortress, 1985), 1.

This article will explore how the questions of Jesus' historical context, self-understanding, eschatology, and intentions have been answered in the contemporary quest by focusing on the words and deeds of Jesus at the Last Supper. On the one hand, in the case of each question, a number of widely accepted conclusions about Jesus in contemporary scholarship are not easily reconciled with evidence preserved in the accounts of the Last Supper (Matt. 26:26–28; Mark 14:24–25; Luke 22:19–22; 1 Cor. 11:23–25). On the other hand, when examined carefully, the words and deeds of Jesus at the Last Supper have a direct bearing upon the four questions of his relationship to his Jewish context, his self-understanding, his eschatological outlook, and his intentions toward the community of his disciples. Indeed, I would contend that to the extent that the contemporary quest has failed to integrate the Last Supper into its overall reconstruction of Jesus' life and teaching—which it often has—then it has also failed to answer adequately the four guiding questions in the quest for Jesus. In the words of the young Albert Schweitzer, written over a century ago: "The problem of the Lord's Supper is the problem of the life of Jesus!"[4]

I. Jesus, Judaism, and the Last Supper

The first question that presents itself to us is that of Jesus' Jewish context. How do the accounts of the Last Supper fit into the context of first-century Judaism? Are their basic contents historically plausible? If so, what might they have meant in Jesus' Jewish context? When we examine such questions in light of recent scholarship on Jesus, something of a paradox emerges.

The Jewish Jesus

On the one hand, nowadays it is all but universally affirmed by scholars that Jesus of Nazareth was born, lived, and died a Jew. Perhaps more than any other result of contemporary Jesus research, the Jewish identity of Jesus has commanded a widespread acceptance, and represents a virtual consensus. Consider, for example, the remarkably categorical statements of several prominent scholars:

> It is with ... Judaism, the Judaism of the first century CE, that we must carry through the task of finding the historical Jesus.[5]

> Virtually no one today disputes or has any reason to dispute that Jesus was a Jew from Galilee.[6]

---

4 Albert Schweitzer, *The Problem of the Lord's Supper*, trans. A. J. Mattill, Jr., ed. John Reumann (Macon, GA: Mercer University Press, 1982 [orig. 1901]), 137.

5 Maurice Casey, *Jesus of Nazareth: An Independent Historian's Account of His Life and Teaching* (London: T. & T. Clark, 2010), 59.

6 Craig S. Keener, *The Historical Jesus of the Gospels* (Grand Rapids: Eerdmans, 2009), 178.

> One of the characteristic pursuits of the latest phase of Jesus-of-history research, namely the so-called Third Quest, has been the serious attempt to locate Jesus within first-century AD Judaism, to seek a Jesus who would be plausible within his Jewish context.[7]

> Jesus had to have made sense in his own context, and his context is that of Galilee and Judea. Jesus cannot be fully understood unless he is understood through first-century Jewish eyes and heard through first-century Jewish ears. ... To understand Jesus' impact in his own setting—why some chose to follow him, others to dismiss him, and still others to seek his death—requires an understanding of that setting.[8]

> [A]ny attempt to build up a historical picture of Jesus of Nazareth should and must begin from the fact that he was a first-century Jew operating in a first-century milieu.[9]

> [I]f there is any enduring gain from the so-called third quest, it is the one hammered home by scholars like Geza Vermes and E. P. Sanders: Jesus first, last, and only a Jew.[10]

> If [Jesus] belongs anywhere in history, it is within the history of first-century Judaism.[11]

Scholars continue to debate exactly what it *means* to say that Jesus was "Jewish" and what Judaism was like at the time of Jesus.[12] Nevertheless, the same general point is made by many recent titles, which go out of their way to emphasize that the Jesus of history is unequivocally a Jewish Jesus.[13] In short, the importance of Jesus' Jewish identity and context has become one of those extremely rare occasions

---

7 Tom Holmén, *Jesus from Judaism to Christianity: Continuum Approaches to the Historical Jesus*, ed. Tom Holmén, Library of New Testament Studies 352 (Edinburgh: T. & T. Clark, 2007), 1.

8 Amy-Jill Levine, *The Misunderstood Jew: The Church and the Scandal of the Jewish Jesus* (San Francisco: HarperCollins, 2006), 20–21.

9 James D. G. Dunn, *Jesus Remembered*, Christianity in the Making, Vol. 1 (Grand Rapids: Eerdmans, 2003), 86.

10 John P. Meier, *A Marginal Jew: Rethinking the Historical Jesus*, 4 vols. (5th vol. forthcoming), Anchor Yale Bible Reference Library (New Haven & London: Yale University Press, 1991, 1994, 2001, 2009), 4:7.

11 Wright, *Jesus and the Victory of God*, 91.

12 See William Arnal, *The Symbolic Jesus: Historical Scholarship, Judaism and the Construction of Contemporary Identity* (Sheffield: Equinox, 2005).

13 For example, Martin Hengel and Anna Maria Schwemer, *Jesus und das Judentum, Geschichte des frühen Christentums*, Vol. 1 (Tübingen: Mohr-Siebeck, 2007); John Dominic Crossan, *The Historical Jesus: The Life of a Mediterranean Jewish Peasant* (San Francisco: HarperCollins, 1991); James H. Charlesworth, *Jesus within Judaism: New Light from Exciting Archaeological*

where virtually everyone in the scholarly realm agrees upon a basic conclusion and treats it as settled.

The Problem of the Last Supper

On the other hand, it is by no means immediately evident how the Jewish Jesus of scholarly consensus can be reconciled with what might be called the "eucharistic Jesus"—that is, the Jesus depicted in the words of institution recorded in the Synoptic Gospels and Paul, as well as the arguably eucharistic elements of the discourse in the synagogue at Capernaum attributed to Jesus in the Gospel of John.

As is well known, according to all four accounts of Jesus' words and deeds at the Last Supper—including what is commonly regarded as the most ancient account in 1 Corinthians—Jesus not only identifies the bread and wine of his final meal with his own body and blood, but also commands his disciples to eat and drink them:

> Now as they were eating, Jesus took bread, and blessed, and broke it, and gave it to the disciples and said, "*Take, eat; this is my body.*" And he took a cup, and when he had given thanks he gave it to them, saying, "*Drink of it, all of you; for this is my blood of the covenant,* which is poured out for many for the forgiveness of sins. (Matt. 26:26–28)

> And as they were eating, he took bread, and blessed, and broke it, and gave it to them, and said, "*Take; this is my body.*" And he took a cup, and when he had given thanks *he gave it to them, and they all drank of it.* And he said to them, "*This is my blood of the covenant,* which is poured out for many." (Mark 14:22–24)

> And he took bread, and when he had given thanks he broke it and gave it to them, saying, "*This is my body which is given for you. Do this in remembrance of me.*" And likewise the cup after supper, saying, "*This cup which is poured out for you is the new covenant in my blood.*" (Luke 22:19–20)[14]

Discoveries, Anchor Bible Reference Library (New York: Doubleday, 1990); Geza Vermes, *Jesus the Jew: A Historian's Reading of the Gospels* (Philadelphia: Fortress, 1973).

14 In some ancient manuscripts of Luke's Gospel, vv. 19b–20 are omitted. An enormous body of text-critical discussion has grown up around this issue, debating whether the so-called "longer version" (including vv. 19b–20) or "shorter version" (omitting vv. 19b–20) is original. In my opinion, the manuscript evidence for the longer version is simply too abundant to maintain the minority position, which has only a single Greek manuscript in its favor. For these and other reasons, I will adopt the longer version herein, referring the reader to the discussion in I. Howard Marshall, "The Last Supper," in *Key Events in the Life of the Historical Jesus*, eds. Darrell L. Bock and Robert L. Webb, Wissenschaftliche Untersuchungen zum Neuen Testament 247, (Tübingen: Mohr Siebeck, 2009), 529–541; Bradly S. Billings, *Do This in Remembrance of Me:*

> For I received from the Lord what I also delivered to you, that the Lord Jesus on the night when he was betrayed took bread, and when he had given thanks, he broke it, and said, "*This is my body which is for you. Do this in remembrance of me.*" In the same way also the cup, after supper, saying, "*This cup is the new covenant in my blood. Do this, as often as you drink it, in remembrance of me.*" (1 Cor. 11:23–25)

Along similar lines, but in a different mode and form, according to the Gospel of John, Jesus said something very similar to this while teaching in the Jewish synagogue at Capernaum, when he declared it necessary to eat the flesh and drink the blood of the Son of man—which he identifies as real food and drink—in order to participate in the resurrection of the dead and eternal life (John 6:53–55):

> Jesus said to them, "Amen, amen, I say to you, *unless you eat the flesh of the Son of man and drink his blood, you have no life in you;* he who eats my flesh and drinks my blood has eternal life, and I will raise him up at the last day. *For my flesh is real food, and my blood is real drink* (John 6:54–55).

The problem with this evidence is that it stands in stark contrast to the express directives of ancient Jewish Scripture. According to the Torah of Moses, it was absolutely forbidden for anyone to consume blood:

> Every moving thing that lives shall be food for you ... Only *you shall not eat flesh with its life, that is, its blood.* (Gen. 9:3–4)[15]

> If any man among the house of Israel or of the strangers that sojourn among them eats any blood, *I will set my face against that person who eats blood, and will cut him off from among his people. For the life of the flesh is in the blood; and I have given it for you upon the altar to make atonement for your souls;* for it is the blood that makes atonement, by reason of the life. Therefore I have said to the people of Israel, *No person among you shall eat*

The Disputed Words in the Lukan Institution Narrative (Luke 22:19b-20): An Historico-Exegetical, Theological, and Sociological Analysis, Library of Biblical Studies (London: T. & T. Clark, 2006). Joseph A. Fitzmyer, S.J. (*The Gospel according to Luke*, Anchor Bible [New York: Doubleday, 1983, 1985], 2:1387–1389) sums up well two of the main arguments favoring the longer version as original: (1) the "overwhelming number" of Greek manuscripts supporting the longer version; (2) "the principle of *lectio difficilior,*" by which Luke's account of multiple cups provides a ready explanation for why a baffled scribe would shorten the longer version.

15 Unless otherwise noted, all translations of Scripture in this article are from the Revised Standard Version (RSV).

> *blood, neither shall any stranger who sojourns among you eat blood.* (Lev. 17:10–12)

> You may slaughter and eat flesh within any of your towns, as much as you desire ... *Only you shall not eat the blood;* you shall pour it out upon the earth like water. (Deut. 12: 15–16)

Clearly, the biblical commandment against drinking blood was gravely serious and absolute: any transgression of this law would result in being "cut off" from God and from the people of Israel. Notice also that the law is universal in scope: the Torah commands that not only Israelites avoid the consumption of blood, but that any Gentile "strangers" living among them do so as well.

In light of such evidence, a fundamental problem emerges. If, for the sake of argument, we assume that the substance of Jesus' words regarding eating his body and drinking blood are historical,[16] then how could he as a first-century Jew have ever commanded his disciples to eat his flesh and drink his blood? If he did, would this not entail explicitly breaking the Torah's repeated commandments against consuming blood? It is precisely this tension between the Jewish Torah and the eucharistic words attributed to Jesus that leads Geza Vermes to contend:

> [T]he imagery of eating a man's body and especially drinking his blood ... , even after allowance is made for metaphorical language, strikes a totally foreign note in a Palestinian Jewish cultural setting (see John 6:52). With their profoundly rooted blood taboo, Jesus' listeners would have been overcome with nausea at hearing such words.[17]

Along similar lines, another major Jewish scholar, Joseph Klausner, writes:

> [I]t is quite impossible to admit that Jesus would have said to his disciples that they should eat of his body and drink of his blood, "the blood of the new covenant which was shed for many." The drinking of blood, even if it was meant symbolically, could only have aroused horror in the minds of such simple Galilean Jews.[18]

Note two points about the views of both Vermes and Klausner. First, both agree that there is simply no way to reconcile the Jewish taboo against blood consump-

16 I deal at great length with the question of the historical plausibility of the substance of the words of institution and the discourse on the manna in the Capernaum Synagogue in the full length monograph. See Brant Pitre, *Jesus and the Last Supper* (Grand Rapids: Eerdmans, 2015), chapters, 2, 3, and 5.

17 Geza Vermes, *The Religion of Jesus the Jew* (Minneapolis: Fortress, 1993), 16.

18 Joseph Klausner, *Jesus of Nazareth: His Life, Times, and Teaching,* trans. Hebert Danby (New York: Macmillan, 1925), 329.

tion with Jesus' command for his disciples to eat his flesh and drink his blood at the Last Supper. The words of institution are thus historically "impossible." Second, both agree that even if Jesus only meant these words *metaphorically*, as many Christian interpreters since the Protestant Reformation have contended, in an ancient Jewish context, such a command would have been completely repugnant. From this point of view, there is no way to reconcile the Jewish Jesus and the Jesus of the Last Supper accounts. Therefore, since the Jewishness of Jesus cannot be called into question, it is the words of institution that must be rejected as unhistorical.

This tension between the Jewish Jesus and the eucharistic Jesus has been felt since the very beginning of the modern quest, and continues to be present in studies of Jesus and the Last Supper. For example, already in the eighteenth century, Hermann Samuel Reimarus found it impossible to reconcile the accounts of the Last Supper with his portrait of Jesus as a Jewish revolutionary. As a result, Reimarus was forced to insist—against the testimony of all the extant evidence—that Jesus celebrated the Last Supper "without the least alteration" from the ordinary Jewish Passover meal. Indeed, Reimarus claimed that "one cannot see that he omitted or changed anything that was customary for this meal."[19] To say the least, this is a questionable interpretation of the data. To the contrary, if anything is certain, it is that all four accounts of the Last Supper agree that Jesus identified the bread and wine of the meal with his own body and blood, and that such an identification was certainly *not* customary Jewish Passover practice (see Matt 26:26-28; Mark 14:22–24; Luke 22:19–20; 1 Cor. 11:23–25). However, Reimarus' assertion helps to make an important point: from the earliest days of the modern quest, in order to maintain the hypothesis that Jesus was thoroughly Jewish, scholars were forced to explain away the eucharistic words. In the figure of Reimarus, the quest begins to exhibit a tendency to dismiss the startling words of Jesus at the Last Supper as "incidental."[20]

Much more recently, this tension between the Jewish Jesus and the eucharistic Jesus manifests itself in another way: entire studies of the Last Supper that pay almost no attention to the Old Testament or to Second Temple Judaism.[21] For example, one searches Jens Schröter's recent monograph on the Last Supper in vain for any detailed discussion of the early Jewish context of the images of blood, covenant, Passover, sacrifice, kingdom of God, etc.[22] Perhaps, unsurprisingly, Schröter

19 Reimarus, *Fragments*, 118–119.

20 See Reimarus, *Fragments*, 118.

21 For example, there is a stunning dearth of discussion of Old Testament and early Jewish sources in Rudolf Pesch, *Das Abendmahl und Jesu Todesverständnis* (Freiburg: Herder, 1978), and Helmut Feld, *Das Verständnis des Abendmahls* (Darmstadt: Wissenschaftliche Buchgesellschaft, 1976). By contrast, Hermann Patsch (*Abendmahl und historischer Jesus* [Stuttgart: Calwer, 1972], 17–39) devotes substantial attention to the Old Testament and early Jewish parallels.

22 Jens Schröter, *Das Abendmahl: Früchristliche Deutungen und Impulse für die Gegenwart*,

ends up concluding that the words of institution, with the sole exception of Jesus' vow about not drinking in the kingdom (Mark 14:25), in all probability do not stem from Jesus, but from the early church (to which he has devoted all his attention).[23]

In sum, there remains an undeniable tension between Jesus the Jew and the Jesus of the Last Supper accounts—a tension that is sometimes not faced head-on. If the substance of the eucharistic words recorded in the Gospels and Paul is historically plausible, then how could Jesus have ever commanded his disciples to eat his body and drink his blood—even if he only meant it symbolically? In a word, how does one reconcile the Jewish Jesus and the eucharistic Jesus?

II. The Self-Understanding of Jesus

When we turn from the question of Jesus' context to the question of his self-understanding, the Last Supper presents us with yet another paradox. On the one hand, much of contemporary biblical scholarship on Jesus concludes that we lack solid evidence that he saw himself as or ever claimed to be the messiah. On the other hand, if the words of institution at the Last Supper are basically historical, then it is rather hard to square them with a Jesus who did not see himself as anything more than just a Jewish teacher or prophet.

The Dogma of the Non-Messianic Jesus

In his massive study on the death of Jesus, Raymond Brown once described the idea that "neither Jesus nor his followers thought he was the Messiah" as a "'dogma' of modern critical scholarship."[24] Roughly around the same time, Martin Hengel used equally strong language: "Today the unmessianic Jesus has almost become a dogma among many New Testament scholars."[25]

To be sure, there are numerous scholars who have argued *in favor of* some kind of messianic self-understanding on the part of the historical Jesus.[26] Indeed, at the end of his life, even Rudolf Bultmann retracted his earlier assertion that Jesus saw himself merely as a rabbi and concluded instead that Jesus appeared as

---

Stuttgarter Bibelstudien 210 (Stuttgart: Katholisches Bibelwerk, 2006).

23 Schröter, *Das Abendmahl*, 132–133.

24 Raymond E. Brown, *The Death of the Messiah*, 2 vols., Anchor Bible Reference Library (New York: Doubleday, 1993), 1:478.

25 Martin Hengel, "Jesus, the Messiah of Israel," in *Studies in Early Christology* (Edinburgh: T. & T. Clark, 1995), 16.

26 Most recently, see Dale C. Allison, Jr., *Constructing Jesus: Memory, Imagination, and History* (Grand Rapids; Baker Academic, 2010), 221–304; Michael F. Bird, *Are You the One Who Is to Come? The Historical Jesus and the Messianic Question* (Grand Rapids: Baker Academic, 2009). I too have made the case for Jesus' messianic self-understanding in Brant Pitre, *Jesus, the Tribulation, and the End of the Exile*, Wissenschaftliche Untersuchungen zum Neuen Testament 2.204 (Tübingen: Mohr Siebeck; Grand Rapids: Baker Academic, 2005), 455–514. See also Wright, *Jesus and the Victory of God*, 477–539; Meyer, *The Aims of Jesus*, 178–180.

a messianic prophet whose proclamation "implies a christology."[27] Nevertheless, it remains true that many scholarly works and introductions to the New Testament reflect the assumption that no historically reliable evidence exists that Jesus saw himself as the Jewish messiah.

For our purposes in this article, one key feature of this so-called "dogma" is the conviction that Jesus did not attribute any redemptive or saving significance to his death.[28] Consider the following remarks from recent works on Jesus:

> The inauthenticity [of Jesus' description of his death as a 'ransom for many'] follows from the fact that it is the 'risen Christ' speaking.[29]

> It's not clear why, exactly, Jesus went with his disciples to Jerusalem. A theologian, of course, might say that it was in order to die for the sins of the world. This view, though, is based on Gospel sayings ... that cannot pass the criterion of dissimilarity, in that they portray Jesus as being fully cognizant of the details of his own fate.[30]

> It is not historically impossible that Jesus was weird ... But the view that he plotted his own redemptive death makes him strange in any century and thrusts the entire drama into his peculiar inner psyche. The other things that we know about him make him a *reasonable* first-century visionary. We should be guided by them.[31]

Perhaps the most influential articulation of this view comes from Rudolf Bultmann, who famously wrote:

> The greatest embarrassment to the attempt to reconstruct a portrait of Jesus is the fact that we cannot know how Jesus understood his end, his death. It is symptomatic that it is practically universally assumed that he understood this as the organic

27 Rudolf Bultmann, "The Primitive Christian Kerygma and the Historical Jesus," in *The Historical Jesus and the Kerygmatic Christ: Essays on the New Quest for the Historical Jesus*, eds. Carl E. Braaten and Roy A. Harrisville (Nashville: Abingdon, 1964), 28–29.

28 For discussion, see Scot McKnight, *Jesus and His Death: Historiography, the Historical Jesus, and Atonement Theory* (Waco: Baylor University Press, 2005), 47–75; Dunn, *Jesus Remembered*, 805–818; Brown, *The Death of the Messiah*, 2:1468–1491 (with bibliography).

29 Gerd Lüdemann, *Jesus After 2000 Years: What He Really Did and Said*, trans. John Bowden (London: SCM; Amherst: Prometheus, 2001), 72.

30 Bart Ehrman, *Jesus: Apocalyptic Prophet of the New Millennium* (New York: Oxford University Press, 1999), 209–210.

31 Sanders, *Jesus and Judaism*, 332–333 (emphasis original).

> or necessary conclusion to his activity. But how do we know this, when prophecies of the passion must be understood by critical research as *vaticinia ex eventu* [foretelling after the event]? ... What is certain is that he was merely crucified by the Romans, and thus suffered the death of a political criminal. This death can scarcely be understood as an inherent and necessary consequence of his activity; rather it took place because his activity was misconstrued as political activity. In that case it would have been—historically speaking—a meaningless fate. We may not veil from ourselves the possibility that he suffered a collapse.[32]

The impact of Bultmann's assessment of the historical question of Jesus' self-understanding is hard to overestimate. As I have shown elsewhere, such sentiments have led to a situation in which many influential scholars on Jesus do not consider it necessary even to discuss the evidence that Jesus saw his death as redemptive, much less to provide arguments for why this evidence should be regarded as unhistorical.[33] As I stated above, while this is certainly not true of all studies on Jesus, it is widespread enough for the most recent full-length study of Jesus and his death to draw the following conclusion: "Many scholars, perhaps a majority today, think Jesus was innocent, that he was righteous, that his death was splendidly exemplary, and/or that he died as a result of his self-claim and his mission, but that his death was not undertaken (consciously and deliberately) as an atonement."[34]

It seems, then, that the "dogma" of the non-messianic Jesus—and its sister, the dogma of the non-redemptive Jesus—has become something of an assumption in the minds of many contemporary scholars.

The Problem of the Words of Institution

A major problem with this dogma is that if the words of institution attributed to Jesus at the Last Supper are basically historical, then it is rather difficult to square them with the non-messianic Jesus.

In all three Synoptic accounts of Jesus' words at the Last Supper, he specifically identifies himself as the "the Son of man" whose death is prophesied in Jewish

---

32 Bultmann, "The Primitive Christian Kerygma and the Historical Jesus," 22–23.

33 For example, the evidence that Jesus saw his death as Son of Man as redemptive (Matt 20:28; Mark 10:45) is ignored in the following reconstructions: Karl Jaros, *Jesus von Nazareth: Geschichte und Deutung* (Mainz: Verlag Philipp von Zabern, 2000); Fredriksen, *Jesus of Nazareth*; Ehrman, *Jesus: Apocalyptic Prophet*; Joachim Gnilka, *Jesus of Nazareth: Message and History*, trans. Siegfried S. Schatzmann (Peabody: Hendricksen, 1997); Crossan, *The Historical Jesus*; Vermes, *Jesus the Jew*; Norman Perrin, *Rediscovering the Teaching of Jesus* (New York: Harper & Row, 1967); Günther Bornkamm, *Jesus of Nazareth*, trans. Irene and Fraser McLuskey with James Robinson (New York: Harper, 1960). See Pitre, *Jesus, the Tribulation, and the End of the Exile*, 419.

34 McKnight, *Jesus and His Death*, 71.

Scripture (Matt. 26:24; Mark 14:21; Luke 22:22). Although the exact meaning of Jesus' usage of the "Son of man" continues to be debated, the expression itself continues to be widely regarded as a positive indicator of historicity. If, as some scholars hold (and I have argued elsewhere), the Son of Man *is* in fact a messianic figure in Daniel and Jesus saw himself as this figure, then this strong linkage between the Last Supper and Jesus' self-understanding as Son of Man poses a serious problem for the dogma of the non-messianic Jesus.[35] Perhaps even more striking is that in all four accounts of the Last Supper, Jesus identifies the wine of the meal with his own "blood" that will establish a new "covenant" between God and his people. In all four accounts, Jesus uses the language of sacrifice to describe his blood as being offered for others:

> And he took a cup, and when he had given thanks he gave it to them, saying, "Drink of it, all of you; for *this is my blood of the [new] covenant,* which is poured out for many for the forgiveness of sins. (Matt. 26:27–28)

> And he took a cup, and when he had given thanks he gave it to them, and they all drank of it. And he said to them, "*This is my blood of the [new] covenant,* which is poured out for many." (Mark 14:23–24)

> And likewise the cup after supper, saying, "This cup which is poured out for you *is the new covenant in my blood.*" (Luke 22:20)

> In the same way also the cup, after supper, saying, "*This cup is the new covenant in my blood.* Do this, as often as you drink it, in remembrance of me." (1 Cor. 11:25)

Numerous scholars have identified in these accounts allusions to the "blood of the covenant" established by Moses (Exod. 24:8), the "new covenant" spoken of by the prophets (Jer. 31:31), as well as the sacrificial death of the suffering servant who offers himself for "many" (Isa. 53:12).[36]

Now, if Jesus understood himself as merely a rabbi, or prophet, or anything less than the messianic redeemer (whether he saw himself as *more* than a messiah is yet another question), then we should not expect to find him saying and doing the

---

35 See Allison, *Constructing Jesus,* 293–303; Bird, *Are You the One Who Is to Come?,* 78–98; Pitre, *Jesus, the Tribulation, and the End of the Exile,* 54–55; Delbert Burkett, *The Son of Man Debate: A History and Evaluation,* Society for New Testament Studies Monograph Series 107 (Cambridge: Cambridge University Press, 1999). In light of these connections, Seyoon Kim (*The Son of Man as the Son of God,* Wissenschaftliche Untersuchungen zum Neuen Testament 30 [Tübingen: Mohr Siebeck, 1983]) holds that the words of institution may be aptly described as "the eucharistic words of the Son of Man."

36 See McKnight, *Jesus and His Death,* 275–292.

kinds of things the evidence claims he said and did at his final meal. Conversely, if the eucharistic words of institution are basically historical, then they make good sense on the lips of a Jesus who saw himself as the messianic deliverer of Israel, one whose death would somehow usher in the age of redemption awaited by many Jews and spoken of by the prophets.

This tension between the dogma of the non-messianic Jesus and the evidence in the accounts of the Last Supper is manifest in the work of scholars who deny that Jesus saw himself as messiah and/or that he attributed any redemptive significance to his death.[37] Consider the following:

> All of the texts which deal with the last supper of Jesus reflect the liturgical concerns of the meal celebrations of the various churches. *No text reports the historical event … The words of institution … [are] reminiscent of Isaiah 53:12, but Jesus cannot have spoken that way …* [W]hen we examine Jesus' message elsewhere, we find nowhere the suggestion that God's gracious acceptance of the lost was dependent in any way on the sacrifice of Jesus' own life.[38]

> If it is certain that according to the accounts of Paul and Mark (the same is probably true of the accounts of Matthew and Luke) Jesus celebrated the first Lord's Supper with his disciples, at which he distributed to them his body and blood and at which they ate his body and drink his blood symbolically, really, or in whatever way, *then it is equally certain that the institution of the supper thus described is not historical … [For] he had said nothing about a saving effect of his death or even his resurrection …* Only Jesus' expectation of the future kingdom of God stands at the centre, not Jesus as savior …[39]

> According to these accounts [of the Last Supper], he told his disciples that the unleavened bread was (or represented) his body that would be broken, and the cup of wine was (or represented) his blood that would be shed (Mark 14:22–25; Matt. 26:26–29; Luke 22:15–20; 1 Cor. 11:23–26). *It's very difficult to know whether this "institution" of the Lord's Supper is historical.* On the one hand, it is multiply attested in independent sources, even

37 See, for example, Jürgen Becker, *Jesus of Nazareth*, trans. James E. Crouch (New York/Berlin: Walter de Gruyter, 1998), 187–197, for an emphatic denial of Jesus' messianic self-understanding.

38 Becker, *Jesus of Nazareth*, 340–342 (emphasis added).

39 Lüdemann, *Jesus After 2000 Years*, 96–97 (emphasis added).

> though they disagree concerning the precise words that were spoken. And one of these sources, Paul, who claimed to know people who had been there at the time, was writing just twenty years after the event. *On the other hand, the accounts seem so heavily "Christianized" with the doctrine of the saving effect of Jesus' death (a doctrine that developed, of course, after he had died), that it is hard to know here what is history and what is later theology.*[40]

In all three of these analyses, the historicity of the words of institution at the Last Supper is rejected, not because of any evidence to the contrary, but because of the assumption that Jesus did not see his death as redemptive. Bart Ehrman's statements are particularly revealing. On the one hand, according to his own criteria of historicity, the words of institution should pass with flying colors, since they are quadruply attested, and since he regards Paul's account as the earliest recorded words of Jesus.[41] On the other hand, when Ehrman is faced with the evidence in the Last Supper accounts that Jesus saw his death as redemptive, he quickly jettisons the very criteria of authenticity which in other cases he utilizes to establish the historicity of a given saying or deed, thus casting doubt on the words of institution. Indeed, he does not seem to consider the possibility that the reason why the words of institution are so solidly attested may be because the idea that Jesus' death had "saving significance" goes back to Jesus himself.

In sum, it is quite common nowadays to assume that Jesus did not see himself as the messiah and, *a fortiori*, did not see his death as redemptive. It is very difficult, however, to see how such conclusions can be reconciled with the words and deeds of Jesus at the Last Supper. In light of this situation, we find ourselves on the horns of yet another historical dilemma: Is it possible to reconcile the non-messianic Jesus and the Jesus of the Last Supper? Is one of them in error? If so, which?

III. The Eschatology of Jesus

A third issue regards the relationship between the accounts of the Last Supper and Jesus' eschatological expectations. On the one hand, one of the most influential theses of the twentieth century is that Jesus' proclamation of the kingdom of God should be understood in light of ancient Jewish beliefs about the end of history, the final judgment, and the destruction and renewal of creation. On the other hand, what often goes unnoted is how difficult it is to integrate the words of institution into the portrait of Jesus as an apocalyptic prophet at the end of history.

---

40 Ehrman, *Jesus: Apocalyptic Prophet*, 215 (emphasis added).

41 Cf. Ehrman, *Jesus: Apocalyptic Prophet*, 85–96.

The Apocalyptic Jesus and the End of History

The pervasive influence of an apocalyptic view of Jesus is commonly credited to Albert Schweitzer's famous book, *The Quest of the Historical Jesus* (1906).[42] In the wake of Schweitzer's work, it became widely accepted that Jesus' expectations were characterized by what Schweitzer referred to as "thoroughgoing eschatology."[43] From this perspective, Jesus acted on the conviction that the end of the present world was imminent and would coincide with the advent of the kingdom of God. In Schweitzer's own words, Jesus "thought the end was at hand."[44] Therefore, he expected "the immediate coming of the last things"—that is, the final tribulation, the last judgment, the resurrection of the dead, etc.—along with "the coming of the new supernatural world."[45]

For Schweitzer, Jesus not only expected the end to take place soon, he also acted on this expectation by going to Jerusalem to die and thereby force the coming of the kingdom to take place. Consider Schweitzer's famous description of how Jesus understood his death with the accounts of the Last Supper in mind:

> There is silence all around. The Baptist appears, and cries: "Repent, for the Kingdom of Heaven is at hand." Soon after that comes Jesus, and in the knowledge that he is the coming Son of Man lays hold of the wheel of the world to set it moving on that last revolution which is to bring all ordinary history to a close. It refuses to turn, and He throws himself upon it. Then it does turn; and crushes Him. Instead of bringing in the eschatological conditions, He has destroyed them. The wheel rolls onward, and the mangled body of the one immeasurably great Man, who was strong enough to think of Himself as the spiritual ruler of mankind and to bend history to His purpose, is hanging upon it still. That is His victory and His reign.[46]

Schweitzer's Jesus does not look beyond his own death precisely because he saw it as the event that would "bring all ordinary history to a close." Consequently, for Schweitzer, Jesus did not expect his disciples to continue the work of his public

---

42 Albert Schweitzer, *The Quest of the Historical Jesus: A Critical Study of Its Progress from Reimarus to Wrede*, trans. William Montgomery, rev. ed. (New York: Macmillan, 1968 [orig. 1906]). The English translation was recently revised and expanded in Albert Schweitzer, *The Quest of the Historical Jesus: First Complete Edition*, trans. William Montgomery, J. R. Coates, Susan Cupitt, and John Bowden (Minneapolis: Fortress, 2001). Given the impact of the first edition on English-speaking scholarship, in what follows, the page references (unless otherwise noted) are to the first English edition.

43 Schweitzer, *The Quest of the Historical Jesus*, 330–397.

44 Schweitzer, *The Quest of the Historical Jesus*, 395.

45 Schweitzer, *The Quest of the Historical Jesus*, 365.

46 Schweitzer, *The Quest of the Historical Jesus*, 371.

ministry after his death: "[The disciples] are not [Jesus'] helpers in the work of teaching; we never see them in that capacity, and *He did not prepare them to carry on that work after His death*."[47] For Schweitzer, then, Jesus was an eschatological prophet in the strictest sense of the word: he proclaimed and expected the end of ordinary history to coincide with his own demise.

In the wake of Schweitzer's work, the view of Jesus as an apocalyptic prophet of the imminent end of the world soon became widely accepted by a large sector of New Testament studies.[48] Over and over again in influential books on Jesus, we find conclusions such as the following:

> Jesus' generation ... passed away. They all tasted death. And it is not the kingdom of God that has come but the scoffers who ask, Where is the promise of his coming? All things continue as they were from the beginning of creation. Jesus the millenarian prophet, like all millenarian prophets, was wrong.[49]

> Jesus appears to have anticipated that the coming judgment of God, to be brought by the Son of Man in a cosmic act of destruction and salvation, was imminent. It could happen at any time. But it would certainly happen within his own generation.[50]

> [T]he great event which Jesus was convinced would happen in his lifetime failed to materialize ...[51]

> We have no saying of Jesus that postpones the end into the distant future ... That raises an extremely serious question: must we not concede that Jesus' expectation of an imminent end was one that remained unfulfilled? Honesty and the demand for truthfulness compel us to answer 'Yes'. Jesus expected the end would come soon.[52]

> [Jesus expected] salvation not from a miraculous change in historical (i.e., political and social) conditions, but from a cosmic catastrophe which will do away with all conditions of the present world as it is.[53]

---

47 Schweitzer, *The Quest of the Historical Jesus*, 371 (emphasis added).

48 On the influence of Schweitzer, see Wright, *Jesus and the Victory of God*, 83–124.

49 Dale C. Allison Jr., *Jesus of Nazareth: Millenarian Prophet* (Minneapolis: Fortress, 1998), 218.

50 Ehrman, *Jesus: Apocalyptic Prophet*, 161.

51 Geza Vermes, *The Religion of Jesus the Jew* (Minneapolis: Fortress, 1993), 211.

52 Joachim Jeremias, *New Testament Theology I. The Proclamation of Jesus*, trans. John Bowden (New York: SCM; London: Charles Scribner's Sons, 1971), 139.

53 Rudolf Bultmann, *Theology of the New Testament*, 2 vols. (New York: Charles Scribner's Sons,

Such examples could be easily multiplied. To be sure, there are voices to the contrary.[54] Nevertheless, when modern scholarship is taken as a whole, it seems as if the Jesus of Schweitzer—the apocalyptic Jesus of the imminent end of history—has convinced many and left an indelible mark on the way in which Jesus' eschatological outlook is conceived.

The Problem of the Words of Institution

One serious problem with the hypothesis of Jesus as an apocalyptic prophet of the imminent end of history is that scholars who adopt this point of view have substantial difficulty making sense of the words of institution recorded in our earliest accounts of the Last Supper. In these words, Jesus apparently looks *beyond* his own imminent suffering and death, in at least two ways. First, as we have already mentioned, in all four accounts of the Last Supper, he speaks of his own "blood" as establishing a new "covenant" between God and his people (Matt. 26:28; Mark 14:24; Luke 22:20; 1 Cor. 11:25). Second, and equally important, he commands the disciples to repeat his actions in "remembrance" of him:

> And he took bread, and when he had given thanks he broke it and gave it to them, saying, "This is my body which is given for you. *Do this in remembrance of me.*" And likewise the cup after supper, saying, "This cup which is poured out for you is *the new covenant in my blood.*" (Luke 22:19–20)[55]

1951–55), 1:4.

54 That is, scholars who reject the idea that Jesus shared the eschatological expectation of an imminent cosmic catastrophe. See Robert J. Millar (ed.), *The Apocalyptic Jesus: A Debate* (Santa Rosa: Polebridge, 2001); John Dominic Crossan, *The Historical Jesus: the Life of a Mediterranean Jewish Peasant* (San Francisco: HarperCollins, 1991). For a very helpful analysis, see also Ben Witherington III, *Jesus the Seer: the Progress of Prophecy* (Peabody: Hendrickson, 1999), 246–292. In recent times a number of scholars differ from Schweitzer in rejecting as unhistorical the three key passages in which Jesus seems to speak of the imminent advent of the kingdom of God (Matt. 10:23; Mark 9:1; 13:30 [and parallels]). With this solution, the difficulty of the imminent end of history disappears, though the problem of exactly what the coming of the kingdom means remains. See, for example, Meier, *A Marginal Jew*, 2:336–348; Gnilka *Jesus of Nazareth*, 147–149; Perrin, *Rediscovering the Teaching of Jesus*, 199–202.

55 In treating the longer version of the words of institution in Luke's Gospel as text-critically authentic, I am following the most recent and exhaustive work on the subject by Bradly S. Billings, *Do This in Remembrance of Me: The Disputed Words in the Lukan Institution Narrative (Luke 22:19b–20): An Historico-Exegetical, Theological, and Sociological Analysis*, Library of New Testament Studies (London: T. & T. Clark, 2006) as well as François Bovon, *Luke* 3, trans. James Crouch (Hermeneia; Minneapolis: Fortress, 2012), 154–155. See also Eldon Jay Epp, "The Disputed Words of the Eucharistic Institution (Luke 22, 19b–20): The Long and Short of the Matter," *Biblica* 90 (2009): 407–416; Marshall, "The Last Supper," 529–541; Fitzmyer, *Luke*, 2:1387–1389. Given the strength and diversity of the manuscripts of Luke that contain the longer form and the circularity of arguments in favor of the shorter version, this seems to be the strongest position.

> For I received from the Lord what I also delivered to you, that the Lord Jesus on the night when he was betrayed took bread, and when he had given thanks, he broke it, and said, "*This is my body which is for you. Do this in remembrance of me.*" In the same way also the cup, after supper, saying, "*This cup is the new covenant in my blood. Do this, as often as you drink it, in remembrance of me.*" (1 Cor. 11:23–25)

Taken together, these passages can be accurately described as words of *institution*, in which Jesus is commanding the disciples to repeat a particular ritual in his absence and after his death.

In light of such texts, T. Francis Glasson, one of the twentieth century's most vocal critics of Schweitzer's reconstruction, makes a case against the apocalyptic Jesus of the immediate end in his small but significant book, *Jesus and the End of the World*.[56] First, Glasson argues that the command to repeat his actions at the Last Supper implies that Jesus did *not* expect the end of history to coincide with his death:

> For seventy years we have been told that Jesus could not have envisaged the Church because his view of the future left no interval of time in which such a community could operate. Yet the evidence ... surely shows that he did count on the continuance of human history after his death ... The words "This do in remembrance of me" occur twice in the oldest account we have, *1 Corinthians* 11:24 and 25 ... However the words are interpreted, they are inconsistent with the view that Jesus expected the world to end immediately after his crucifixion ...[57]

Second, and perhaps even more important, Glasson points out that Jesus' words about establishing a new "covenant" in his blood not only shows that he did not think the world would end immediately, but rather, when interpreted in light of the Jewish Scriptures, that the era of Jesus' new covenant would endure for some time:

> [Even a] "short interval" does not appear to do justice to the conception of a new covenant and a period in which it would operate ... The words "my blood of the covenant" (Mark 14:24) and "This cup is the new covenant in my blood" (1 Corinthians 11:25) look back, as the commentators remind us, to Exodus

56 T. F. Glasson, *Jesus and the End of the World* (Edinburgh: St. Andrew, 1980). See also the important essay, T. Francis Glasson, "Schweitzer's Influence—Blessing or Bane?," *Journal of Theological Studies* 28 (1977): 289–302.

57 Glasson, *Jesus and the End of the World*, 65–66.

> 24 ... Jesus knew that the covenant at Sinai had been instituted many centuries before. Is it conceivable that he envisaged only a "short interval" before the Last Judgment and a supernatural new world? ... When Jesus in the upper room referred to this [the covenant], surely he cannot at the same time have thought that a catastrophic kingdom was imminent, bringing history to an end, and touching off the resurrection of the dead, the last judgment, a new heaven and earth. This just does not make sense. Judas had departed, and Jesus knew that in all probability he had not many hours to live. Was the new covenant to operate for merely a few hours, or a few days, or a "short interval"?[58]

This is a powerful argument, one that to my knowledge has never been rebutted by advocates of Schweitzer's reconstruction. If Jesus did indeed think that the end of the world would coincide with his death, or even that it would take place a few days thereafter, then it would be nonsense—especially in a Jewish context—for him to compare his actions to the covenant established by Moses at Sinai, which had lasted for well over a thousand years. By contrast, once we dispense with the idea that Jesus expected the immediate end of the world and entertain the possibility that he expected history to continue after his death—however long that may be—then both his commands to repeat his actions in memory of him and his establishment of a new covenant make good sense.

Should there be any doubt about the problems caused by the words of institution for the hypothesis of Jesus as an apocalyptic prophet of the immediate end, it is striking to note how, over the course of the last century, scholarly advocates of Schweitzer's hypothesis consistently *ignore* the words of institution in their reconstruction of Jesus' eschatology.[59] For example, in Schweitzer's famous work, *The Quest of the Historical Jesus,* he dismisses the words of institution with a single sentence.

> The mysterious images which He used at the time of the distribution concerning the atoning significance of His death do not

58 Glasson, *Jesus and the End of the World,* 67–68.

59 This tendency to downplay the words of institution can already be found in the seminal work of Johannes Weiss, *Jesus' Proclamation of the Kingdom of God,* trans. R. H. Hiers and D. L Holland (Philadelphia: Fortress, 1971 [orig. 1892]), 83–84. To be fair, there are some scholars indebted to Schweitzer's outlook who give attention to the Last Supper, such as Wright, *Jesus and the Victory of God,* 553–563; Jeremias, *New Testament Theology I,* 288–292; idem, *The Eucharistic Words of Jesus,* trans. Norman Perrin (London: SCM; New York: Charles Scribner's Sons, 1966). That said, even these scholars do not often make clear how to reconcile the command to repeat Jesus' actions and the imagery of a new covenant fit into the overall picture of Jesus' eschatology.

> touch the essence of the celebration, they are only discourses accompanying it.[60]

Notice here that Schweitzer does not argue that the words of institution are unhistorical—the evidence for them is too strong for that—he just dismisses them as insignificant, not touching the "essence" of the Last Supper.

Along similar lines is the work of E. P. Sanders, who follows Schweitzer's basic reconstruction of Jesus as a Jewish eschatological prophet for whom "the end was at hand."[61] Remarkably, when it comes to the Last Supper, Sanders concludes it is "almost equally certain" in historical plausibility to Jesus' act of cleansing of the Temple, which he considers certain.[62] However, while Sanders devotes two long chapters to Jesus' words and deeds regarding the temple, *he completely ignores the Last Supper* and never explains how the words of institution can be reconciled with his overall reconstruction of Jesus' eschatology.[63]

Last, but certainly not least, there is the work of Dale Allison, one of the most brilliant and persistent advocates for Schweitzer's apocalyptic Jesus. In his most comprehensive study to date, Allison makes a powerful case for Jesus as an apocalyptic prophet of the immediate end of the world.[64] While Allison capably shows that eschatological concepts such as the kingdom of God and the Son of man are front and center in the accounts of the Last Supper (Matt. 26:24–29; Mark 14:21–25; Luke 22:14–22), he gives no detailed discussion of the words of institution.[65] Indeed, in Allison's many writings on Jesus and eschatology, he never explains how the words of institution do or do not fit into his overall reconstruction of Jesus' eschatology.[66]

In short, it seems that the apocalyptic Jesus of the immediate end of history has proven very hard to square with the Jesus of the Last Supper. This is an interesting situation. Given the importance in Jesus research of the question of

---

60 Schweitzer, *The Quest of the Historical Jesus*, 380.

61 Sanders, *Jesus and Judaism*, 334. (For his differences with Schweitzer, see Sanders, *Jesus and Judaism*, 327–330).

62 Sanders, *Jesus and Judaism*, 307.

63 See Sanders, *Jesus and Judaism*, 131–133.

64 See Allison, *Constructing Jesus*, 31–220.

65 The Last Supper texts are listed, but not discussed, in Allison, *Constructing Jesus*, 41, 79, 178, 403.

66 See for example, Dale C. Allison, Jr., *The Historical Christ and the Theological Jesus* (Grand Rapids: Eermdans, 2009); Dale C. Allison Jr., "Jesus and the Victory of Apocalyptic," in *Jesus & the Restoration of Israel: A Critical Assessment of N. T. Wright's Jesus and the Victory of God*, ed. Carey C. Newman (Downers Grove: InterVarsity, 1999), 126–141; Dale C. Allison Jr., *Jesus of Nazareth: Millennarian Prophet*; Dale C. Allison Jr., "The Eschatology of Jesus," in *The Encyclopedia of Apocalypticism: Volume I: The Origins of Apocalypticism in Judaism and Christianity*, ed. John J. Collins (New York: Continuum, 1998), 267–302; Dale C. Allison Jr., "A Plea for Thoroughgoing Eschatology," *Journal of Biblical Literature* (1994): 651–668.

his eschatological expectations, it seems that any worthwhile reconstruction of Jesus' eschatology must take into account his words and deeds at the Last Supper. To be sure, the words of institution can be dismissed as unhistorical; they can be reinterpreted so as to accommodate an imminent eschatology; but they should not simply be ignored.

IV. Jesus and the Early Church

The fourth and final issue has to do with the question of Jesus' intentions and the origin of the early church. On the one hand, in contrast to popular Christian belief, many scholars conclude that Jesus himself did *not* intend to found a church. Indeed, any talk of such an intention on his part is commonly viewed as anachronistic. For example, the famous text in which Jesus speaks of building his "assembly" or "church" on Peter (Matt. 16:18–19) is widely ignored or regarded as unhistorical by most works on Jesus.

On the other hand, several scholars have argued that the eucharistic words of institution, when situated in the context of ancient Jewish hopes for the restoration of Israel, *do* reveal an intention on Jesus' part both to replace the Jerusalem Temple cult with his own sacrificial meal and, in this way, to begin a new community. From this perspective, a case can be made that at the Last Supper Jesus deliberately founded a new cult, one focused on the sacrifice of his own body and blood that would establish a new "covenant."

The Question of Jesus and the Church

The first of these two positions—that Jesus did not intend to found any kind of enduring community and that it is anachronistic to speak of him instituting the church—is widely attested. In 1902, it found its classic formulation in the work of the French biblical scholar Alfred Loisy, who famously asserted:

> It is certain, for instance, that Jesus did not systematize beforehand the constitution of the Church as that of a government established on earth and destined to endure for a long series of centuries ... *Jesus foretold the kingdom, and it was the Church that came.*[67]

Although this last line has often been taken out of context, it became, over the course of the twentieth century, an influential way of summing up the discontinuity between the intentions of the historical Jesus and the actual effects of his ministry. Indeed, many recent studies, if they take up the question of Jesus and the church at all, often declare—usually in no uncertain terms—that he did not intend to found

67 Alfred Loisy, *The Gospel and the Church*, trans. Christopher Home (London: Isbister & Co., 1903), 166.

any kind of community that would live on after his death. Consider, for example, the following:

> [T]here arise most serious doubts as to whether the historical Jesus himself really did speak these words [to Peter about the building of the church]. This is not only because they have no parallel in the other Gospels, and because this is the only place in the whole synoptic tradition where the word "*ekklēsia*" appears in the sense of the church as a whole ... But the authenticity of the passage in Matthew xvi is questioned chiefly because it is not easily compatible with Jesus' proclamation of the imminent coming of the kingdom of God.[68]

> [L]et it be re-stated for a last time, if [Jesus] meant and believed what he preached ... namely, that the eternal Kingdom of God was truly at hand, he simply could not have entertained the idea of founding and setting in motion an organized society intended to endure for ages to come.[69]

> [*E*]*kklēsia* in Matt. 16:18 comes from the usage of the early church, and not from the historical Jesus ... It is difficult to imagine such a usage in the mouth of the historical Jesus.[70]

> Jesus cannot have spoken these words [in Matt. 16:18–19] as he did not found a church.[71]

> In two famous passages in Matthew, Jesus is reported as speaking of his *ekklēsia* ... Both passages are probably redactional and indicative of later developments.[72]

It should be clear from statements such as these that many modern biblical scholars, even those who are otherwise disposed to affirm many of the sayings of Jesus in the Synoptic Gospels as historically reliable, reject the notion that the Jesus of history intended to found a church of any kind. Note in particular that Bornkamm and Vermes (see above quotes) reject the idea that Jesus instituted any kind of ecclesial community because they believe that Jesus expected an imminent coming of the kingdom of God (similar to the view of Loisy).

---

68 Bornkamm, *Jesus of Nazareth*, 187.

69 Vermes, *The Religion of Jesus the Jew*, 214.

70 Meier, *A Marginal Jew*, 3:232, 233.

71 Lüdemann, *Jesus After 2000 Years*, 198.

72 Dunn, *Jesus Remembered*, 513.

Indeed, many recent books on the historical Jesus show their allegiance to the idea that Jesus did not intend to found a church by simply ignoring the question altogether. One searches the indexes of a remarkable number of major works on Jesus in vain for any discussion of whether or not he intended to found a community in the wake of his death.[73] Hand in hand with the apocalyptic Jesus of the imminent end of history, the non-ecclesial Jesus also seems to have largely won the day.

The Problem of the Cultic Words of Jesus

One problem with this "non-ecclesial" view is that it fails to take seriously the evidence for Jesus' intentions implicit in the accounts the Last Supper. For example, in all four accounts, Jesus explicitly speaks of a "covenant" that is centered on the sacrifice of his own blood, not the covenant sacrifices of the Jerusalem Temple (Matt. 26:28; Mark 14:24; Luke 22:20; 1 Cor. 11:25). Moreover, in the Synoptic accounts this covenant is not established with just anyone, but with "the twelve" disciples who represent the nucleus of a new Israel that is bound together by the blood of Jesus rather than the blood of Jacob the patriarch (Matt. 26:20; Mark 14:17; Luke 22:14, 28–30).[74]

In light of this evidence, a number of studies over the course of the last century have concluded that Jesus did in fact intend to establish a new covenant in his own blood and a new community in the persons of the twelve disciples. Although the following articulations are lengthy, they are worth citing in full:

---

73 For example, in many reconstructions of Jesus' life, the famous passage in which Jesus speaks of "building" the "church" (*ekklēsia*) on the disciple Peter (Matt. 16:16–19) is treated almost as if it did not exist. The following major works on Jesus simply ignore the evidence that Jesus intended to "build" his *ekklēsia* on Peter and his disciples, leaving the reader to come to his or her own (negative) conclusion: Allison, *Constructing Jesus*; David R. Flusser, with R. Steven Notley, *The Sage from Galilee: Rediscovering Jesus' Genius* (Grand Rapids: Eerdmans, 2007); Fredriksen, *Jesus of Nazareth: King of the Jews*; Ehrman, *Jesus: Apocalyptic Prophet*; Sanders, *The Historical Figure of Jesus*; Becker, *Jesus of Nazareth*; Allison, *Jesus of Nazareth*; Crossan, *The Historical Jesus*; Vermes, *Jesus the Jew*; Perrin, *Rediscovering the Teaching of Jesus*, etc. Other scholars will briefly mention Matt. 16:16–19 as the source of Simon's being renamed "Peter," but either dismiss or ignore Jesus' express statements about building his *ekklēsia* on Peter. See, for example, Gnilka, *Jesus of Nazareth*, 186–187; Sanders, *Jesus and Judaism*, 146–147; Bornkamm, *Jesus of Nazareth*, 186–187. As always, there are exceptions. See, for example, Michael J. Wilkins, "Peter's Declaration concerning Jesus' Identity at Casearea Philippi," in *Key Events in the Life of the Historical Jesus*, eds. Darrell L. Bock and Robert L. Webb, Wissenschaftliche Untersuchungen zum Neuen Testament 247 (Tübingen: Mohr Siebeck, 2009), 292–381; Michael F. Bird, *Jesus and the Origins of the Gentile Mission*, Library of New Testament Studies 331 (Edinburgh: T. & T. Clark, 2007), 155–161.

74 On Jesus and the restoration of the twelve tribes of Israel, see Meier, *A Marginal Jew*, 3:153; Allison, *Jesus of Nazareth*, 101–102; Wright, *Jesus and the Victory of God*, 300; Sanders, *Jesus and Judaism*, 97; Jeremias, *New Testament Theology*, 234. See also Pitre, *Jesus, the Tribulation, and the End of the Exile*, throughout.

> If Jesus understood his Messiah-ship in the sense of Daniel 7, this will open up new vistas when we are considering the nature and the importance of his founding of the Church. For the Son of Man in Daniel is not a mere individual: he is the representative of 'the people of the saints of the Most High' and has set himself the task of making this people of God, the *ekklēsia*, a reality. *From this point of view, the so-called institution of the Lord's Supper can be shown to be the formal founding of the Church.*[75]

> The decisive saying for the connection of the message of a crucified Messiah with the reconstituted People of God is to be found in the words of institution at the Last Supper, and particularly in the use of the word *diatheke* ["covenant"] ... *If we may look for any one moment wherein the new Israel was constituted, it would be in the act of Jesus at the Last Supper.*[76]

> In the time of Jesus the sectaries of Qumran regarded themselves as the people of the new covenant. The idea, therefore, of a covenant as the foundation charter (so to speak) of the people of God was very much alive at the time, and *there can be no doubt what Jesus had in mind when he invited his followers to drink of the cup of the covenant: he was formally installing them as foundation members of the new people of God.*[77]

> *By the command 'Do this'* (Luke 22.19; cf. 1 Cor. 11:25) *he enjoined the continuation of this fellowship in his absence and endowed it with a distinctive social and cultic act.* This was to be the visible unifying factor of a community otherwise remaining scattered throughout Israel ... Until the definitive gathering of the saved at the end of time the aims of Jesus would be incarnated in this community, at once the remnant and the first fruits of messianic Israel.[78]

> [T]he twelve disciples were probably looked upon by Jesus as the nucleus of the restored people of God in an eschatological sense. The choosing of the twelve took place during Jesus' Galilean

75 Karl Ludwig Schmidt, *The Church*, trans. J. R. Coates (London: SCM, 1950 [orig. 1935]), 39–40 (emphasis added). Here Schmidt is following F. Kattenbusch, "Der Quellort der Kirchenidee," in *Festgabe von fachgenossen und freunden A. von Harnack zum siebzigsten geburtstag dargebracht* (Tübingen: Mohr-Siebeck, 1921), 143–172, espec. 171.

76 R. Newton Flew, *Jesus and His Church* (London: Epworth, 1938), 71, 76 (emphasis added).

77 C. H. Dodd, *The Founder of Christianity* (London: Macmillan, 1970), 96.

78 Ben F. Meyer, *The Aims of Jesus* (London: SCM, 1979), 219 (emphasis added).

> ministry. The interesting point now to note is that the *definitive* constitution of this new people of God *in nuce* was done in proleptic manner *at the Last Supper*.[79]

> The symbolic action against the temple cult was complemented by *Jesus' symbolic action at the last supper in founding a cult,* though he did not intend to found a cult which would last through time. He simply wanted to replace provisionally the temple cult which had become obsolete: *Jesus offers the disciples a replacement for the official cult in which they could either no longer take part, or which would not bring them salvation—until a new temple came.* This 'substitute' was a simple meal. By a new interpretation, the last supper becomes a substitute for the temple cult—a pledge of the eating and drinking in the kingdom of God which is soon to dawn.[80]

Three aspects of these proposals are worth highlighting.

First, the question of Jesus' self-understanding and the question of his intentions are inextricably bound up with one another.[81] For if Jesus saw himself as the messianic head of a "new" Israel, then one of his key tasks will be to gather the eschatological community.

Second, insofar as the Last Supper was intended to function as a unifying event among the twelve disciples, it would have the effect of creating an eschatological community. In other words, the Last Supper is not just a sign of the restoration of Israel, but to a certain extent, the very *means* by which Jesus unifies the community of followers that would exist in his absence.[82]

Third, the presence of the language of a "covenant" at the Last Supper is implicitly but undeniably cultic. In a Jewish context, such language would have enormous implications. Indeed, as a number of scholars have suggested recently, when Jesus' demonstration in the Temple and the Last Supper are taken together, they may suggest that he intended to replace the atoning cult of the Jerusalem Temple with the atoning cult of his own sacrifice, embodied in the eucharist.[83] In

---

79 Kim Huat Tan, *The Zion Traditions and the Aims of Jesus*, Society for New Testament Studies Monograph Series 91 (Cambridge: Cambridge University Press, 1997), 217.

80 Gerd Theissen and Annette Merz, *The Historical Jesus: A Comprehensive Guide*, trans. John Bowden (Minneapolis: Fortress, 1998), 434 (emphasis added).

81 As Schmidt says elsewhere: "The question whether Jesus himself founded the Church is really the question concerning his Messiah-ship." Schmidt, *The Church*, 41.

82 See also Gerhard Lohfink, *Jesus and Community*, trans. John P. Galvin (Philadelphia: Fortress; New York: Paulist, 1984), 9–12, 23–26; Jeremias, *New Testament Theology*, 167–170.

83 See, for example, Brant Pitre, "Jesus, the New Temple, and the New Priesthood," *Letter & Spirit* 4 (2008): 47–83, espec. 63–82; McKnight, *Jesus and His Death*, 325–328; Jostein Ådna, *Jesu Stellung zum Tempel*, Wissenschaftliche Untersuchungen zum Neuen Testament (Tübingen:

short, the messianic Jesus, as head of a new community, and the eucharistic Jesus, as the founder of a new cultic rite, lead directly to the ecclesial Jesus, the founder of a community unified by his leadership and his covenant.

If any of the suggestions listed above are correct, then Jesus' actions at the Last Supper do not cohere well with the overly simplistic (but quite common) picture of an eschatological prophet who had no intentions of establishing any community that would survive him. To the contrary, when the words and deeds of Jesus are interpreted within the context of ancient Judaism, a case can be made that he not only awaited the eschatological restoration of the people of Israel, he deliberately established the nucleus of a new Israel precisely by means of the Last Supper. At the very least, the question of Jesus' intentions cannot simply be decided on the basis of an evaluation of Jesus' words to Peter at Caesarea Philippi; the accounts of the Last Supper must be taken into account. As A. J. B. Higgins aptly stated in his study of the Lord's Supper:

> *The cleavage of opinion as to whether Jesus did or did not 'found' the Church has its counterpart in the debate on the origin of the Eucharist.* Was it deliberately 'instituted' by Jesus himself, or is it a natural and perhaps inevitable development which began in the earliest days of the Church, but which Jesus had neither foreseen nor intended? These two questions of the Church and the Eucharist are inseparably connected, just as it is impossible to isolate Israel and the Passover from one another.[84]

In other words, if Jesus did indeed institute a new cultic ritual to be performed after his death by his twelve disciples as the sign of a new covenant with the new Israel, then, on some level, he certainly envisioned a community that would perform the ritual. And if he did indeed intend to replace the Jerusalem Temple cult with the sacrificial banquet of the coming kingdom of God, then the whole question of the opposition between the kingdom and the church posed by Loisy at the start

---

Mohr-Siebeck, 2000), 2.119; Jostein Ådna, "Jesus' Symbolic Action in the Temple (Mark 11:15-17): The Replacement of the Sacrificial Cult by His Atoning Death," in *Gemeinde ohne Tempel*, eds. Beate Ego, Armin Lange, and Peter Pilhofer (Tübingen: Mohr Siebeck, 1999), 461–473; Bruce D. Chilton, *Rabbi Jesus* (New York: Doubleday, 2000), 248–257; Wright, *Jesus and the Victory of God*, 557–563; Bruce Chilton, *The Temple of Jesus* (University Park: Pennsylvania State University, 1992); Jacob Neusner, "Money-Changers in the Temple: The Mishnah's Explanation," *New Testament Studies* 35 (1989): 287–290 (here 290).

84 A. J. B. Higgins, *The Lord's Supper in the New Testament* (Chicago: Alec R. Allenson; Alva: Robert Cunningham and Sons, 1952), 9. For similar sentiments, see Vermes, *The Religion of Jesus the Jew*, 15: "[T]he historical authenticity of the establishment of the eucharist as a permanent institution depends not only on whether the meal was really a Passover supper celebrated on the correct date ..., but also on whether [Jesus] ever envisaged the creation of an enduring church." See also Rudolf Pesch, "Das Abendmahl, Jesu Todesverständnis und die Konstitution der Kirche," in *Das Abendmahl und Jesu Todesverständnis* (Freiburg: Herder, 1978), 112–125.

of the century needs to be reexamined. If what Jesus intended for his followers is important, then the quest for the historical Jesus must pay serious attention to the question of what he did and said—and hence, what he intended—at the Last Supper.

Conclusions

Although contemporary Jesus research is dominated by the four questions of Jesus' relationship to Judaism, his self-understanding, his eschatological outlook, and his intentions toward the community of his followers, and while the words and deeds of Jesus at the Last Supper have a direct bearing on each of these questions, a remarkable number of major scholarly reconstructions have failed to integrate the Last Supper into their overall portraits of the historical figure of Jesus.

If the accounts of the "eucharistic" words and deeds of Jesus in the Gospels are historically plausible, then at least four preliminary implications follow for contemporary research.

First, scholarship needs to clarify how it is that the Jewish Jesus and the eucharistic Jesus can be reconciled with one another. One way forward—keeping in mind the patently Jewish context of the scene—is to recognize elements of both *continuity* and *discontinuity* in Jesus' words and deeds at the Last Supper. To take but one example: the very *Jewish* belief that "the life is in the blood" (Lev. 17:11), which is the rationale behind the prohibition of drinking animal blood in the Old Testament, provides a plausible explanation for why drinking the blood of Jesus is necessary. Unless one drinks the "blood" of the "Son of man," one has no *eschatological* "life" (John 6:53–56). In other words, far from undermining the Jewish Jesus, the complex combination of continuity and discontinuity in an eschatological context has a great deal of explanatory power in clarifying how Jesus the Jew could have ever uttered such words. It is only as a Jew that his eucharistic words makes sense.

Second, along similar lines, if contemporary Jesus research wants to take the accounts of the Last Supper as actual history, it needs to seriously reconsider what Martin Hengel and Raymond Brown referred to as the "dogma" of the "non-messianic Jesus." No mere *prophet* of Israel, however great, ever saw his own "blood" as having the power to establish the eschatological "covenant" that would inaugurate the year of the forgiveness of sins (see Jer. 31:31–33; Ezek. 16:59–63). Far more plausibly, the Jesus of the Last Supper accounts is, christologically speaking, a *self-referential* Jesus. He not only proclaims the coming of the kingdom, he places himself and his own sacrificial death at the center and head of that coming kingdom. This makes perfect sense if Jesus sees himself as the king of the kingdom of God (see Dan. 7:13–15); it makes no historical sense whatsoever if Jesus thinks of himself as merely its herald.

Third, the now aging, exegetically myopic portrait of Jesus the "apocalyptic prophet" of the imminent "end of the world" made so influential by Albert

Schweitzer and Rudolf Bultmann not only needs to be reconsidered, it needs to be completely retooled. On the one hand—as I have argued at length elsewhere—it is certainly the case that Jesus drew upon and spoke in the language of Jewish "apocalyptic"—especially as found in the book of Daniel.[85] On the other hand, the evidence in the Last Supper accounts where Jesus saw himself as instituting a new "covenant" (Matt. 26:28; Mark 14:24; Luke 22:20; 1 Cor. 11:25) simply cannot be reconciled with the simplistic reconstruction in which he expected the destruction of the cosmos and final judgment to coincide with or happen shortly after his own death. Instead, as T. F. Glasson showed some time ago, Jesus' words about instituting a new covenant presuppose at the very least a "substantial interim period" during which this new covenant, like the old covenants before it, would function.[86]

Fourth and finally, but by no means least significantly, the widespread assumption that it is almost historically meaningless to ask whether Jesus intended to found an "assembly" (Greek *ekklēsia*; Hebrew *qahal*) needs to be radically called into question by the undeniably *cultic* character of Jesus' words of institution (drawing, as he does, upon the temple language of sacrifice; see Matt. 26:28; Mark 14:24; Luke 22:20; 1 Cor. 11:25). If Jesus' actions at the Last Supper are understood as a deliberate effort to establish a new "temple," then it seems equally clear that he expected his disciples to be united in the cultic offering of sacrifice in a manner akin to the people of the old temple. Like the Passover of old offered as a "memorial" that both united and constituted Israel (Exod. 12:14), he expected the assembly that he left behind to repeat the inaugural sign performed at the Last Supper as an act of "remembrance" (Luke 22:19; 1 Cor. 11:23–24).

To the extent that contemporary Jesus scholarship continues to explore the four *historical* questions of his relationship with Judaism, his self-understanding, his eschatological outlook, and his ecclesial intentions, it can also provide insights useful to the *theological* study of typology, christology, eschatology, and ecclesiology. In this way, one can say that Albert Schweitzer was right: "The problem of the Lord's Supper *is* the problem of the life of Jesus!"[87]

---

85 See Brant J. Pitre, "Apocalypticism and Apocalyptic Teaching," in *Dictionary of Jesus and the Gospels*, 2nd ed., eds. Joel B. Green, Jeannine K. Brown, and Nicholas Perrin (Downers Grove: IVP Academic, 2013), 23–33.

86 Pitre, "Apocalypticism," 29.

87 Schweitzer, *The Problem of the Lord's Supper*, 137.

Letter & Spirit 9 (2014): 105-123

"All Things in Wisdom"
Reading the Prologue to the Gospel of John with St. Augustine

~: **William M. Wright IV** :~

Duquesne University

Introduction

The first eighteen verses of the Gospel according to John, more commonly known as the Prologue, envision all things in relation to the Word (or Son) of God.[1] The Prologue's opening words, "In the beginning" (John 1:1), are a deliberate allusion to the beginning of the Book of Genesis, and through this allusion, the Prologue signals to its audience that it is providing a "re-reading" of things in several respects.[2]

First, given that the Book of Genesis opens the biblical canon, the Prologue's allusion to Genesis 1:1 indicates that it is offering a summarized version of the whole biblical drama in light of the Incarnate Word. The Prologue moves from the creation of all things through the Word (1:1–5), the prophetic witness to that Word (1:6–8, 15), to the presence and activity of the Word in creation generally and in the history of Israel specifically (1:9–13), and it culminates in the incarnation of the Word and the gifts made available to humanity through him (1:14–18).

Second, as Genesis 1:1 introduces the creation accounts in Genesis, the Prologue envisions the whole of creation in relation to God's Word. Making use of biblical traditions about God's Word and Wisdom (for example, Wisd. 9:1–9), the Prologue presents all created reality existing in relation to and by virtue of the Divine Word.

Third, the Prologue goes beyond the canonical narrative and the whole of creation to provide a glimpse of the inner-life of the Godhead as an eternal

1 For a fuller exposition of John's Prologue, see Francis Martin and William M. Wright IV, *The Gospel of John* (Grand Rapids: Baker Academic, *forthcoming*), chapter 1; C. K. Barrett, *The Gospel according to St. John*, 2nd ed. (Philadelphia: The Westminster Press, 1978), 149–170; Daniel Boyarin, "The Gospel of the *Memra*: Jewish Binitarianism and the Prologue to John," *Harvard Theological Review* 94 (2001): 243–284; Raymond E. Brown, S.S., *The Gospel according to John*, Anchor Bible 29–29A (New York: Doubleday, 1966–1970), 1.1–37; Francis J. Moloney, S.D.B., *The Gospel of John*, Sacra Pagina 4 (Collegeville: Liturgical Press, 1998), 33–48; Gail R. O'Day, "The Gospel of John," in *New Interpreter's Bible* 9 (Nashville: Abingdon, 1995), 515–524; Rudolf Schnackenburg, *The Gospel According to St. John*, trans. by Kevin Smyth et al., 3 vols. (New York: Crossroad, 1968–1982), 1.221–281.

2 In this article, when Scriptural texts are being quoted in their own right, the translations will be my own from the original text. However, when they are being quoted in the context of Augustine's exegesis, I will quote from Augustine's Latin text of Scripture as it is rendered in Hill's translation of Augustine.

exchange of life and love between God and his Word (or, the Father and the Son; compare 1:1, 14, 18).

The basis of the Prologue's envisioning or "re-reading" of these three things—the canonical narrative, the whole of creation, and the inner-life of God—is the revelation given in the Divine Word made flesh: Jesus of Nazareth.

The subject matter of John's Prologue is most profound, and quite appropriately, this text and its contents have been contemplated by saints and scholars throughout the history of the Church. Consistent with longstanding tradition, the Second Vatican Council states that the Church "strives to reach day by day a more profound understanding of the sacred Scriptures, in order to provide her children with food from the divine words."[3] The Council goes on to specify that in order to move into "a more profound understanding" of Scripture, the Church "duly fosters the study of the Fathers, both Eastern and Western, and of the sacred liturgies."[4] The Council here reaffirms that the biblical interpretation of the Church Fathers constitutes a valuable resource and guide for progressing into a deeper understanding of Scripture.

These hermeneutical prescriptions of Vatican II's *Dei Verbum* [The Word of God] coincide (to an extent) with some interests of the growing scholarly field of biblical reception history. Biblical reception history is the scholarly study of periods, trends, and instances of interpretation throughout the course of the Bible's reception, which itself includes "every single act or word of interpretation of that book (or books) over the course of three millennia."[5] Reception history is "a scholarly enterprise, consisting of selecting and collating shards of that infinite wealth of reception material in accordance with the particular interests of the historian concerned, and giving them a narrative frame."[6] Biblical reception history is a highly diverse and eclectic field, and its practitioners undertake this scholarly research for a variety of different reasons and ends.

In this essay, we will seek—in concert with the teachings of *Dei Verbum*—a deeper understanding of John's Prologue by examining it in light of its interpretation by one of its most important and consequential readers: St. Augustine. Focusing on Augustine's *Tractates on the Gospel according to John* 1–3 (henceforth *Tract. Ev. Jo.*), I will attend to the ways in which Augustine develops the Prologue's unifying vision

---

3 Second Vatican Council, *Dei Verbum* [The Word of God], Dogmatic Constitution on Divine Revelation, (November 18, 2965), §23, in *Vatican II: The Conciliar and Post Conciliar Documents*, New Revised Edition, gen. eds. Austin Flannery, O.P. (Boston: St. Paul Books & Media, 1992), 763.

4 *Dei Verbum* §23, *Vatican II: The Conciliar and Post Conciliar Documents*, 763.

5 Jonathan Roberts, "Introduction," in *The Oxford Handbook of the Reception History of the Bible*, eds. Michael Lieb, Emma Mason, and Jonathan Roberts (Oxford and New York: Oxford University Press, 2013 [2011]), 1.

6 Roberts, "Introduction," 1.

of things in relation to God's Word or Wisdom.[7] What emerges from Augustine's interpretation is a synthetic account of "all things in Wisdom," wherein all created realities, and human beings in particular, creation and redemption, revelation and reason, the Old and New Covenants, are all inter-connected with one another by virtue of their relation to Christ, the Word and Wisdom of God.[8]

I. The Divine Word

John begins the Prologue with the mystery of God: "In the beginning was the Word and the Word was with God and the Word was God. He was in the beginning with God" (1:1–2). Drawing on biblical imagery for God's Word or Wisdom as being present with or involved when God creates (see Prov. 8:22–31; Wisd. 9:1–9), John's Prologue sets forth the life of God as constituted by unity and distinction: "the Word was with God" (there is distinction) and "the Word was God" (there is unity and identity) (1:1). The divine life, or "identity," is a relationship between God and his Word, or, to use the register introduced at 1:14, the Father and the Son.[9]

Throughout his ministry, Jesus speaks of the Father as the source of his life and mission. Jesus is the Son, the one whom the Father has sent into the world for its salvation (3:16–17). Jesus' unique and eternal relationship with the Father as his only Son makes him the only one who can reveal the Father to the world (1:18; 6:44; 14:9–10). All of Jesus' words and deeds are given him to do by the Father (5:19–20; 8:38–39; 14:11), and he carries out his mission in perfect love and obedience (10:17–18). The Father gives his everything to the Son (5:24), and as is made manifest in the gift of his life on the cross, the Son in turns gives his everything back to the Father. Jesus acts with the Father's power and authority (10:30), and a response to Jesus is the same as a response to the Father who sent him (5:20–23).[10] Thus, when viewed in light of the Gospel narrative, these opening

---

7 English citations of Augustine's *Tract. Ev. Jo.* will be taken from Augustine, *Homilies on the Gospel of John 1–40*, trans. Edmund Hill, O.P. (Hyde Park: New City Press, 2009). Citations of Augustine's Latin texts will be taken from the editions in *Patrologia latina*, ed. J. P. Migne, 217 vols. (Paris, 1844–1864); henceforth abbreviated as PL.

8 The phrase "all things in wisdom" comes from Augustine's quotation of Ps. 103:24 in *Tract. Ev. Jo.* 1.16 (Hill 51).

9 The use of "divine identity" as a means for understanding New Testament claims about Jesus vis-à-vis the God of Israel is set forth in Richard Bauckham, *Jesus and the God of Israel: God Crucified and Other Studies on the New Testament's Christology of Divine Identity* (Grand Rapids: Eerdmans, 2008). The Fourth Gospel does not explicitly speak of the Holy Spirit as "God" as it does of the Word. However, the Fourth Gospel does speak of the Spirit as "holy" (1:33; 14:26; 20:22)—a modifier which John reserves only to the divine (the Father, in 17:11; the Son, in 6:69). Moreover, in the Farewell Discourse, Jesus speaks of the Spirit as being sent by (and thus closely related to) the Father and himself and never acting independently of them (16:13–15). In subsequent doctrinal statements and Trinitarian theology, the Holy Spirit is identified (by analogy) with the eternal love existing between the Father and the Son, and when the Prologue is read in light of subsequent Christian doctrine, the Spirit's inclusion within the Godhead could be taken as implied.

10 This identification of a response to Jesus as a response to the Father likely reflects ancient Jewish

words of the Prologue invite us to think of the relationship of God (the Father) and the Word (the Son) as turned towards each other in an infinite exchange of life and love: the divine communion.

Confronted with this glimpse into the mystery of God, Augustine opens his homiletic exposition of John's Prologue not by delving immediately into the Gospel but by putting his congregation into an appropriate context for thinking properly about God. He begins by pointing out that the members of his congregation have different capacities to understand spiritual realities. On the one hand, with reference to 1 Corinthians 2:14, Augustine states that many among his hearers are "merely natural, still of a materialist cast of mind and still not able to raise themselves to a spiritual understanding."[11] On the other hand, Augustine also acknowledges that others in his congregation are more intellectually capable of understanding both the Gospel and Augustine's interpretation. Although Augustine's hearers may differ in their abilities to understand spiritually, they will all benefit (no matter their intellectual capacities) from the Scriptural teaching by the grace of God: "Ultimately, the mercy of God will be present, so that all may be satisfied and each one will grasp what he can."[12]

Augustine develops this distinction between those more and less capable of spiritual understanding by interpreting it through Psalm 71:3 ("*May the mountains receive peace for your people and the hills justice*"): "Mountains are lofty souls; hills are ordinary souls."[13] The lofty souls (or mountains), among whom Augustine counts John the Evangelist and John the Baptist, are those who have been illumined according to their respective capacities by God's Wisdom (they "receive peace") so that they might pass on "justice" (which Augustine identifies as faith by way of Rom. 1:17) to those ordinary souls (the hills) with lesser capacities to understand.[14]

Part of the theological payoff of this homiletic opening is to highlight the limits of human beings for grasping spiritual realities and especially God. While Augustine acknowledges that his congregants have different capacities to understand, he speaks of any measure of spiritual understanding as a gift from God, and, in doing so, he effectively levels these differences between his congregants. Both lofty souls and ordinary souls stand in need of illumination by God and any understanding of spiritual realities comes by way of God's grace and mercy—a point

---

understandings of sender and envoy; see Peder Borgen, "God's Agent in the Fourth Gospel," in *Religions in Antiquity: Essays in Memory of Erwin Ramsdell Goodenough*, ed. Jacob Neusner (Leiden: Brill, 1968), 137–148; repr. in *The Interpretation of John*, 2nd ed., ed. John Ashton (Edinburgh: T & T Clark, 1997), 83–95.

11 Augustine, *Tract. Ev. Jo.* 1.1 (Hill 39). The translation of 1 Cor. 2:14 in Augustine's sermon reads "*a merely natural human being does not grasp what pertains to the spirit of God.*"

12 Augustine, *Tract. Ev. Jo.* 1.1 (Hill 39). See also *Tract. Ev. Jo.* 1.7, 13.

13 *Tract. Ev. Jo.* 1.2 (Hill 40).

14 *Tract. Ev. Jo.* 1.2 (Hill 40). Augustine quotes Rom. 1:17 ("*the just person lives by faith*") in *Tract. Ev. Jo.* 1.2 (Hill 40).

to which I will later return. The incomprehensibility of God is, as Lewis Ayres puts it, a fundamental principle of Augustine's "Trinitarian grammar"—before the ineffable mystery of God, all people fall short of understanding and stand in need of God's assistance.[15]

Augustine's teaching about divine incomprehensibility informs his exegesis of John 1:1. He remarks that the opening of the Prologue treats "Christ's inexpressible divinity—and it was spoken almost inexpressibly. Who, in fact, will ever comprehend *In the beginning was the Word, and the Word was with God?*"[16] Augustine calls attention to the use of the verb "to be" (given in the imperfect tense as "was") with reference to the Word in John 1:1. The use of this verb in connection with the Divine Word indicates that the Word, simply, *is*.[17] The Word is eternal, unchanging "Being itself [Latin: *Idipsum est*]... it is the same, ever in the same way; as it is, so it always is; it cannot change; that is what *is* means."[18] As such, the Word is distinct from and transcends all created realities, especially the material and changeable. Thus, Augustine speaks of John the Evangelist, a great mountain, as soaring high above creation, "above and beyond all these created things ... things that were made through the Word" so to contemplate the Divine Word.[19]

II. The Creator Word

Continuing its "re-reading" of Genesis 1, the Prologue teaches that the Divine Word is the agent by which the world was created: "all things came to be through him and apart from him, not one thing came to be" (John 1:3; see also 1:10). All creation exists in relation to the Divine Word, and accordingly, as Raymond Brown writes, "the Word's role in creation means that Jesus has a claim on all."[20] All creation owes its existence to the Divine Word, and, consistent with the broad biblical tradition, the Prologue affirms the radical distinction between the transcendent Creator God and the created world (that is, God and everything-that-is-not-God).[21]

---

15 Lewis Ayres, "The Fundamental Grammar of Augustine's Trinitarian Theology," in *Augustine and His Critics: Essays in Honour of Gerald Bonner*, eds. Robert Dodaro and George Lawless (London and New York: Routledge, 2002 [2000]), 51–76.

16 Augustine, *Tract. Ev. Jo.* 2.2 (Hill 55).

17 Ayres observes that Augustine often regards the Latin *est* ["he, she, or it is"] as a name for God. See Lewis Ayres, *Augustine and the Trinity* (Cambridge and New York: Cambridge University Press, 2010), 201–202.

18 Augustine, *Tract. Ev. Jo.* 2.2 (Hill 55–56); Latin text from PL 35:1389. On Augustine's analysis of *idipsum*, see Ayres, *Augustine and the Trinity*, 200–208.

19 *Tract Ev. Jo.* 1.5 (Hill 42). Elsewhere, Augustine speaks of the eagle as the symbol befitting John the Evangelist because John "flies like an eagle above the clouds of human weakness and looks upon the light of unchanging truth with the sharpest and steadiest eyes of the heart"; quotation from Augustine, *De consensu evangelistarum* [*On the Agreement of the Evangelists*] 1.6.9; translated from PL 34:1047.

20 Brown, *Gospel according to John*, 1.25.

21 A masterful explication of this essential doctrine for all Christian thinking is Robert Sokolowski,

John articulates the distinction by a careful use of two Greek verbs in 1:1–14. When referring to God in himself, John uses the Greek verb *eimi* ("to be") in the imperfect tense: "the Word *was* God." John also uses the Greek verb *ginomai* ("to become") when articulating the "coming to be" of the created world through the Divine Word. In doing so, the Prologue resembles the Septuagint text [LXX] of Genesis 1, which uses the same Greek verb (*ginomai*) in the "Let there be ..." commands spoken by God throughout the days of creation. The dual reservation of the verbs "to be" for God and "to become" for the world continues throughout the Prologue until 1:14 when John sets forth the incarnation of the Word wherein the Divine, Creator Word becomes part of his creation: "the Word *became* flesh and tabernacled among us."

For Augustine, a proper understanding of the Creator/creation relationship is essential for a correct understanding of the Prologue's teachings. Augustine's homilies raise the question of how human beings might understand these statements about God and the Word in the Prologue, given God's radical transcendence and incomprehensibility.

Augustine frames his response by first instructing his congregation to resist thinking about the Divine Word as a thing or within the categories proper to created realities. For instance, Augustine contrasts his own words, which he is presently speaking in his sermon, with God's Word. Augustine's verbalizations sound out and pass away, and thus they are unlike God's Word which is eternal. God's Word is not like Augustine's spoken words, and thus he rhetorically asks, "What kind of Word can it be then, that is both spoken and does not come to an end?"[22] To assist in appropriate thinking about God's Word, Augustine offers the created analogy of the inner, spiritual word.[23] Before a person vocalizes speech, he or she first conceives an inner, immaterial word in the mind (something like an idea, intention, or meaning). A person then conveys this spiritual word to another through the medium of a spoken word. This inner word, Augustine says, "is the word which is really spoken in the spirit, that which you understand from the sound but which is not itself the sound."[24] The spoken word comes to be and then passes away, but the spiritual word remains in the minds of both the speaker and the hearer.[25] Hence, the inner

---

The God of Faith and Reason: Foundations of Christian Theology (Notre Dame: University of Notre Dame Press, 1982), espec. 12–19. For this teaching in Second Temple Judaism, see Bauckham, *Jesus and the God of Israel*, 8–11.

22 Augustine, *Tract. Ev. Jo.* 1.8 (Hill 45).

23 See Lewis Ayres, "Augustine on the Trinity," in *The Oxford Handbook of the Trinity*, eds. Gilles Emery, O.P. and Matthew Levering (New York: Oxford University Press, 2011) 124; Lewis Ayres, *Augustine and the Trinity*, 194–195, 290–293; Gerard Watson, "St. Augustine and the Inner Word: The Philosophical Background," *Irish Theological Quarterly* 54 (1988): 81–92.

24 Augustine, *Tract. Ev. Jo.* 1.8 (Hill 45).

25 Augustine (*Tract. Ev. Jo.* 1.8) states: "The word that sounds out loud dies away and ceases; but what the sound signifies remains both in the thought of the speaker and in the understanding of the hearer; that is what remains when the sounds die away" (Hill 46).

word provides a limited measure of insight into how God's Word could be thought of intelligently as both spoken and enduring. And yet, while the analogy of the inner word has some merit, Augustine reminds his congregation of the limitations of all created analogies, for God's Word cannot be defined or adequately grasped in terms of created realities, including human speech.[26]

The reason why created analogies have even a small measure of legitimacy for talking about God is the relationship which exists between the Divine Word (Being itself) and the creation which exists through him. Augustine explicates the Creator/creation relationship in terms of God's Wisdom, a title interchangeable with God's Word, and he does so by using two similar analogies.[27]

First, Augustine elaborates on the analogy of the inner, spiritual word by likening it to a builder's design (Latin: *consilium*).[28] Just as a person conceives an inner word in the mind, so too does a builder devise a mental plan for a building to be constructed. Once the building has actually been built, Augustine says, "People notice the admirable building and admire the builder's plan; they are surprised by what they can see [that is, the building] and in love with what they do not see [that is, the builder's mental plan]."[29] Augustine's point is that the building is a sensible expression of the mental plan which exists in the builder's mind. By observing the material building, a person can obtain a measure of insight into the builder's mental plan.

Augustine uses this analogy of the builder to explain how human beings can obtain some insight into God on the basis of the created world. Just as a building reveals something of the mental design which exists in the builder and from which it derives its existence, so too does the created world reveal something of God's Wisdom which made it and from which it is derived. Augustine says, "Take a look at the structure of the world, observe what has been made through the Word, and then you will have some idea of what the Word is like."[30] God's Word/Wisdom is Being itself, and therefore everything that exists derives its existence from God. Things exist because they participate derivatively in God's Being, and this ontological participation allows for some manner of analogous speech and thought about God.

Augustine elaborates on how creation derives its existence from God's Wisdom in his exegesis of John 1:3c–4a: "*What was made in him is life*."[31] Augustine

26 See *Tract. Ev. Jo.* 1.10 (Hill 47).

27 On these analogies, see Ayres, *Augustine and the Trinity*, 193–194.

28 Augustine, *Tract. Ev. Jo.* 1.9; Latin from PL 35:1384.

29 *Tract. Ev. Jo.* 1.9 (Hill 46).

30 Augustine, *Tract. Ev. Jo.* 1.9 (Hill 46). He later (*Tract. Ev. Jo.* 1.9) adds, "From this structure [i.e. heaven and earth], then, think about what the Word must be like through which it was made" (Hill 47).

31 Augustine, *Tract. Ev. Jo.* 1.16 (Hill 51). A critical issue in the interpretation of John's Prologue is how to punctuate 1:3b–4a—an issue which Augustine himself points out in *Tract. Ev. Jo.* 1.16.

interprets this statement in tandem with the claim of Psalm 104:24, "*You have made all things in wisdom.*"[32] Combining the claims of John's Prologue and that of Psalm 104, Augustine states, "So if Christ is the Wisdom of God, and the Psalm says, *You have made all things in wisdom*, then just as all things were made through him, so all things were made in him."[33] All things exist not only *through* God's Wisdom, but also, somehow, *in* God's Wisdom.

To explain, Augustine employs a second, related analogy: a craftsman who builds a wooden chest.[34] Once again, he makes a distinction between the immaterial chest, which exists in the craftsman and from which a material wooden chest is constructed. Augustine speaks of the immaterial chest existing in the craftsman's "art" [Latin: *ars*], which "refers to the learnt and active knowledge or knowing of an artist who creates."[35] The immaterial chest is that from which the material, wooden chest originates. These two chests are related in one respect, but distinct in another—for one chest exists conceptually and invisibly in the craftsman and the other chest has a derivative, sensible existence as the wooden box. For Augustine (with a certain indebtedness to Platonism), the immaterial chest has a stronger mode of existence (it is more "alive") than the wooden chest because it is not subject to material corruption: "For the one can rot and decay, but the other one, which remains in the mind, can fashion another chest."[36] In this light, Augustine says, "The chest he made is not living; but the chest in his mind is alive, because the soul of the craftsman, where all these things are before they are in fact produced, is living."[37]

As the immaterial chest, which exists *in* the craftsman's creative "art," is a source for the life and existence of the material wooden chest, so, by analogy, can the Wisdom of God be said to contain the intelligible forms (the Life) of all things which Wisdom creates.[38] Augustine states, "the Wisdom of God, through whom all things were made, contains all things in the mind before she fashions them; consequently, all the things that are made through such a design are not thereby

---

The issue is whether to take the Greek phrase "what has come to be" (*ho gegonen*) as completing what comes before it in 1:3 (thus, "apart from him there came to be not one thing which has come to be") or as leading into what follows the phrase in 1:4 (thus, "what came to be in Him was life"). Augustine chooses the latter articulation.

32 Augustine, *Tract. Ev. Jo.* 1.16 (Hill 51).

33 Augustine, *Tract. Ev. Jo.* 1.16 (Hill 51).

34 Augustine, *Tract. Ev. Jo.* 1.17.

35 Augustine, *Tract. Ev. Jo.* 1.17 (PL 35:1387). Quotation from Ayres, *Augustine and the Trinity*, 194 n. 60.

36 Augustine, *Tract. Ev. Jo.* 1.17 (Hill 52).

37 Augustine, *Tract. Ev. Jo.* 1.17 (Hill 52).

38 See Wayne J. Hankey, "*Ratio*, Reason, Rationalism," in *Augustine through the Ages: An Encyclopedia*, gen. ed. Allan D. Fitzgerald, O.S.A. (Grand Rapids: Eerdmans, 1999), 696–702, at 697–698.

life, but whatever has been made is alive in him."[39] All created realities derive their existence and life from God's Wisdom. In this way, Augustine develops the Prologue's account of Creator and creation into his account wherein all things are ontologically related in that they all share a common relation to God's Word/Wisdom, who made and contains all things: "All things came to be through him, and apart from him, not one thing came to be. What has come to be through him was life" (John 1:3–4).

III. The Enlightening Word

After identifying the Divine Word as the agent of creation and source of life, John's Prologue continues, "the life was the light of human beings" (1:4). The Fourth Gospel, as well as the First Letter of John, employs the symbolism of light in its presentation of Jesus.[40] More specifically, the Gospel uses light symbolism with regard to three key aspects of Jesus and his work: Jesus the revealer, Jesus the giver of eternal life, and the coming of Jesus as the occasion of judgment.

First, John uses light symbolism to present Jesus as the revealer. On two occasions, Jesus identifies himself as "the Light of the world" (8:12; 9:5). He is the one sent into the world by the Father to reveal God as Father and himself as Son and to accomplish the divine work of salvation. The pre-eminent moment of the revelation of God is at the cross, where the Father's giving of the Son (his all) and the Son's laying down his life out of love and obedience to the Father (his all) reveals God as an eternal exchange of radical, self-giving love (John 8:28; 1 John 4:8–10).

Second, Jesus as the light is also the giver of life. After first identifying himself as the Light of the World, Jesus adds "the one who follows me will not go about in the darkness but will have the light of life" (John 8:12). As the one who reveals the Father and accomplishes his saving work, Jesus offers eternal life to those who receive him in faith and discipleship (3:16–17). The Fourth Gospel teaches that eternal life is a participation in the relationship of the Father and the Son—the divine communion—entered into by receiving a share in Jesus' own life as the Son (and thus sharing in his relationship with the Father). At the close of his public ministry, Jesus exhorts his hearers, "believe in the Light so that you may become sons of the light" (12:36). These words recall the Prologue, which speak of an anthropological aspect of salvation: "to as many as did receive him, he gave them the power to become children of God" (1:12).

Third, John associates the coming of Jesus as the light with judgment (3:19–21). In John's Gospel, "the world" (when used with a negative connotation)

---

39 Augustine, *Tract. Ev. Jo.* 1.17 (Hill 52).

40 For more on John's use of light symbolism, see Brown, *Gospel according to John*, 1.515–516; C. H. Dodd, *The Interpretation of the Fourth Gospel* (Cambridge: Cambridge University Press, 1998 [1953]), 201–205; Craig R. Koester, *Symbolism in the Fourth Gospel: Meaning, Mystery, Community* (Minneapolis: Fortress Press, 1995), 123–154.

indicates human beings and their world as they are in a willful rebellion against God and his Word—hence, it has turned away from the spiritual light and into spiritual darkness.[41] Jesus was sent as the Light into this spiritually darkened world, and the very presence of the Light necessarily provokes a response from people. All people must make a decision whether to receive or reject Jesus and his revelation.[42] Those who receive him in faith are delivered from the spiritual darkness and are given the light of life (8:12; 12:35); those who knowingly and willfully refuse the Light choose to remain in the spiritual darkness.

Augustine's interpretation of the Prologue's teaching about the Word as "light" (1:4) follows closely upon his analysis of 1:3b–4a ("*what was made in him is life*") in terms of God's Wisdom.[43] According to Augustine, the Prologue speaks of "life" being "*in*" God's Wisdom because the intelligible forms of all things, which he creates, exist primarily in God's Wisdom. For Augustine, the Prologue's further claim, "the life was the light of human beings" (1:4b), speaks to the Wisdom of God as the source of illumination of human beings in particular.[44]

The claim that the Light illumines human beings in particular leads Augustine to consider what makes human beings distinct from other creatures and thus capable of being illumined. After ruling out qualities such as strength, speed, and beauty, Augustine claims that human uniqueness and superiority to the animals lies in the human possession of a rational mind capable of understanding.[45] Augustine identifies the rational mind as that aspect of human nature where human beings bear the image of God: "the human being, *made to the image of God* (Genesis 1:27), does have a rational mind, with which wisdom may be perceived."[46] The rational mind seeks to be illumined by and contemplate Wisdom, which also created all things and contains their intelligible forms. In this way, Augustine explains how the Life "*in*" the Wisdom of God is also "the Light" which illumines the rational human mind, seeking understanding: "the light of human beings is the

41 Donatien Mollat thus describes "the world" as used negatively in John: "at the heart of this world, the author of the Gospel uncovers an irreducible core of resistance to God. He has the intuition of a formidable power of negation and refusal, which exceeds the limits of humanity and plunges its roots into a hidden home of hate and deception." Quoted from Donatien Mollat, "S. Jean L'Évangéliste," in *Dictionnaire de Spiritualité*, ed. Marcel Viller, S.J. et al., 17 vols. (Paris: Beauchesne, 1974), 8.199 [my translation].

42 This is a point classically highlighted in Rudolf Bultmann, *Theology of the New Testament*, trans. Kendrick Grobel, 2 vols. (New York: Charles Scribner's Sons, 1951–1955), 2.33–40.

43 Augustine, *Tract. Ev. Jo.* 1.16 (Hill 51).

44 Augustine (*Tract. Ev. Jo.* 1.18) says of John 1:4, "it is from life that human beings are enlightened" (Hill 53). On the complex topic of "illumination" in Augustine, see R. A. Markus, "Augustine: Reason and Illumination," in *The Cambridge History of Later Greek and Early Medieval Philosophy*, ed. A. H. Armstrong (Cambridge: Cambridge University Press, 1967), 362–373; Etienne Gilson, *The Christian Philosophy of St. Augustine*, trans. L. E. M. Lynch (New York: Random House, 1960), 77–96; Hankey, "*Ratio*, Reason, Rationalism," 698–699.

45 *Tract. Ev. Jo.* 1.18; 3.4.

46 *Tract. Ev. Jo.* 1.18 (Hill 53).

light of minds. The light of minds is above minds and surpasses minds. That is the life through which all things were made."[47]

Augustine's interpretation of God's Wisdom as the source of illumination for human minds gives perspective on his (previously mentioned) remarks about the different human capacities to understand spiritual realities, that is, "the mountains" and "the hills." Augustine cites John the Evangelist as the highest of mountains, for "he was contemplating the divinity of the Word."[48] These heights of contemplation were not an achievement of John himself, but rather a gift of divine grace. Like the other mountains, John was "enlightened by Wisdom herself."[49] But Augustine asks how John could ascend to contemplate the ineffable Wisdom of God, which 1 Corinthians 2:9 describes as that "*which no eye has seen nor ear heard, nor has it entered in the heart of man.*"[50] He answers that Wisdom so entered into John's heart such that he was ceasing to be a man and "had begun to be an angel," that is, John became a messenger proclaiming God.[51] Augustine cites holiness and that which accompanies people becoming "more than human," for "all the saints—because they are announcers of God—are angels."[52] God's Wisdom transforms John spiritually and morally by grace and elevates him to contemplate the divinity of the Word. Augustine thus praises the Evangelist for his holiness and humility, which coincide with the elevating and illuminating activity of God's Wisdom, and so encourages his congregation: "We will become more than merely human if we acknowledge in the first place that we are in fact human, that is, so that we might rise up to that lofty height by humility."[53]

The goal of such divinely worked illumination is that the one illumined (a "mountain") should pass on what they have received to others, especially to ordinary people ("the hills"). John the Evangelist did this by passing on the fruits of his illumination through his Gospel. Referencing the scene where the Beloved Disciple leaned back upon Jesus' chest at the Last Supper (John 13:23), Augustine says of John the Evangelist: "he laid his head on the Lord's breast and from the Lord's breast drank in what he would give us to drink."[54] John received wisdom and illumination from the Lord, and he in turn "gave us words to drink" in his Gospel.[55] However, Augustine is quick to point out that both the Evangelist and the Scriptures are not

47 *Tract. Ev. Jo.* 3.4 (Hill 71).

48 *Tract. Ev. Jo.* 1.5 (Hill 42).

49 *Tract. Ev. Jo.* 1.2 (Hill 40).

50 As quoted in Augustine, *Tract. Ev. Jo.* 1.4 (Hill 41).

51 *Tract. Ev. Jo.* 1.4 (Hill 41).

52 *Tract. Ev. Jo.* 1.4 (Hill 41).

53 *Tract. Ev. Jo.* 1.4 (Hill 41).

54 *Tract. Ev. Jo.* 1.7 (Hill 44). See also Augustine, *De consensu evangelistarum* [On the Agreement of the Evangelists] 1.4.7.

55 *Tract. Ev. Jo.* 1.7 (Hill 44).

luminous of their own accord but are mediators of light. As Augustine says of John the Baptist (another one of the "mountains"), "if … he had not been enlightened, he would have been darkness."[56] The mountains, like John the Evangelist and John the Baptist, are lights, but they only shine because they have been illumined by and mediate "the true Light" (John 1:9): "a person who has been enlightened is also called light, but the true light is the one who enlightens."[57] Accordingly, Augustine instructs his congregation to look beyond such "mountains" and lesser "lights" to the true light (that is, God's Word/Wisdom) who illumines them.

Augustine also maintains that such divinely inspired illumination as that granted to John the Evangelist is not the only way by which human beings can attain some insight into God's Wisdom. Appealing to Romans 1:20–22, Augustine argues that human beings can arrive at some knowledge of the Creator by means of philosophical reflection on the created world.[58] The possibility of knowing something of God from creation arises from a combination of two previously mentioned factors: first, human beings possess rational minds capable of perceiving Wisdom, and second, created realities derive their existence from (and thus participate in) God's Wisdom, Being itself. The (limited) powers of human reasoning can attain something of divine Wisdom by rational reflection on the created order which comes from and exists in the same divine Wisdom.

Augustine places this discussion of knowing something of the Creator from reasoned reflection on creation within a metaphorical description of the human condition. He likens it to a person who can see his homeland from afar and desires to reach its secure confines but is separated from it by a vast, presently uncrossable sea.[59] The homeland which people long for is eternal Wisdom. Some people ("The great minds of the mountains") are able to see across the waters to view their destination, but others (the "little") cannot.[60] While "the great" by philosophical reasoning may be able to recognize Wisdom as the longed-for homeland, both they and "the little" are equally unable to cross the sea on their own. Both the great and the little have the same identical means for crossing the sea: "no one can cross the sea of this world unless carried over it on the cross of Christ."[61]

---

56 *Tract. Ev. Jo.* 2.6 (Hill 60).

57 *Tract. Ev. Jo.* 2.6 (Hill 59).

58 Augustine (*Tract. Ev. Jo.* 2.4) says, "Certain philosophers in this world have sought the creator through the creature—because he can indeed be found through the creature, as the apostle clearly tells us …" (Hill 57). For a sketch of Augustine's account of the knowledge of God from creation, see R. A. Markus, "Augustine: Reason and Illumination," in *The Cambridge History of Later Greek and Early Medieval Philosophy*, ed. A. H. Armstrong (Cambridge: Cambridge University Press, 1967), 395–405, at 395–397.

59 *Tract. Ev. Jo.* 2.2–3.

60 *Tract. Ev. Jo.* 2.3 (Hill 57).

61 *Tract. Ev. Jo.* 2.2 (Hill 56).

Once again, Augustine presents God's Wisdom as bringing diverse realities together. Both John the Evangelist and the philosophers are "mountains," who have as their object of contemplation God's eternal Wisdom. By placing these two "mountains" in a similar position vis-à-vis God's Wisdom, Augustine brings together revelation and reason, theological contemplation and philosophical inquiry. They are inter-connected as diverse ways in which human beings are given to know Wisdom.

But whereas Augustine praises John the Evangelist for his humility, he indicts the philosophers for their pride and sin. This brings us to Augustine's interpretation of "the darkness" (John 1:5). The Fourth Gospel teaches that the world, although created good by the Divine Word (in light of Gen. 1), has been plunged into spiritual darkness on account of its sin. The Gospel locates the core of sin in creatures' knowing and willful rebellion against God's Word, but Augustine focuses his discussion of sin in terms of pride and worldly attachments. He does so by citing three groups as examples.

First, like Paul in Romans 1:20–21, Augustine castigates the philosophers, who could see across the metaphorical waters to the destination of eternal Wisdom, but their pride prevented their crossing: "They saw where they were to go, but, being ungrateful to the one who set what they saw before them, they wanted to take all the credit for the sight themselves; and, grown thus proud, they lost what they saw and turned away from there to idols ... and disdaining the creator."[62] These philosophers boast in their achievements and mock the humility of the incarnate and crucified Word as the only means of reaching their goal.[63]

A second group, whom Augustine singles out as inhabiting the darkness, are heretics and schismatics.[64] These people may have the great minds of mountains, but instead of passing on "peace," they bring division and sunder the Church.

A third group whom Augustine indicts are the "lovers of the world."[65] In his discussion of this group, Augustine says that to love something is "to live from within [it]"—or, one might say, to seek one's happiness and fulfillment in it and thereby rest in it.[66] The lovers of the world are people "who put the world first in their affections; for their heart dwells in the world."[67] In this way, Augustine interprets the Fourth Gospel's use of "the world" with different connotations. On the one hand, the world can mean God's good creation as such, but when the

62 *Tract. Ev. Jo.* 2.4 (Hill 58). Augustine here reads John's Prologue in light of Rom. 1:20–21.

63 *Tract. Ev. Jo.* 2.4 (Hill 58).

64 *Tract. Ev. Jo.* 1.3.

65 See *Tract. Ev. Jo.* 2.11; 3.5.

66 *Tract. Ev. Jo.* 2.11 (Hill 63). Compare Augustine's distinction of "use" and "enjoy" in Augustine, *De doctrina christiana* [*On Christian Teaching*], 1.3.3–1.4.4; 1.22.20–1.33.27.

67 *Tract. Ev. Jo.* 2.11 (Hill 63).

Gospel speaks of the world as wicked, it is because of these "lovers of the world" and not on account of its creation by God.[68]

Human beings have withdrawn from the Light by their sins, and the sin of human beings has left them in a woeful, wounded state.[69] Augustine frequently describes this state of fallen humanity in terms of diseases and ailments of the eyes. Sin has left humans spiritually blind to God's ever-present Wisdom: "just as a blind person, placed in the sun, has the sun present to him, even though he is absent from it [that is, he cannot see the sun], in the same way every [sinner] is blind in heart."[70] Similarly, Augustine will speak of the eyes of the heart as being weakened and incapable of seeing clearly.[71] So, wounded and blinded, the fallen human race stands in need of a healer, and, in this way Augustine explicates the Prologue's teaching on the economy of salvation worked by the Divine Word.

IV. The Healing Word

John's Prologue famously speaks of the Divine Word, who created the world, as becoming incarnate: "And the Word became flesh and tabernacled among us" (1:14). The Prologue goes on to speak of him as the source of "grace upon grace" (1:16) as well as "grace and truth" (1:17). The Incarnate Word (or Son) is the sole revealer of the Father, for only he exists from before creation "upon the Father's heart" (1:18).

Less clear is how much of the Prologue speaks of the work of the *incarnate* Word—that is, Jesus' life and work in the flesh—and more specifically, how 1:10–13 should be understood.[72] For instance, many Johannine scholars see the first mention of John the Baptist in 1:6 as indicating that all the material from 1:6–18 pertains to the work of the Word made flesh in Jesus.[73] Taken in this light, 1:10–13 speaks to the incarnation of the Word in Jesus and the mixed (but largely negative) response which he received from his Jewish contemporaries.

Other scholars, however, locate the discussion of the Incarnate Word only in 1:14–17[74] and so take 1:10–13 as speaking of the activity of the Divine Word prior to his Incarnation—that is, his presence and activity in the world generally

68 Augustine (*Tract. Ev. Jo.* 3.5) uses the example of a "bad house" to illustrate this point: "the world is bad, because those who live in it are bad, just as a house is bad—not because of its walls, but because of its inhabitants" (Hill 72–73). See also *Tract. Ev. Jo.* 2.11.

69 *Tract. Ev. Jo.* 2.7.

70 *Tract. Ev. Jo.* 1.19 (Hill 54); compare *Tract. Ev. Jo.* 3.5.

71 *Tract. Ev. Jo.* 2.8.

72 The text of John 1:10–13 reads: "He was in the world, and the world came to be through him. Yet the world did not know him. He came to his own, and his own did not receive him. But as many as did receive him, he gave them, to those who believe in his name, power to become children of God, those who were not born from blood, nor from the will of the flesh, nor from human will, but from God."

73 See, for example, Brown, *Gospel according to John*, 1.28–30; Moloney, *Gospel of John*, 37–39.

74 "And the Word became flesh and dwelt among us… & etc."

and in Israel specifically.[75] Support for this second interpretation comes from the Fourth Gospel's subtle affirmation of the presence of the Divine Word in the history of Israel. For example, when a heated exchange between Jesus and his opponents reaches its climax in 8:57, Jesus claims to have had a relationship with Abraham. His opponents are incredulous and ask, "You are not yet fifty years old and you have seen Abraham?" Jesus then speaks of his divine identity and that he actually existed before Abraham: "before Abraham came to be, I AM" (8:58). In another instance, the evangelist identifies the Divine Word as the one seen by the prophet Isaiah when Isaiah saw the Lord at his prophetic call (John 12:41; compare Isa. 6:1–4). Augustine's exegesis of the Prologue coheres with this second line of interpretation.

Augustine understands the economy of redemption as an overarching sequence of activity in which the Eternal Word condescends, or accommodates Himself, to human beings into order to heal the wounds of sin and draw them into eternal life.[76] In his exposition of the economy in *Tract. Ev. Jo*, 1–3, Augustine continues to show the inter-connectedness of distinct realities by virtue of their relationship to God's Word/Wisdom. To bring these inter-connections into clearer focus, I will focus this treatment of Augustine's exegesis in terms of divine agency. That is, Augustine identifies the Eternal Word as the agent who is at work in both creation and redemption, in both the biblical history of Israel and in the Incarnation. The one divine agent, who is at work in these realities, binds them all together in himself.

Consistent with longstanding Christian orthodoxy, Augustine maintains the intrinsic unity between the orders of creation and redemption. One way in which he does so is by specifically identifying the Eternal Word as both the Creator and the Savior. Some of his clearest affirmations of this identification in *Tract. Ev. Jo.* 1–3 appear in places where Augustine speaks polemically against Arian Christology and warns his congregation against such heretical thinking.[77] In the course of his anti-Arian polemic, Augustine identifies the Eternal Word as both the Creator and Redeemer (or Re-creator) of humanity: "if you were once made through the Word, you still need to be remade through the Word."[78] In doing this, Augustine brings to light the unity between the orders of creation and redemption, since the same divine agent (the Word) acts in each.

For Augustine, this continuity of divine agency also underlies the deep unity between the Old and New Testaments. On several occasions, Augustine speaks

75 See, for example, Martin and Wright, *Gospel of John*, chapter 1; Schnackenburg, *Gospel according to St. John* 1.255–265; Boyarin, "Gospel of the *Memra*," 264–275.

76 For an overview of key aspects of Augustine's Christology, see Brian E. Daley, S.J., "The Humble Mediator: The Distinctive Elements in Saint Augustine's Christology," *Word and Spirit: A Monastic Review* 9 (1987): 100–117.

77 *Tract. Ev. Jo.* 1.11–12.

78 *Tract. Ev. Jo.* 1.12 (Hill 48).

of the presence and activity of the Eternal Word in Old Testament events. As we have seen, Augustine interprets the use of the verb "to be" in John 1:1 ("In the beginning *was* the Word") to indicate that the Divine Word is "Being itself," eternal and unchanging.[79] Augustine then associates the Word as "Being itself" with the revelation of God's sacred name to Moses in Exodus 3:14: "That is the name he declared to his servant Moses: *I am who am*; and *He who is sent me* (Exod. 3:14)."[80] Significant here is that Augustine identifies the one who appeared and spoke to Moses in Exodus 3 as the Eternal Word.[81]

Augustine's identification of the saving actions of God in the Old Testament as actions of the Eternal Word continue in his remarks about the election of Israel. Augustine interprets the reference to "his own" in John 1:11 as referring to the Jews. They are the "people he made: the Jews whom, in the beginning, he made to be over all the nations."[82] The Eternal Word is the one who brought the Israelites out of Egypt and formed them as a nation of his own. This special relationship between the Eternal Word and the people of Israel, which was forged in the covenant promises to Abraham and at Sinai, extends into the Word's incarnation in Jesus the Jew. Augustine states, "[the Jewish] people were born of the seed of Abraham, and they are supremely his own, because they are related to him through the flesh which he was good enough to take to himself."[83]

Augustine also speaks of the Eternal Word as the one who gave Israel "the law through Moses" and also became incarnate in Jesus to give "grace and truth" (John 1:17).[84] Augustine draws out the interrelationship between the Torah and the incarnation (and thus the Old and New Covenants) by speaking of them as both having roles in the Word's activity to heal a spiritually blind, wounded humanity. In *Tract. Ev. Jo.* 3.14, Augustine introduces the example of a sick person, who does not think that he is sick and thus does not desire a cure. Redolent of Paul's characterization of the Law as a "pedagogue" (Gal. 3:24–25), Augustine interprets the Law as a slave or nurse who assists and prepares for the doctor's arrival. He states, "a doctor who wants to cure someone first sends along his slave so that the doctor might find the patient bandaged up."[85] Continuing his Pauline-inspired reading of John's Prologue, Augustine speaks of the Law as this nurse-slave, who bandaged up (that is, bound) the patient by laying bare his guilt and weakness but who also could not cure the patient of the illness of sin, inherited from Adam.[86] It

79 *Tract. Ev. Jo.* 2.2 (Hill 55).

80 *Tract. Ev. Jo.* 2.2 (Hill 56).

81 Compare Augustine, *De trinitate* [*On the Trinity*] 2.5.23.

82 *Tract. Ev. Jo.* 2.12 (Hill 64).

83 *Tract. Ev. Jo.* 2.12 (Hill 64).

84 *Tract. Ev. Jo.* 3.2, 17.

85 *Tract. Ev. Jo.* 3.14 (Hill 78–79).

86 *Tract. Ev. Jo.* 3.2, 11–12, 14.

is the work of "our Lord Jesus Christ," whom Augustine says "is our one and only doctor," to heal a wounded and spiritually blinded humanity.[87]

Augustine speaks of the incarnation of the Divine Word in Jesus as medicine or healing for fallen humanity.[88] He pays special attention to the healing role of the Incarnate Word's humanity and humility.[89] Augustine spoke of the woundedness of fallen humanity as caused by and exemplified in sinners' misguided love for worldly realities (that is, the "lovers of the world"). These misguided loves for worldly things leave sinful humanity spiritually blinded to their true homeland in God's Wisdom: "The soul … had become fleshly-minded by giving its consent to fleshly-minded inclinations, and that is how the eye of the heart had been blinded."[90] Correspondingly, the Eternal Word became "flesh" (that is, he came to exist in a material way as a man) in order to deliver human beings from their love for and attachment to "the flesh" (that is, material things). Augustine states that the Word "became a medicine for us, so that as we had been blinded by the earth we might be healed by the earth."[91]

Augustine cites the humility of the Eternal Word in condescending to take flesh and then to embrace the humiliation of the cross as an antidote to human pride and arrogance. Within the context of his metaphor of the vast sea, which separates people from their homeland, Augustine says the following: "why was he crucified? Because you were in need of the wood of his humility. You had swollen up with pride … and you have no means of crossing over to the home country, unless you are carried there on the wood [of the cross]."[92] The incarnation of the Word in the man Jesus means that to perceive God's Wisdom, one must humble oneself and look towards the humble flesh of Jesus.[93]

After stating that "the Word became flesh," John's Prologue adds "and we saw his glory" (1:14). Augustine capitalizes on this association between the Word becoming flesh and people being given to see the divine glory. According to Augustine, the Incarnate Word heals the blinded eyes of the heart in order that they might be able to see (that is, contemplate) God. He says of the Incarnate Word, "by his very birth he made an ointment with which the eyes of our hearts could be cleaned that we might see his majesty through his humility."[94] The humility of God's Word/

87 *Tract. Ev. Jo.* 3.3 (Hill 70).

88 So too Augustine, *De doctrina christiana* [*On Christian Teaching*] 1.12.12–1.14.13.

89 See John C. Cavadini, "Pride," in Fitzgerald, *Augustine through the Ages*, 679–684, at 682–683.

90 *Tract. Ev. Jo.* 2.16 (Hill 67).

91 *Tract. Ev. Jo.* 3.6 (Hill 73).

92 *Tract. Ev. Jo.* 2.4 (Hill 58).

93 Robert E. Cushman, "Faith and Reason," in *A Companion to the Study of St. Augustine*, ed. Roy W. Battenhouse (New York: Oxford University Press, 1955), 287–314, at 287–288.

94 *Tract. Ev. Jo.* 2.16 (Hill 66).

Wisdom serves to heal a fallen, prideful humanity, whose spiritual vision has been impaired, so they might be elevated to contemplate God.

Augustine follows the Prologue's sequence by associating the two following statements—"*from his fullness we have all received grace for grace*" (1:16) and "*grace and truth have come about through Jesus Christ*" (1:17)—as further descriptions of the Incarnate Word's saving work.[95] Augustine takes "grace for grace" as signifying two distinct but related gifts of the Incarnate Word. The first "grace" is faith and the forgiveness of sins.[96] Augustine arrives at this interpretation by reading John 1:17 through Romans and Paul's exposition of the grace of justification. This first grace of the remission of sins is the precondition for the second "grace" which is the gift of eternal life.[97]

Elsewhere in *Tract. Ev. Jo.* 1–3, Augustine speaks of the same sequence of gifts (forgiveness and then eternal life) and makes clear that eternal life *is* the grace of divine adoption. Commenting on John 1:12, Augustine states, "the only-begotten Son came to forgive sins, those sins which had us so tied up that they were an impediment to his adopting us; he forgave those he wished to make his brothers and sisters and made them co-heirs."[98] The Eternal Word, therefore, is the source of both mercy and of eternal life. The coming of the Word as a human being in Jesus gives confirmation that human beings can in fact become God's adopted children.[99]

Augustine links these two "graces" (mercy *and* eternal life) in 1:16 to the "grace and truth" that came through Jesus (1:17). The singular mention of "grace" in 1:17 summarizes the two "graces" spoken of in 1:16. The "truth" in 1:17 names the faithfulness of the Divine Word, who fulfilled the promises spoken through the prophets. Augustine thus says, "God had promised [mercy] through the prophets; and when he came to give what he had promised, he gave not only grace, but truth as well. How was truth demonstrated? Because he did what was promised."[100] Through his interpretation of the Incarnate Word's "grace and truth," Augustine unites the Old and New Covenants in the person of the Divine Word. What the Divine Word promised through the prophets in the Old Testament, he accomplished in the New by taking flesh in Jesus.

V. Conclusion

From its opening presentation of the pre-existent relationship of God and the Word, the Prologue of the Gospel according to John sets forth a comprehensive vision of

95 Scripture quotations taken from *Tract. Ev. Jo.* 3.8 (Hill 74) and 3.16 (Hill 79) respectively.

96 *Tract. Ev. Jo.* 3.8–9.

97 *Tract. Ev. Jo.* 3.9.

98 *Tract. Ev. Jo.* 2.13 (Hill 64).

99 *Tract. Ev. Jo.* 2.15; 3.6.

100 *Tract. Ev. Jo.* 3.8 (Hill 75); see *Tract. Ev. Jo.* 3.13.

all things in relation to the Divine Word. Augustine develops this comprehensive vision through a complex exegesis of John's Prologue. In these homilies, Augustine articulates the inter-relationships between Creator and creation, all human beings as both bearing the image of God and in need of divine healing, between revelation and reason, creation and redemption, and the Old and New Covenants. All of these diverse realities are deeply inter-related with each other because they are all related to one common subject: God's Eternal Word. Augustine's exegesis of John's Prologue is truly an account of "all things in wisdom."

How, in light of *Dei Verbum* §23, might we think of Augustine's exegesis as helping us to arrive at "a more profound understanding" of John's Prologue? Francis Martin makes a key distinction between two related aspects of biblical interpretation: "what the text *says*" and "what the texts are *talking about*."[101] The biblical texts are the divinely inspired points of access by which readers encounter the realities about which the texts speak. But there are more to these realities than their verbal articulations in the Bible, and thus these realities can be understood as transcending (but not denying) their historically and linguistically particular presentations in the biblical texts.

Taken in this light, Augustine attends carefully to the plain sense of John's Gospel ("what the text says"), even though he is not concerned to explicate the Prologue in its context of origins like a modern historical-critical exegete. Compared with most modern exegetes, Augustine operates with a different understanding of what constitutes the literal sense of Scripture. Augustine's larger concern lies with an intellectual exploration of "what the text is about" (its reality, or *res*).

For Augustine, the ultimate goal of proper biblical interpretation is the contemplation of eternal Wisdom, such as that passed on by John the Evangelist in his Gospel, rather than the valuable, but limited, knowledge of history and philology.[102] It is the reality given in the text, not the text proper, which is the ultimate object of biblical interpretation. Therefore, Augustine can bring his theological intelligence to consider the biblical *res* in ways that transcend, but do not deny, what the text may say. For in contemplating the realities given in Scripture, we encounter God's Word and Wisdom, who heals the eyes of the heart, breaks down arrogant pride, and illumines the mind to contemplate his eternal glory.

---

101 Francis Martin, "Mary in Sacred Scripture: An Ecumenical Reflection," *The Thomist* 72 (2008): 525–569, here 561.

102 Augustine makes the distinction between knowledge (which is concerned with historical and temporal things and is ordered to action) and wisdom (which is concerned with eternal things and is ordered to contemplation) in *De trinitate* [*On the Trinity*] 12.4.22–25; 13.1.1–4.

Letter & Spirit 9 (2014): 125-152

Covenant Fulfillment in the Gospel of John

∼: **Vincent P. DeMeo** :∼
International Theological Institute

Within the scholarly investigation of the presence and function of a covenant theology in the Johannine writings, a lacuna exists in regard to its association to the divine kinship relations that are present in the foreground of the gospel. This study will attempt to fill this lacuna.

Following Frank M. Cross and others,[1] I have argued elsewhere[2] that the covenant institution in the ancient Near East was the legal means by which kinship relationships were extended beyond the natural kinship sphere. They generated sacred bonds of kinship with those who are outside one's blood kinship group. Covenants, at any level (individual, tribal, international; either secular or divine), utilized kinship language to disclose that blood kinship relations (and their consequent obligations) have been extended across family lines to non-relatives (that is, "kinship-by-covenant").

The purpose of this article is to demonstrate that a covenant theology is operative in the background of John 13–17 (which functions as an adequate representative of the entire Johannine tradition). This will be accomplished by showing that the kinship-by-covenant principle disclosed in the Old Testament (OT) is employed as a formative and controlling principle with respect to how Jesus, and through him the Father, relates and guides his community of disciples. In other words, my aim is to point out that in the actions and discourses of his final meal narrated in John 13–17, Jesus established the new covenant with his eschatological

---

1 Frank Moore Cross offers the following definition of "covenant": "Oath and covenant, in which the deity is witness, guarantor, or participant, is ... a widespread legal means by which the duties and privileges of kinship may be extended to another individual or group." *From Epic to Canon: History and Literature in Ancient Israel* (Baltimore: Johns Hopkins University Press, 1998), 8. See also G. Quell, "διαθήκη," in *Theological Dictionary of the New Testament*, trans. G. Bromiley, eds. G. Kittel and G. Bromiley, Vol. II (Michigan: Eerdmans, 1964), 106–124; Gordon P. Hugenberger, *Marriage as a Covenant: A Study of Biblical Law & Ethics Governing Marriage, Developed from the Perspective of Malachi*, Vetus Testamentum Supplements 52 (Leiden: Brill, 1994), 168–215; Scott W. Hahn, *Kinship By Covenant: A Canonical Approach to the Fulfillment of God's Saving Promises*, Anchor Yale Bible Reference Library (New Haven: Yale University Press, 2009), 28–31; Mark Smith, "'Your People Shall Be My People': Family and Covenant in Ruth 1:16–17," *Catholic Biblical Quarterly* 69 (2007): 242–258; Duane A. Smith, *Kinship and Covenant: An Examination of Kinship Metaphors for Covenant in the Book of the Prophet Hosea*, Ph.D. Diss. (Harvard University; Cambridge, Massachusetts: University Microfilms, 1994), 28. Of vital importance are the works of Dennis J. McCarthy, *Treaty and Covenant* (Rome: Biblical Institute Press, 1978) and Paul Kalluveettil, *Declaration and Covenant* (Rome: Biblical Institute Press, 1982).

2 Vincent P. DeMeo, *Covenantal Kinship in John 13–17: A Historical-Narrative Approach*, Vol. 22 (Roma: Ateneo Pontificio Regina Apostolorum, 2012), 43–109.

community and, in doing so, generated a divine kinship relation (with corresponding familial obligations) with them. They are the definitive children of God (see John 1:12; 11:52; 13:33; 14:18). My intent is, therefore, to further and deepen the recent research on the covenant tradition in the gospel by explaining how Israel's covenantal kinship relation and obligations with their God are, according to the gospel of John, fulfilled with a realism that is heightened in an unexpected manner.

I. Covenantal Relation: Generation of the Children of God

Covenant Meal

Jesus' discourses with his disciples in John 13–17 take place within the setting of a meal.[3] One characteristic of this meal that emerges is that it is shared between members of kin. Not only does John 13–17 contain a detailed discourse about Jesus' Father and his own divine sonship, but his disciples are referred to as "his own" (13:1)—a phrase with familial connotations—and as his "children" (v. 33) who possess a dwelling place in his "Father's house" (14:2).[4] They will not be "orphans" (14:18) but will be called by the name of the Father (17:6, 11, 12, 26). This particular meal seems to adhere to the principle commonly found in banquets of the ANE, namely, only members of the same kin, broadly understood, ate together.[5]

Another indicator of the character of this supper is that it is associated in some manner with the Passover feast (see 13:1). The Passover celebration was a festival of kin and for kin celebrated in the home. Jesus' disciples constituted a type of kinship community known as a *ḥabhurà* (חבורה — that is, a fictive family unit who together celebrate the Passover). It is possible that Jesus was acting as the *paterfamilias* (father of the family) whose duty it was to bring to mind the redemptive events of God in the Passover and exodus events (Exod. 12:24, 26–27).

The Passover context is also the first hint that this meal could be associated with the covenant between God and Israel. Not only was God's election of Israel in the Passover-Exodus and Israel's acceptance of sonship sealed by a shared meal at the covenant ratification ceremony on Mt. Sinai (Exod. 24:9–11), but two parties sharing a meal together when establishing a covenant was a standard practice within the ancient Near East and ancient Israel.[6] A banquet eaten in the context

---

3 See John 13:2, 4, 18, 26–30.

4 All English quotations of Scripture are taken from the *Revised Standard Version* (1952). Modifications of this translation are my own. All Hebrew quotations of the Old Testament reflect the Masoretic Text (MT), while all Greek quotations reflect the Septuagint translation (LXX).

5 See Jan G. Van Der Watt, *Family of the King: Dynamics of Metaphor in the Gospel according to John* (Leiden: Brill, 2000), 339; Joachim Jeremias, *Eucharistic Words* (New York: Charles Scribner's Sons, 1966), 204; DeMeo, *Covenantal Kinship*, 69–81.

6 See, for instance, Gen. 26:26–30; 31:43–54; Deut. 27:6–7.

of a covenant expressed their belonging to one family and the sharing of a common life. Especially in light of the other traditions of the OT divine covenant found throughout John 13–17 (which will be discussed below), it is probable that this meal functions analogously to the common practice of sharing a banquet at a ratification or renewal of a covenant.[7]

His Own

According to John 13:1, Jesus' disciples are considered to be "his own" (τοὺς ἰδίους). The phrase "his own" is powerfully evocative of Israel being given the status of God's own possession in their covenant: "If you will obey my voice and keep my covenant, you shall be my own possession among all peoples" (Exod. 19:5). In the midst of the renewal of this divine covenant in Exodus 34:9–10, Moses begs God to "take us as your own possession." Both of these texts are rooted in God's overall plan with Israel as revealed in the covenant formula of Exodus 6:7 which has as an essential aim God's active "taking" of Israel as his own possession: "I will take you for my people, and I will be your God."[8] In a similar vein Deuteronomy 7:6 states, "For you are a people holy to the Lord your God; the Lord your God has chosen you to be a people for his own possession."[9] This verse highlights the relationship between mutual possession (Israel has given themselves to their God and he has chosen Israel as his own) and covenant belonging ("The Lord your God" expresses the covenant relationship).

The prophets, too, foretold that God would establish mutual possession and belonging in the covenant given on the eschatological day. According to the prophet Malachi, when the "messenger of the covenant" comes (3:1–2) those Israelites who fear God shall be possessed by him as his covenantal sons: "They shall be mine, says the Lord of hosts, my special possession on the day when I act, and I will spare them as a man spares his son who serves him" (3:17). The hope of this eschatological day for mutual possession in a covenant relationship was previously disclosed in 3:7: "Return to me, and I will return to you, says the Lord of hosts." This mirrors the covenant formula: "I will be yours and you will be mine."[10]

---

7 Other New Testament traditions support this conclusion. The Synoptic gospel tradition explicitly states that this final meal is a covenant meal: "This cup which is poured out for you is the new covenant in my blood" (Luke 22:20; see also Mark 14:24; Matt. 26:28). The Pauline tradition also confirms the meal's covenantal character: "In the same way also the cup, after supper, saying, 'This cup is the new covenant in my blood. Do this, as often as you drink it, in remembrance of me'" (1 Cor. 11:25).

8 The prophet Ezekiel reiterates the motif of personal possession in the OT divine covenant: "I swore an oath to you and entered into a covenant with you; you became mine, says the Lord" (Ezek. 16:8).

9 Deut. 26:17–18 reads: "You have declared this day concerning the Lord that he is your God, and that you will walk in his ways, and keep his statutes and his commandments and his ordinances, and will obey his voice; and the Lord has declared this day concerning you that you are a people for his own possession, as he has promised you, and that you are to keep all his commandments." See also Deut. 4:20; 9:26; 14:2; 26:18; 33:12; Ps. 135:4.

10 See also Hos. 1:9; 2:1, 25 for further insights into the notions of possession, covenant, and

The status of being God's "own," which is deeply inherent to the OT divine covenant, is taken up and applied to the relationship between the Father, the Son, and the disciples. A covenantal understanding of Jesus' "own" is supported by John 10:1–2. Here the relationship between Jesus and his own is depicted through the shepherd-sheep imagery, suggestive of the OT covenant between God and Israel.[11] The fundamental characteristics of this relationship are present: divine initiative, a redeeming intervention, careful providence, election and possession, obedience and love towards the divine word and commandment, and knowledge that is significantly interior, personal, and decisive.[12] Jesus depicts his reciprocal relationship to his own in a manner identical to the OT covenant formula: "I know my own and my own know me" (John 10:14).

Furthermore, as with the other usages of "his own" in the gospel,[13] the phrase in John 13:1 has a familial character and refers to relations between kin. Jesus' "own" are those disciples who have been definitively taken by Jesus as his personal possession. He has taken them to himself in the fullness of love ("he loved his own ... he loved them to the end," v. 1), which implies that they have given themselves to him. Because they have been loved by him and have given themselves to him in belief and love they have been granted the definitive status of those "who received him" (John 1:12a). In receiving him, they receive what he alone has the authority to give—they become like him.[14] According to the logic of 1:12, this likeness is one of sonship in relation to the Father: as those "who received him" (1:12a), the disciples are like the Son by having been given the grant of the status of "children of God" (1:12c). Such status is explicitly confirmed in 13:33 where Jesus himself calls them "children." Jesus' "own" are, in fact, those who have been given to him by the Father: "they were yours, and you gave them to me" (17:6; see also v. 9). They are the Son's "own" as they are the Father's "own"—they are the children of God. In sum, in being given the status as Jesus' "own," the disciples have not rejected the new covenant offered by their God,[15] but, on the contrary, have been generated as children of God in the new covenant.

---

divine sonship.

11 See, for example, Jer. 31:1, 10, 31–34; Ezek. 34:15–16, 23–25, 30–31; 37:23–28.

12 Jesus' "own" who responded positively to him are "defined as those who heed his message (10:3–4), those who were truly in covenant relationship with him." See Craig S. Keener, *The Gospel of John: A Commentary* (Massachusetts: Hendrickson Publishers, Inc., 2003), 399.

13 See, for example, John 1:11; 4:44; 7:53; 10:3, 4; 19:27.

14 There appears to be a general principle functioning in the background of the use of the phrase "his own" in 13:1 that was operative in later Israelite traditions, namely, the principle that like generates and loves its like. This principle is exemplified in Ps. 115:8 and Sir. 13:15 respectively: "Those who make them are like them" and "Every creature loves its own like."

15 Unlike "his own" who received him not (John 1:11), namely, some of his own Israelite kinsman.

The Status of Children

The kinship relationship that is implicit in the phrase "his own" is explicitly expressed in 13:33 where Jesus calls his disciples "children" (τεκνία). The significance of this title is highlighted since this first-time usage occurs within the context of the ushering in of Jesus' decisive hour which has finally come, when his love for his own has reached eschatological fulfillment ("to the end," 13:1). Moreover, "children" appears immediately following the mutual glorification of God and the Son of man (vv. 31–32). In a gospel which places such emphasis on the divine kinship motif,[16] this first-time designation of "children" functions as a climactic high-point within the gospel as a whole.

Τεκνία in 13:33 recalls the use of τέκνα in 1:12 and 11:52 and ought to be understood in light of them.[17] John 11:52 discloses the meaning of Caiaphas' prophecy regarding Jesus' death: he will die "to gather into one the children of God (τέκνα τοῦ θεοῦ)." Regardless of the exact referent of the phrase "children of God" (the Gentiles, the diaspora Israelites, or both),[18] the notion that Jesus has gathered his disciples into one is implied in the phrase "his own" (13:1). John 17:1–26 explicitly states that the Father, the Son, and Jesus' own will be "one" (vv. 21, 22, 23). In deeming them "his own" (13:1) and "children" (13:33), Jesus is fulfilling his mission (at least in principle) to gather into one the children of God.

If the gospel is strongly influenced by the thought world of biblical Israel and Judaism—as I believe it is[19]—the reference to a gathered group of people claiming to be God's "children" is significant. Such Jewish groups thought of themselves, in one way or another, as the remnant of Israel and that God was performing his eschatological interventions of restoration and vindication through them.[20] The reason for this is that divine childhood or sonship is a central feature of Israel's covenant relationship to their God.[21] Israel's designation in the covenant as God's

---

16 See DeMeo, *Covenantal Kinship*, 133–140.

17 See Mary Coloe, "Welcome into the Household of God: The Foot Washing in John 13," *Catholic Biblical Quarterly* 66 (2004): 409. The difference between τεκνία and τέκνα is insignificant. See Keener, *John*, 921; Matthew Vellanickal, *The Divine Sonship of Christians in the Johannine Writings* (Rome: Biblical Institute Press, 1977), 91. We fully agree with Bruce Vawter that John 13–17 functions as a commentary on 1:12: "to all who received him, who believed in his name, he gave power to become children of God." See Bruce Vawter, "The Gospel according to John," in *The Jerome Biblical Commentary* (New Jersey: Prentice Hall Inc., 1968), 2:450.

18 See the discussion in John Dennis, *Jesus' Death and the Gathering of True Israel: The Johannine Appropriation of Restoration Theology in the Light of John 11:47–52*, Wissenschaftliche Untersuchungen zum Neuen Testament (Tubingen: Mohr-Siebeck, 2006), 258–259.

19 See DeMeo, *Covenantal Kinship*, 140–144.

20 See R. Alan Culpepper, "Pivot of John's Prologue," *New Testament Studies* 27 (1980): 25.

21 See Exod. 4:22; Deut. 14:1; 32:18–19; Isa. 63:8, 16; 64:8; Jer. 3:19; 31:9; Hos. 11:1, 10; Ezek. 16:21; 2 Sam. 7:14; Ps. 89:26–27; etc. Raymond Brown concurs with our conclusion: "the status of Israel as God's son or child is a covenantal relationship." See Raymond Brown, *The Epistles of John*, The Anchor Bible 30 (New York: Doubleday and Co., 1982), 389. See also DeMeo, *Covenantal Kinship*, 64–108.

"people" (עם) implies a kinship relation.[22] Israel is explicitly given the status of "first-born son" in Exodus 4:22–23 which is confirmed in the Sinai covenant's blood and meal rituals[23] and later described in Deuteronomy.[24] Within the ratification of the covenant with David, God promises that "I will be his father, and he shall be my son" (2 Sam. 7:14; see also Ps. 89:26–27 where God deems David his "first-born son"). Finally, the grant of the prophetic new covenant includes, as a vital component, the promise of the restoration of the Father-son relationship between God and Israel: "At that time, says the LORD, I will be the God of all the families of Israel, and they shall be my kin (עם)" (Jer. 31:1). According to the Septuagint, Jeremiah 31(8):8 relates how God will gather a remnant of Israel from the ends of the earth to the feast of the Passover where a great multitude will be begotten. Jeremiah 31:9 states that such a restorative gathering is rooted in the re-establishment of God's fatherhood and Israel's consequent first-born sonship: "I have become a father to Israel, and Ephraim is my firstborn" (v. 9). Jeremiah 31:20 echoes 31:9 by underlining their restored father-son relationship: "Ephraim is a beloved son, a pleasing child to me." The "new covenant," explicitly stated in Jeremiah 31:33, is the proximate setting for the restoration of God's fatherhood and Israel's divine sonship.[25]

Kinship language is utilized in John 13:33 (and elsewhere in John 13–17) for the same reasons as in the examples of covenant making in the OT, namely, for the sake of indicating that family ties have been furthered across family bloodlines. In giving his disciples the title of "children" at his final Passover meal, Jesus is signifying that a chief promise of the OT divine covenant—namely, the establishment of intimate, personal bonds of divine kinship between God and his people—has been fulfilled. According to Brown, "Jesus was proclaiming the arrival of the eschatological times when men would be God's children."[26] Commenting on 11:52, he holds

---

22 See Cross, "Kinship and Covenant," 13; Vellanickal, *Divine Sonship*, 14; Johannes Pedersen, *Israel: Its Life and Culture* (London: Oxford University Press, 1926), 1:55–57; Norbert Lohfink, "The People of God," in *Great Themes from the Old Testament* (Edinburgh: T. & T. Clark Ltd., 1982), 122; Dennis J. McCarthy, "Israel, My First-Born Son," *The Way* 5 (1965): 187.

23 John W. Pryor highlights the birth of Israel at the covenant of Sinai as reflected in Rabbinic tradition: "Song of Songs 8:2 read: 'I would lead you and bring you to my mother's house …' The interpretation of this Cant r. 8:2 reads: 'I will lead you': I [Israel] will lead you [God] from the world above to that below [i.e., God will come down]. 'I will bring you to my mother's house': that is, Sinai. R. Berekiah said: Why was Sinai called 'the house of my mother'? Because there the Israelites were made like a newborn child." *John: Evangelist of the Covenant People* (Illinois: InterVarsity Press, 1992), 174.

24 In the context of election and covenant, Deut. 14:1 LXX exclaims, "You are the children of the Lord your God."

25 The writings of Qumran, the Pseudepigrapha, and certain Rabbinical texts utilized the title "children of God" in one form or another in reference to the covenant institution. See DeMeo, *Covenantal Kinship*, 144–169.

26 Raymond Brown, *The Gospel According to John I-XII*, The Anchor Bible 29a (New York: Doubleday and Co., Inc., 1966), 139. In his commentary on 1 John he writes, "one of the tasks

that "John has rephrased the covenant saying, 'I will be your God, and you shall be my people,' into 'I will be your God, and you shall be my children.'"[27] He sums up the principle at work in the conferral of the status of children to his disciples in John 13:33: "where sonship is mentioned, it is the result of covenant choice."[28]

Conferral of Inheritance

In John 13:8, Jesus grants his own the gift of inheritance: "If I do not wash you, you have no inheritance with me." "Inheritance" (μέρος) signifies the grant of participation in Jesus' life. It makes explicit what is implicit in the phrase "his own" (13:1), namely, a relationship or communion of mutual belonging and abiding—the disciples share in Jesus' life in such a manner as to be with him (and therefore he with them). This inheritance is familial in that it is a gift passed down from kin to other members of kin.[29] Analogous to the double-portion of inheritance received by the first-born son in the ancient Near East, Jesus, the only Son (μονογενής, see 1:14, 18; 3:18),[30] has received "all things" from the Father (13:3) and authority over "all flesh," (17:2). In sum, "all that the Father has" belongs to Jesus (16:15).

As the only Son "coming" from God and "sent" by the Father,[31] Jesus is the agent or envoy who speaks in the name of the Father and acts as his representative.[32] As the Father has life in himself, so he has also given the Son to have life in himself (5:26; see also 5:21) for the sake of perpetuating it for the future prosperity of Jesus' own: "from his fullness have we all received" (1:16). Jesus stands in the Father's stead as a kind of "father-figure" to his "children" (13:33)[33]—or, as St. Au-

---

of the Messiah will be to distinguish the true children of Israel; for *Ps. Sol.* 17:28–30 says of the Son of David: 'he shall gather together a holy people whom he shall lead in justice ... He shall know them, that they are all sons of God.'" He concludes, "divine childhood is part of the New Covenant." *Epistles*, 389–390. See also Sherri Brown, *Gift Upon Gift: Covenant through Word in the Gospel of John* (Oregon: Pickwick Publications, 2010), 228.

27 Brown, *Epistles*, 391. See the related text in Rev. 21:7, "I will be his God and he will be my son."

28 Brown, *John I-XII*, 139.

29 See Raymond Brown, *The Gospel According to John XIII-XXI*, The Anchor Bible 29b (New York: Doubleday and Co., Inc., 1970), 566.

30 Jesus is considered to be the "first-born" (πρωτότοκος) in other NT traditions such as Rev. 1:5; Luke 2:7; Rom. 8:29; Col. 1:15, 18; Heb. 1:6; 12:23.

31 See John 13:3; 13:20; 14:24; 15:21; 16:5; 17:3, etc.

32 According to Jewish rabbinic tradition, "the One who is sent is like the one who sent him." See Brown, *John XIII-XXI*, 632; Marinus De Jonge, "The Son of God and the Children of God in the Fourth Gospel," in *Saved by Hope: Essays in Honor of Richard C. Oudersluys*, ed. J. Cook (Grand Rapids: Eerdmans Publishing Co., 1978), 48; Marianne M. Thompson, "The Living Father," *Semeia* 85 (2001): 27; Jan A. Bühner, *Der Gesandte und sein Weg im 4. Evangelium*, Wissenshaftliche Untersuchungen Zum Neuen Testament 2 (Tübingen: Mohr-Siebeck, Taschenbuch, 1977), 210, 233.

33 See St. Thomas Aquinas, *Commentary on the Gospel of John*, §1922 [*Super Evangelium Johannis*, caput 14, lectio 5].

gustine says, to the "begotten of the only begotten" (*invenies unigeniti genitorem*),[34]—and "younger brethren" (20:17) granting his disciples an "inheritance" in his very own power to become children of God who are "born … of God" (1:12–13). In other words, "inheritance" in 13:8 signifies a grant of participation in Jesus' inheritance in such a manner that the disciples share *in him*—they are "sons in the Son"—and are drawn into his destiny as Son of the Father. They have a prepared place for them in the "Father's house" (14:2). Jesus has brought Israel's disinheritance to an end.[35] This marks the fulfillment of the eschatological promise: the Father himself is now, in Jesus, the inheritance of Israel.

Lastly, the inheritance that Jesus gives to his own in John 13:8 is acutely appropriate in a covenant context, for, according to many OT and NT traditions, the divine covenant and the reception of inheritance are integrally related. As Israel was promised in the covenant to receive God himself and the ancestral land of Canaan as an inheritance,[36] so now Jesus' own are given an inheritance with him in the new covenant.[37] Such inheritance is a central effect of the formation of sacred kinship bonds via the ratification of the new covenant at this final meal. It denotes a mutual sharing of a common life within a covenant relationship. Such an understanding of inheritance as familial communion in covenant relation is found in another Johannine text, namely, Revelation 21:7, "He who overcomes will inherit these things, and I will be his God and he will be my son."

Blessed and Chosen Ones

According to John 13:17–18, Jesus' disciples have received the status as the "blessed" and "chosen" ones.[38] Such a status is quintessential to the OT divine covenant. To be "blessed" in the OT is practically equivalent to being in a right covenant relationship with God.[39] For instance, as a final declaration of their divine covenant relationship, God swears a covenant oath to Abraham to bless him, his future seed, and all the nations: "I will indeed bless you … and by your descendants shall all the nations of the earth bless themselves" (Gen. 22:17–18). Likewise, in the midst of the ratification of the Deuteronomic covenant a promise of blessing is given: "And

34 St. Augustine, *Gospel of John*, 49.2 quoted in St. Thomas Aquinas, *Catena Aurea-The Gospel of John* (New York: Preserving Christian Publications, 2000), 433 [*Catena Aurea in Joannem*, caput 13, lectio 3].

35 For Israel's disinheritance see Exod. 32:7–9; 34:9; Num. 14:12; Deut. 32:5–26; Jer. 16:18, 19.

36 See, for instance, Exod. 32:13; 34:9; Lev. 20:24; Num. 18:20; 26:53ff.; 34:2ff.; Deut. 12:10; 1 Chron. 16:7–18; Jer. 10:16; Isa. 57:13; Ezek. 44:28; 57:13; Sir. 24:8–12; 45:20.

37 See the connection between covenant and inheritance in several NT traditions such as Gal. 3:8–29; 4:21–31; Heb. 6:13–18; 9:15; 11:7–9; 1 Pet. 1:4–2:10.

38 John 13:17–18 reads: "If you know these things, blessed are you if you do them. I am not speaking of you all; I know whom I have chosen; it is that the scripture may be fulfilled, 'He who ate my bread has lifted his heel against me.'"

39 For instance, Gen. 9:1–26; 17:16; 22:17–18; Deut. 11:26–28; 23:5; 28:2–6, 8; Jos. 24:10; 2 Sam. 7:29.

all these blessings shall come upon you and overtake you, if you obey the voice of the LORD your God" (Deut. 28:2; see also vv. 3–6). For that matter, in the whole of Deuteronomy the term "blessing" seems to be a technical word indicating favor within the covenant relationship.[40] Similarly, the divine blessing is emphatically solicited by David in the covenant that God granted him in 2 Samuel 7:29.[41] The logic of being "blessed" in the divine covenant is as follows: similar to a father blessing his son because of the latter's loyalty and filial obedience, so those of Israel who rightly live out their covenant position in faithfulness and love as divine sons were blessed by God their Father.[42]

Hence, in obeying Jesus' teaching and imitating his example as his own who believe and love him, the disciples are the blessed ones (John 13:17).[43] Such a blessing not only acknowledges the divine sonship of the disciples, it indicates that they are successfully living out their covenant relationship with the Father and the Son.[44]

John 13:18 relates that Jesus has conferred upon his disciples the relational status of being his "chosen" ones.[45] As the chosen ones of the "chosen one of God" (1:34),[46] Jesus' disciples participate in his relation to the God who chooses. Being chosen by Jesus is comparable in meaning to the disciples' status of being "his own" (v. 1). According to v. 18, Jesus is fulfilling the scripture in choosing his disciples by inserting them into the theological history of Israel's covenant election.[47] Among other texts,[48] the intimate association between being "chosen" in the covenant is poignantly expressed in Deuteronomy 7:6–7, 9:

> For you are a people holy to the Lord your God; the Lord your God has *chosen* you to be a people for his own possession ... the Lord set his love upon you and *chose* you ... Know therefore that

40 It is opposed to the term "curse" reserved for those who are disobedient to the covenant commands.

41 Pedersen writes, "Those who have peace with one another impart a mutual blessing, and if one gives blessing, then one creates peace and covenant," and "to make a blessing ... is the same as to make a covenant ... because the covenant consists in mutual blessing." *Israel*, 1:303–304.

42 See DeMeo, *Covenantal Kinship*, 46–63.

43 See John 16:27, 30; 20:29 and the connections between them.

44 See Charles H. Dodd, *The Interpretation of the Fourth Gospel* (Cambridge: Cambridge University Press, 1968), 403.

45 A similar statement is given in John 15:16, "You did not choose me, but I chose you and appointed you." Also 6:70; 15:16, 19; Rev. 17:14. See Alf Corell, "The Idea of Election in the Fourth Gospel," in his *Consummatum Est: Eschatology and Church in the Gospel of St. John* (New York: The Macmillian Company, 1958), 166–200.

46 According to some manuscripts—Codex Sinaiticus, OL, OS, and some Church Fathers—John 1:34 states that Jesus himself is the "chosen one of God." See Brown, *John I-XII*, 57.

47 See Francis Moloney, *Gospel of John*, Sacra Pagina (Minnesota: The Liturgical Press, 1998), 380.

48 See, for instance, Exod. 6:2–8 in conjunction with Ezek. 20:5 (which appears to be a commentary on God's intervention with Israel in Egypt).

> the Lord your God is God, the faithful God who keeps *covenant* and steadfast love with those who love him.

God's choice of David as his representative king and temple master was utterly fundamental to Israel's divine covenant.[49] In Psalm 89:3 God states, "I have made a covenant with my chosen one, I have sworn to David my servant." Later in the same text, it is said that David, the chosen one, will cry to his God, "You are my father, my God" (v. 26). God replies, "I will make him the first-born" (v. 27). David has been adopted through covenant election to be the first-born of God.[50] Lastly, Isaiah prophesizes about a servant-son (παῖς) "chosen" by God who will be a "covenant to the people" (Isa. 42:1, 6; see also 43:10; 49:7–8). Therefore, we agree with the conclusion of Mendenhall that "the religious meaning of God's 'choosing' must be looked for within the framework of the religious bonds which held early Israel together. This can only be the covenant tradition."[51]

In this eschatological hour of Jesus' final meal (13:1), Israel's theological history of covenant election is fulfilled: Jesus' own are the definitive "chosen" ones of God (13:18). According to the covenant logic found in the OT, this grant of the status of being Jesus' elect coincides with the disciples' adoption as children of God in the new covenant. As the ones "chosen" by the Son, they participate in the divine sonship of the Son as his children and they eat his bread at his table as his kin (vv. 18, 28, 33).

Friendship With Jesus

The relational status granted to the disciples by Jesus is further qualified in a remarkable way in John 15:13–15. They are "friends" (φίλος) with Jesus. Their friendship consists in sharing a common life, namely, in Jesus' filial life that he lays down in love for his own (see v. 13). Furthermore, Jesus shares everything that he has heard from the Father with them (v. 15; see also v. 16); the Father's life is also commonly possessed. Thus, their friendship finds its ultimate referent in the Father. As friends, therefore, they share a quasi-familial life together, a communion comparable to kinship.[52] The meaning of their status as "friends" and their

---

49 See 2 Sam. 7:1–29; Ps. 132:1–18.

50 See Ps. 2:1–12; 2 Sam. 7:14.

51 George Mendenhall, "Election," in *The Interpreter's Dictionary of the Bible* (New York: Abingdon Press, 1962), 79.

52 See Watt, *Family*, 365; Sandra Schneiders, *Written That You May Believe: Encountering Jesus in the Fourth Gospel* (New York: The Crossroad Publishing Company, 2003), 54; Sjef V. Tilborg, *Imaginative Love in John*, Biblical Interpretation Series 2 (New York: E.J. Brill, 1993), 128; Dorothy Lee, "Friendship, Love, and Abiding in the Gospel of John," in *Transcending Boundaries: Contemporary Readings of the New Testament*, eds. R. Chennattu and M. Coloe (Roma: Lireria Ateneo Salesiano, 2005), 71.

status as "brothers" (see 20:17) is similar.[53] This is an illustration of how, in the ancient world, friendship was analogous to kinship relations.[54]

The use of the term "friends" in John 15:13–15 also supports the covenantal status of Jesus' own. In the OT, the status of friendship was commonly linked to the covenant relationship. According to Psalm 25:14, friendship and covenant are interrelated: "The friendship (סוד)[55] of the LORD is for those who fear him, and he makes known to them his covenant." In the midst of the renewal of the Sinai covenant it is disclosed that Moses is a friend of God (Exod. 33:11). Also, the friendship between David and Jonathan, whose souls were bound together in mutual love and "steadfast love," is sealed with a covenant (1 Sam. 18:1–3; 20:3, 8, 17; 23:16–18).[56] Furthermore, Wisdom 1:16 states that the ungodly not only consider death to be "a friend," but "they made a covenant with him." According to Qumran, Abraham, Isaac, and Jacob possessed friendship with God that was equivalent to their covenant relationship with him: "Abraham ... was counted as a friend for keeping God's precepts ... And he passed them on to Isaac and to Jacob, and they kept them and were written up as friends of God and as members of the covenant forever" (Cairo Damascus Document 3:2–4).

In conclusion, the conferral of the status of friendship to Jesus' disciples in John 15:13–15 is analogous to a kinship relation: since a friend is another "self," then it follows that a friend of Jesus the Son will be another "son" who shares in his filial life with the Father. Moreover, this grant of friendship is a grant of a covenantal relation akin to the OT covenantal friendship shared between Abraham, Moses, and God. Altogether, then, the kinship-by-covenant principle is operative in this grant of friendship. Tilborg summarizes, "Jesus knows that he is in the service of the oikos of his heavenly father. Choosing disciples and making them his friends he enlarges the oikos [house] of his heavenly father. He allows these people to enter into the covenant of love."[57]

---

53 See Lee, "Friendship," 68–69.

54 According to Watt, "friends were regarded as a part of the extended family." *Family*, 360. See also Tilborg, *Imaginative Love*, 149; Lee, "Friends," 70; Philip A. Harland, "Familial Dimensions of Group Identity: 'Brother' (ΑΔΕΛΦΟΙ) in Associations of the Greek East," *Journal of Biblical Literature* 124/3 (2005): 513.

55 The Hebrew term סוד suggests a gathering of a secret council or inner circle. In Ps. 25:14 it is possible, then, to consider "those who fear" God as those who possess his friendship.

56 According to McCarthy, in ancient Near Eastern treaty-covenants "the obligation to friendship is commonplace." *Treaty and Covenant*, 43. See also Dennis J. McCarthy, *Old Testament Covenant: A Survey of Current Opinions* (Oxford: Basil Blackwell, 1972), 44; Johns Varghese, *The Imagery of Love in the Gospel of John*, Analecta Biblica 177 (Roma: Gregorian & Biblical Press, 2009), 216; DeMeo, *Covenantal Kinship*, 48–52, 56–61.

57 Tilborg, *Imaginative Love*, 150.

Bestowal of The Father's Name

Multiple texts throughout John 13–17 relate that Jesus' own definitively know the Father's name and are invited to invoke it.[58] Hence, they share in it: they possess his name, are under his name, and resemble various features of the meaning of his name. Such sharing resembles a child being given the same name by his father and, therefore, possessing it. The familial unity shared between the Father, the Son, and the disciples is made manifest by their mutual possession of one "name" (17:11).

That Jesus grants his disciples knowledge of the Father's name and the right to invoke it clearly echoes the OT tradition where God's name was manifested and called to be known and incanted within the covenant relationship. In the renewal of the Sinai covenant Moses petitioned God to restore his name (Exod. 33–34). In fact, the mutual knowledge of each of their respective names signified their covenant relationship itself (33:12, 17, 19). Moreover, this covenant renewal took place through the proclamation of the divine name (34:5–7). By revealing his name in covenant, God desires his people to claim it for themselves, so that he can be their God and they can be his people.

In their covenant, both God and David mutually knew each other's name (2 Sam. 7:9, 13). At the heart of the Davidic covenant was God's promise that a son of David would "build a house for my name" (v. 13) so that God will "make himself a name" (v. 23) and that his name will be "magnified forever" (v. 26).[59] The grant of his name to Israel signified that he will be "God over Israel."

The vindication and knowledge of God's holy name was a vital element in the eschatological covenant as foretold by the prophets. According to Isaiah 42, in the eschatological time God will give over the Servant as a "covenant to the people" (42:6), so that his name may be manifested: "I am the Lord, that is my name" (42:8). Isaiah 56 relates how the foreigner and eunuch who "hold fast my covenant" (56:4) will be granted "a name better than sons and daughters; I will give them an everlasting name which shall not be cut off" (56:5). Moreover, the prophet Jeremiah foretells that the new covenant relationship will be the locus of the definitive revelation of the divine name (Jer. 31:35). The gift of the covenant and the revelation of God's name go hand in hand.[60] According to the prophet Ezekiel, the vindication of the holy name will take place through a new covenant (Ezek. 36:24–28; see also vv. 29, 33).

According to John 17:6, 23, and 26, the Father's name is central to the generation and formation of Jesus' own as the children of God, and their subsequent

---

58 John 14:13, 14; 15:16; 16:24, 26; 17:6, 11, 12, 26.

59 This covenant was renewed (1 Kings 8:20–21, 23–26, 54–63) when Solomon dedicated the temple as "the house of the name of the Lord" (1 Kings 8:16, 17, 18, 19, 20, 29, 43, 44; see 35, 41).

60 Jer. 33:14–26 expresses something similar, for, in a discussion about the perpetuity of the covenant with creation, the covenant with David, and the covenant with the Levites, God discloses his name: "And this is the name by which it will be called: 'The Lord is our righteousness'" (v. 16).

relationship of love with the Father and the Son. This is a significant indicator that the Sinaitic, Davidic, and prophetic promises regarding the divine name and the covenant relationship with Israel are fulfilled. Knowledge of the Father's name and the invitation to incant Jesus' name signifies that the Father is "God over Israel." According to 17:11, because the children of God possess the Father's name, and because they are protected by it, they will be one as the Father and the Son are one. To be unified in the divine name in a manner analogous to the unity found in God is the simultaneous fulfillment of the prophetic promise of a reunified Israel (and the gathering of the nations) and the unprecedented escalation of interpersonal, interfamilial communion.[61]

II. Covenantal Obligations For Kinship Relation

Commandment to Love

In John 13:34–35, Jesus presents his "new commandment." Commandments were characteristic or typical of the OT covenant relationship; where you find commandments, you usually find a covenant.[62] For instance, the promulgation of the Decalogue (Exod. 20:1–17) expressed the essence of the Sinai covenant. It was a gracious revelation of God's will defining Israel's status and relation to him. Deuteronomy 4:13 notes the link between commandments and this covenant: "And he [the Lord] declared to you his covenant, which he commanded you to perform, that is, the ten commandments." Deuteronomy 4:13 is a specific case of the general rule, namely, the OT divine commandment is "a relational term which can be understood only within the covenantal context."[63]

That love is the essential content of Jesus' commandment is undoubtedly evocative of the OT divine commandment given in the divine covenant.[64] Few passages in the OT illuminate as fully the relation of covenant, commandments, and love as Deuteronomy 7:6–13. According to this text, love lies at the heart of the covenant relationship between God and Israel (vv. 7, 8, 9) and is the principal core

61 In addition, the holiness of the Father's name is affirmed by Jesus: "Holy Father" (17:11). This is in accord with Ezekiel's prophecy regarding the vindication of the holiness of God's name in the new covenant.

62 See Gen. 2:16–17; 9:1–17; 17:1–14; Exod. 19–24; Lev. 26; Deut. 6:1–25; 7:9; 26:17–19; 27:9; Josh. 24:25; Jer. 31:31–34. See Kalluveettil, *Declaration and Covenant*, 18; Matthew O'Connell, "The Concept of Commandment in the Old Testament," *Theological Studies* 21 (1960): 379; Urban C. von Wahlde, *The Johannine Commandments: 1 John and the Struggle for the Johannine Tradition* (New York: Paulist Press, 1990), 227.

63 Raymond F. Collins, "A New Commandment I Give to You, That you Love One Another..." (John 13:34)," in *These Things Have Been Written: Studies on the Fourth Gospel* (Leuven: Peeters Uitgeverij, 1990), 234. For other examples of the relation between commandment and covenant in the OT and Qumran see DeMeo, *Covenantal Kinship*, 257–258.

64 On the relation of covenant and love in the ancient Near East and ancient Israel see William L. Moran, "The Ancient Near Eastern Background of the Love of God in Deuteronomy," *Catholic Biblical Quarterly* 25 (1963): 79–80.

of the covenant commandments (v. 9). Love is the reason for their covenant relationship; it explains why God chose Israel and bound himself by a sworn covenant oath to Israel (vv. 7–8, 13). In addition, it is the indispensable obligation required to maintain their covenant relationship. From this text, and others (for instance, Exod. 20:5–6), we can conclude, along with Stauffer, that in the OT "the concept of love is the ultimate foundation of the whole covenant theory."[65]

Jesus' commandment to love is the primary indicator that John 13–17 presents a relationship between the Father, the Son, and the disciples that can be deemed "covenantal." Its vital content and function is unmistakably identical to the OT covenant commandments: as the OT commandments disclosed the will of God for Israel and in doing so defined their covenant relationship, so Jesus' new commandment definitively discloses the will of his Father for his own for the sake of defining their covenant relationship.[66] In other words, Jesus' commandment is the core obligation required of the disciples' newfound status in the new covenant: in keeping it, Jesus' own are securing their relationship and shared life with the Father and the Son as children of God.

However, Jesus' commandment is noticeably dissimilar to its OT counterpart. The uniqueness of the commandment is appropriate for the uniqueness of the event: Jesus' commandment is qualitatively new because it is promulgated for a new, effective covenant[67] which is ratified by a new sacrifice that is bound up with his efficacious love—"as I have loved you" (13:34c)—that does not remain alone, but bears much fruit (12:24–25). In laying down his life for his friends in great love (see 15:13; 10:15, 17–18), Jesus has loved them with the fullness of sacrificial love—"to the end" (13:1)—and in doing so the power of divine love is "given to" them (13:34a; also 15:9) in order to keep his commandment.[68] Jesus' command-

---

65 Stauffer, "ἀγαπάω," in *Theological Dictionary of the New Testament*, trans. G. Bromiley, eds. G. Kittel and G. Bromiley (Michigan: Eerdmans, 1964), 1:27 where he notes further, "There can be no doubt that the thought of covenant is itself an expression in juridical terms of the experience of the love of God."

66 Mendenhall writes, "The Gospel of John ... has a reference to a 'new commandment' appropriate to a 'new covenant' (John 13:34). The commandment to love thus corresponds to the very nature of the covenant itself ... [It is a] stipulated obligation assumed by those who enter the covenant community." See also George Mendenhall, "Covenant," in *The Interpreter's Dictionary of the Bible* (New York: Abingdon Press, 1962), 1:722; Brown, *John XIII-XXI*, 644; G. R. Beasley-Murray, "The Community of True Life," *Review and Expositor* 85 (1988): 476.

67 See Brown, *John XIII-XXI*, 614; Charles H. Talbert, *Reading John* (New York: Crossroad Publishing Company, 1994), 199. See also Pryor, *John*, 163; O'Connell, "Concept of Commandment," 351–403. This qualitative newness is implied in 1 John 2:8, "I am writing you a new commandment, which is true in him and in you," and 1 John 5:3, "his commandments are not burdensome."

68 Although the OT covenant commandments were given by God as their source and, therefore, were good and holy, Israel's history manifests that they were ineffective and insufficient to overcome their spiritual blindness and deafness (see Deut. 29:2–4; Isa. 6:10). Such disobedience to the commandments, caused by a deficient belief and love for their God, not only led to the administration of the covenant curse (for instance, exile—Deut. 27:26; 28:15), but

ment to love is, therefore, the living principle by which the children of God can accomplish the Father's will and live with him in a mutual covenant.[69] In this way, the OT eschatological expectation of an intimate, reciprocal covenant relationship rooted in keeping the divine commandment of love is fulfilled and surpassed in an unforeseen manner.

Belief

In this hour of plain revelation of the Father (John 16:25, 29), Jesus' own make a solemn profession of belief in the divine sonship of the Son who has his origin and end in the Father: "now we know that you know all things ... we believe that you came from God" (v. 30). Through their profession of belief in the sonship of the Son, which was anticipated by Jesus in v. 27b ("you have loved me and have believed that I came from God"), they also declare their belief in the fatherhood of the Father: God is their Father and they believe that "the Father himself loves" them (16:27). This fulfills the logic of John 1:12–13, namely, their belief marks that they have received the Father and the Son (see 17:8 "they received") and their reception manifests that they are children of God.[70] By receiving him in belief, they will not only participate in the very life of the Father and the Son (14:10–11), but also in the future will imitate the Son as children of God ("he who believes in me will also do the works that I do," 14:12a).

The function of "believing" in John 13–17 generates and maintains a relationship with God which the OT would consider to be distinctly covenantal in character. God's dealings with Israel in the Exodus (see Exod. 4:4–5, 7–8; 14:31) and in his theophany on Mount Sinai (see Exod. 19:9; also 34:10–12) were ordered to empower Israel to firmly believe in him for the sake of entering into a covenant relationship with him. In a similar manner, Jesus is appealing to the heart of his disciples to empower them to fidelity and faithfulness to God. Furthermore, as the dangers of disbelief and apostasy were usually addressed during ratifications and renewals of the OT divine covenant, so Jesus' appeal to believe is underlined by the real danger that the disciples may forsake their covenant God by not believing in him (see 16:1).

Lastly, their profession of belief is comparable to the manner in which a covenant oath was sworn at covenant making ceremonies and it bears an analo-

---

also generated prophetic, eschatological expectations for a divine grant of interior power and assistance to keep his covenant commandments (see, for example, Deut. 30:6–7; Jer. 31:31–34; Ezek. 11:20; 36:27; 37:24). John 13–17 presents the unprecedented fulfillment of these expectations in the person of Jesus and his love.

69 See Edward Malatesta, *Interiority and Covenant: An Exegetical Study of the* εἶναι ἐν *and* μένειν ἐν *Expressions in 1 John*, Analecta biblica (Rome: Biblical Institute Press, 1978), 105–106.

70 See also the link between belief, being born from above, water/Spirit, and eternal life in 3:3–18 and belief, being "out of God," and being a son who abides in the house forever in 8:31–59.

gous function to it, namely, it ratifies a covenant.[71] For example, at the ratification ceremony of the divine covenant at Sinai, Israel swears a verbal oath of allegiance to the covenant: "Then he [Moses] took the book of the covenant, and read it in the hearing of the people; and they said, 'All that the Lord has spoken we will do, and we will be obedient'" (Exod. 24:7; see also 24:3). Likewise, in the renewal of the divine covenant in the land of Canaan, Israel professes its allegiance to their covenant God: we "will serve the Lord, for he is our God" (Josh. 24:18; also 24:21, 24). An equivalent occurrence is happening in John 13–17. The profession of the disciples' present belief in the Father and the Son, therefore, manifests their being bound to the relationship they have with them in the new covenant.[72]

III. Covenantal Interiority of the Father, Son, and Children of God

The covenantal kinship status with God that is conferred upon the disciples by Jesus in John 13–17 is further qualified as a relationship of deep interiority which surpasses all traditional and prophetic expectations of Israel.

In 14:1 Jesus reassures and encourages his disciples not to fear his imminent departure: "let not your hearts be troubled; believe in God, believe also in me." Interior belief is that which will grant courage to the "heart," which refers to the very depths of the person and is the "organ of interiority."[73] Throughout the OT, the heart was the reference point for Israel in their covenant with their God (see Deut. 30:1–20)—he continually called and appealed to their heart.[74] It is precisely a relationship of the heart, of great interiority, that Jesus grants his own during his final meal. Their relationship to the Father and the Son will be one of in-being and mutual indwelling, and mutual indwelling generated by the Spirit of truth.[75]

---

71 See Gen. 15:17–18; 22:16; Exod. 19:8; 24:3, 6–8; Deut. 26:17–18; 27:14–26; 29:12; Josh. 24:18, 21–22, 24; 2 Sam. 7:11; Ps. 132:2, 11. The OT covenant relationship is a permanent relationship because it is essentially based on an immutable oath made in God's unchanging, holy name (see Heb. 6:13–18). See Donald L. Magnetti, *The Oath in the Old Testament in the Light of Related Terms and in the Legal and Covenantal Context of the Ancient Near East*, Ph.D. Diss., Johns Hopkins University (Michigan: University Microfilms, 1969), 55–65, 83–85; Quell, "διαθήκη," *Theological Dictionary of the New Testament*, 2:114–115; Mendenhall, "Covenant," 1:720.

72 See Rekha M. Chennattu, *Johannine Discipleship as a Covenant Relationship* (Peabody, MA: Hendrickson Publishers, Inc., 2006), 129–130; Aelred Lacomara, "Deuteronomy and the Farewell Discourse (John 13:3–16:33)," *Catholic Biblical Quarterly* 36 (1974): 75.

73 See Malatesta, *Interiority*, 70; idem, "Covenant and Indwelling," *The Way* 17 (1977): 25. In the OT, the heart is the center of the personality, the source of intelligence and decisions, as it is the seat of memory. See Schnackenburg, *St. John*, 3:58.

74 The covenant, whose law will be written on the heart (Jer. 31:33; Ezek. 36:26), was, as McCarthy states, "an affair of free choice and therefore pre-eminently human ... [which] could become a true and a conscious union of minds and hearts." McCarthy, "Israel, My First-Born Son," 191.

75 Their relationship of interiority is also expressed as permanent "abiding" together. Especially with its association with the "vine and the branches" in John 15:1–17, abiding can be deemed "covenantal." Unlike Israel who "abode not in my covenant" (Jer. 38:32, LXX), the covenant

Spirit of Truth

As the representative of Jesus who speaks in his name (14:26; 16:13), the Spirit-Paraclete helps in bringing to completion the mission of the Son to die for the nation of Israel so as to gather into one the scattered children of God (11:51–52; 7:39; 16:7). The Spirit "gives life" (6:63). As the one who comes from above (1:32, 33), the Spirit is a source and agent of eschatological,[76] divine birth "from above" (3:3, 7) resulting in participation in the familial life of the Father and the Son, "eternal life" (3:15, 16).[77]

At the hour of glorification of the Son (13:31–32; 17:1–5; 12:23, 28), the Spirit of truth is presently given to the disciples (see 7:39) as Jesus discloses: "you know him, for he abides with you, and is in you" (14:17).[78] The role of the Spirit in generating the children of God is explicitly referred to in the next verse: "I will not leave you orphaned" (v. 18). In being sent by the Father through the mediation of the Son (14:16; 3:34), the Spirit manifests the caring, protective action of the Father for the children of God—they will not be left without the Father. The manifestation of the generation of Jesus' own as his children through the Spirit is the long awaited fulfillment of the promise of covenant restoration, especially as foretold by the prophet Ezekiel (see Ezek. 36–37, 39) who foresees the Spirit of God (36:26–27; 37:5–6, 9, 14) as the agent of the vindication and unification of Israel (37:16) through cleansing water (36:25, 33; 37:23) for a renewed covenant relationship (36:28; also 37:23, 26–27).[79]

---

established at Sinai, the abiding relationship in John 15 seems to fulfill the new covenant foretold by Jer. 38:33–34. The Johannine covenant formula makes this manifest: "abide in me and I in you" (15:4). See also: "God is love, and he who abides in love abides in God, and God abides in him" (1 John 4:16; also 3:24; 4:13, 15). See DeMeo, *Covenantal Kinship*, 360–377.

76 See Aune, *The Cultic Setting of Realized Eschatology in Early Christianity* (Leiden: E. J. Brill, 1972), 103.

77 Alan Kerr remarks: "What we are given in Christ are family relationships generated by the Holy Spirit." *The Temple of Jesus' Body* (London: Sheffield Academic Press, 2002), 302.

78 Several important early manuscripts, such as P^{66} B D* W f^{1} many OL MSS $syr^{c,p,pal}$, have the present tense ἐστιν rather than the future ἔσται. In light of the definitive, eschatological nature of the events and discourses of Jesus' final meal, the present tense coheres better with the realized eschatology of the scene as a whole (John 13-17) than does the future tense. See the discussion in Moloney, *Gospel of John*, 406–407; Beasley-Murray, *John*, 243; Brown, *John XIII–XXI*, 639.

79 According to Gary T. Manning, the fulfillment of Ezekiel's prophecies in John 13–17 has the "same function as the Lukan announcement of the 'new covenant in my blood' (Luke 22:20). Luke uses language from the giving of the Mosaic Covenant (Exod. 24:8) and from Jeremiah's prophecy of a new covenant (Jer. 31:31–34) to announce the inauguration of a new covenant between God and his people. John uses language from the creation accounts [see Gen. 2:7] and from Ezekiel's prophecy of a new covenant for essentially the same purpose." *Echoes of a Prophet: The Use of Ezekiel in the Gospel of John and in the Literature of the Second Temple Period* (New York: T&T Clark International, 2004), 170. See also Dennis, *Jesus' Death*, 288.

In-Being

The covenantal relation of the children of God to the Father and the Son is a specific kind, namely, one of "being-in-another." Not only do the Father and the Son share a relation of in-being, "I am in the Father and the Father in me" (14:10, 11),[80] but their in-being relationship is extended to Jesus' own, "I am in my Father, and you in me, and I in you" (14:20). While maintaining a distinction between persons, this relationship suggests a union of wills and activity resulting in a total, reciprocal belonging to the other. It is the father-son relationship which characterizes this mutual in-being relationship: because the Father is the father of the Son and the Son is he who comes from the Father, they are "in" one another. By way of extension, because the Son is in his own, the Father is also in them. In this manner, their status as children of God is highlighted by this interiority.

The triple in-being expression found in John 14:20 is equivalent, in both form and content, to the OT divine covenant formula which expressed the very heart of the covenant relationship, namely, mutual being-together and belonging: "You shall be my people, and I shall be your God."[81] The covenant formula was grounded in the understanding that God was in the midst of his people. Deuteronomy 6:15 states, "The Lord your God in the midst of you is a jealous God."[82] In this text, as in others, the Septuagint translates the Hebrew "in your midst" (קרב) as "in you" (ἐν σοί). "His very presence in the midst of them signifies that he is in a covenant relationship with them."[83] The depth of interiority, force of interchange of mutual presence, and extent of familial intimacy of the in-being presence of the Father and the Son in the children of God and they in them marks the fulfillment of the OT divine covenant with a hitherto unexpected escalation of divine in-being.[84]

Indwelling

The interiority of the covenantal kinship relationship is further qualified as a relation of mutual indwelling: the disciples will mutually dwell with their God within the "many dwellings" (μοναί) in the "Father's house" (John 14:2, 23). Beyond the multiple chambers within the physical temple building, "many dwellings" signify the dwelling of persons in mutual relationship and communion as emphasized in 14:23: "If anyone loves me, he will keep my word, and my Father will love him, and we will come to him and make our dwelling with him."[85] The Father and the Son are dwelling with the children of God in such a reciprocal fashion as to share their life with

80 See also John 1:1–2, 18; 5:19–20; 6:57ab; 10:38; 17:21, 23.

81 See Exod. 6:7; Lev. 26:12; Deut. 29:13; Song 6:3, "I am my beloved's and my beloved is mine."

82 See also Exod. 34:9–10; Hos. 11:9; Joel 2:27; Zeph. 3:17.

83 Varghese, *Imagery*, 344.

84 See Malatesta, "Covenant and Indwelling," 31.

85 See Brown, *John XIII–XXI*, 618–619; Frederich Hauck, "μονή," *Theological Dictionary of the*

them in a manner analogous to how life is shared within a dwelling place or house.[86] Hence, through such mutual indwelling their divine sonship will flourish—they will not be left "orphans" (14:18).

The temple reference contained in "my Father's house" (John 14:2) indicates that Jesus is establishing a new covenant. This is evident because the temple (and the mountains associated with it), which was the "cosmic center of the universe" where "heaven and earth converge,"[87] was the place where covenants were made.[88] The close association between the dwelling place of God and the covenant with his people is disclosed in 1 Kings 8:21 where the tabernacle is the covenant: "And there I have provided a place for the Ark, in which is the covenant of the Lord which he made with our fathers, when he brought them out of the land of Egypt."[89] His concrete presence with his people in the tabernacle and temple expressed the mutual dwelling together in the peace of their covenant relationship.

More specifically, the temple was "the embodiment of the covenant of David."[90] In this divine covenant God requested that the son of David build "a house for my name" (2 Sam. 7:13) or, as 1 Chronicles 17:12 relates, a "house for me." Building this temple "house" is closely associated with the divine paternity of God and the divine sonship of the Davidid that was promised in their covenant: "I will

---

New Testament, 4:579–581; Jerome H. Neyrey, *The Gospel of John in Cultural and Rhetorical Perspective* (Michigan: Eerdmans, 2009), 77.

86 See Keener, *John*, 976; Robert H. Gundry, "In My Father's House Are Many Μοναί (John 14:2)," *Zeitschrift für die neutestamentliche Wissenschaft und die Kunde der älteren Kirche* 58 (1967): 70; James McCaffrey, *The House with Many Rooms: The Temple Theme of John 14, 2–3* (Roma: Editrice Pontificio Istituto Biblico, 1988), 184; Johannes Beutler, *Habt Keine Angst: Die erste johanneische Abschiedsrede (Joh 14)* Stuttgarter Bibelstudien 116 (Stuttgart: Verlag Katholisches Bibelwerk, 1984), 31–32.

87 Carol Meyers, "Temple, Jerusalem," in *The Anchor Bible Dictionary*, ed. David Noel Freedman (New York: Doubleday, 1992), 6.359. See also Delbert Hillers, *Covenant: The History of a Biblical Idea* (Baltimore: The Johns Hopkins Press, 1969), 74.

88 John M. Lundquist, "The Legitimizing Role of the Temple in the Origin of the State," in *Temples of the Ancient World*, ed. D. Parry (Utah: Deseret Book Company, 1994), 220. See Jon Levenson, "The Temple and the World," *Journal of Religion* 64 (1984): 275–298; Meyers, "Temple, Jerusalem," 360; John M. Lundquist, "Temple, Covenant, and Law in the Ancient Near East and in the Old Testament," in *Israel's Apostasy and Restoration: Essays in Honor of Roland K. Harrison*, ed. A. Gileadi (Grand Rapids, Michigan: Baker, 1988), 293.

89 John Welch concludes, "the Temple in Israel was a shrine of the covenant, the home of the ark of the covenant, and the place where the covenant was renewed and perpetuated. There the priest acted as a mediator between God and his covenant people Israel, offering the sacrifices of Israel up to God and instructing the people in God's name." *The Sermon on the Mount in the Light of the Temple* (Farnham, England: Ashgate Publishing Limited, 2009), 35.

90 Toomo Ishida, *The Royal Dynasties in Ancient Israel. A Study on the Formation and Development of Royal-Dynastic Ideology*, Beiheft zur Zeitschrift für die Alttestamentliche Wissenschaft 142 (New York: W. de Gruyter, 1977), 145, quoted in Hahn, "Temple, Sign and Sacrament: Towards a New Perspective on the Gospel of John," *Letter & Spirit* 4 (2008): 109. See also Tom Holmén, *Jesus and Jewish Covenant Thinking* (Boston: Brill, 2007), 277. See 2 Sam. 7//1 Chron. 17; 2 Sam. 23:5; 2 Chron. 7:18; 13:5; Pss. 89 and 132; Isa. 55:3.

be his father, and he shall be my son" (1 Chron. 17:13). Following the kinship-by-covenant principle, 1 Chronicles 17:14 manifests the relationship between God's house and the Davidic divine son: "I will confirm him in my house … forever." A permanent dwelling place will be established and confirmed for the Davidic divine son within God's house which is, subsequently, his "Father's house." This takes place in the fulfillment of their divine covenant.[91]

John 14:2–3, 23 signifies analogously the expected restoration and fulfillment of two necessary traditions of the Davidic covenant, namely, divine sonship and the house-temple as expressed in 2 Samuel 7/1 Chronicles 17.[92] Jesus is the Davidic divine son who not only dwells forever with the Father in the "Father's house," but, as John 2:21 relates, he is the Father's house.[93] Having a dwelling place prepared for them by the Son (14:2–3), the disciples participate in the filial life of the Son to the Father within the Father's house as children of God.[94]

Knowledge and Sight

"Knowing" in the gospel of John suggests more than intellectual apprehension and is an existential, active, concrete experience where one has profound contact with another's presence and their family, occurring at the heart of a personal relationship. It seems to extend to recognition and discernment of another person, and to will or to choose another person, leading to personal communion.[95] John 10:14–15 attests to such a meaning: "I know my own and my own know me, as the Father knows me and I know the Father." "Seeing" in the Fourth gospel is different than knowledge, but is intrinsically bound up with it, for knowledge determines the content of what is seen, that is, the content of the personal presence that we interiorly see and behold through perception.[96]

---

91 It is important to note that the Davidic king is the representative of Israel as a whole. Therefore, through the son of David, who is the covenanted son of God, Israel is promised in this Davidic covenant the opportunity to permanently abide in their Father's house as his covenantal sons.

92 See W. H. Oliver and A. G. Van Aarde, "The Community of Faith as Dwelling Place of the Father: βασιλεία του θεοῦ as 'Household of God' in the Johannine Farewell Discourse(s)," *Neotestamentica* 25 (1991): 393–394. Besides discovering the link between 2 Sam. 7 and John 14:2, 23, they also claim that 2 Sam. 7, John 14:2, 23, and the establishment of the new covenant by Jesus in Luke 22:28–30 share similar traditions. See also Sverre Aalen, "'Reign' and 'House' in the Kingdom of God in the Gospels," *New Testament Studies* 8 (1962): 237–238.

93 On the Johannine royal Davidic messianism/christology see Margaret Daly-Denton, *David in the Fourth Gospel* (Leiden: Brill, 2000), especially 108–110.

94 The close association between the divine dwelling and the divine covenant is reiterated in a different Johannine tradition, namely, Rev. 21:3, "I heard a loud voice from the throne saying, 'Behold, the dwelling of God is with men. He will dwell with them, and they shall be his people, and God himself will be with them.'"

95 See Rudolf Schnackenburg, *The Gospel According to St. John*, 3 vols. (New York: Herder and Herder, 1968), 3:67; George Beasley-Murray, *John*, Word Biblical Commentary, vol. 36, 2d Edition (Nashville: Thomas Nelson, 1999), 257; Schneiders, *Written*, 13.

96 See Keener, *John*, 247–251; Brown, *John I–XII*, 501–503; G. L. Phillips, "Faith and Vision in

These particular aspects of the knowledge and sight of God in the gospel are almost identical to knowledge and sight of God associated with the OT covenant relationship.[97] For instance, to "know" God and to "see" him face to face in a profoundly personal manner was a chief promise manifested in the Sinai covenant (Exod. 24:9–11; 33:18ff.). At the ratification of this covenant the representatives of Israel "saw the God of Israel" (24:10) and "beheld" him (v. 11; see Deut. 5:1–4). Instead of taking away their life because they saw him (v. 11a), God rather granted them the gift of an exclusive participation with him.

Similarly, within the context of the renewal of the Sinai covenant in Exodus 33, God "knows" Moses and has found favor with him "in his sight" (33:12; see vv. 13, 17). Moses was then granted the gift of seeing God "face to face" (v. 11)[98] so that he may "know" and, according to the Septuagint, "see" (ἴδω) him and receive his favorable glance in return (vv. 13, 14). In vv. 18–19, Moses boldly requested, "show me your glory" and God remarked, "I will make all my goodness pass before you, and will proclaim before you my name, 'the Lord.'" Thus, within the context of the renewal of the divine covenant with Israel (see 34:6–32), God confirmed the covenant faithfulness of Moses and demonstrated the purpose of the covenant relationship, namely, to see the face of God, to behold his glory, and to know his name and his ways. To "see," to "behold," and to "know," therefore, manifest the interpersonal communion and friendship promised in the divine covenant.

Furthermore, in his prophecy of the eschatological covenant, Ezekiel included the knowledge and sight of God as vital components to it. Israel will "know that I am the Lord" (36:6–11; see v. 38; 39:6–7, 22) and "the nations will know that I am the Lord" (36:23; see v. 36; 37:28; 39:6–7, 13, 21). This definitive knowledge of God is linked to a newborn communion of persons within a new covenant (36:25–28; also 39:22). Through his jealousy for his holy name, Israel's God will mercifully restore their fortunes again for the purpose of generating an effective covenant communion through the fullness of eschatological divine knowledge where they will "see" his face: "then they shall know that I am the Lord their God ... and I will not hide my face any more from them" (39:28–29).

The intimately personal bond generated by knowledge and sight in the OT divine covenant relationship is indistinguishable from the knowledge and sight given to Jesus' own in the gospel of John. For instance, in John 10:14–15 an interior,

---

the Fourth Gospel," in *Studies in the Fourth Gospel*, ed. Frank M. Cross (London: A. R. Mowbray & Co., 1957), 85.

97 Herbert B. Huffmon argues that ידע, the OT Hebrew equivalent to the verbs γινώσκω and οἶδα, refers to "mutual legal recognition" that occurs frequently in covenants ("covenant recognition"). See Huffmon, "The Treaty Background to Hebrew *YĀDA'*," *Bulletin of the American Schools of Oriental Research* 181 (1966): 31–37. See DeMeo, *Covenantal Kinship*, 55–58, 69–81; Charles K. Barrett, *The Gospel According to St. John* (Philadelphia: Westminster Press, 1978), 504. For these Hellenistic influences see Keener, *John*, 234–239.

98 See also Num. 12:8; 14:13–14; Deut. 5:1–4; 34:10.

mutual knowledge is central to the relationship between Jesus and his own (notice that the structure of these statements is similar to the OT covenant formula): "I know my own and my own know me, as the Father knows me and I know the Father."[99] Furthermore, in John 13–17 the disciples presently possess definitive knowledge and sight of their God as Jesus reveals: "you know him and have seen him" (14:7) and "he who has seen me has seen the Father" (14:9; also 12:45). They have seen his glory (13:31–32; 17:1–5; 1:14). Through their interior, mutual knowledge and sight of God they have been granted the gift of participation in the eternal life of the Father and the Son (17:3; 6:40). This radically fulfills the promise and expectation of eschatological knowledge and sight of God foreshadowed in the Sinai covenant and foretold in the prophecies about the new covenant.[100] Within the new covenant relationship between the Father, Son, and disciples, Israel knows definitively "the one true God" (17:3) and has at long last seen their God "face to face" (14:9; 12:45).[101]

Peace

In having received the gift of covenantal interiority with the Father and the Son, the disciples have received the gift of peace: "Peace I leave with you; my peace I give to you" (John 14:27; also 16:33). This consoling gift of peace is not any ordinary, worldly peace but rather it is precisely the peace that only Jesus gives—it is his personal peace ("my peace"); it is intrinsic to him and represents the "all-embracing sphere of his life (see 14:19), his love (14:21, 23), his joy (15:11; 16:22; 17:13)."[102] Being "in" him (16:33), the disciples have entered into a communion of peace with the Son and, subsequently, into the familial harmony and peace that he shares with the Father.[103] Especially by possessing the protection of the Father (17:11, 12, 15),[104] the children of God dwell in the "Father's house" (14:2–3) in spiritual tranquility and peace with him.

---

99 See Keener, *John*, 234.

100 Brown, *John XIII–XXI*, 614, 752. See Keener, *John*, 1054.

101 See Alexander Tsutserov, *Glory, Grace, and Truth: Ratification of the Sinaitic Covenant according to the Gospel of John* (Oregon: Pickwick Publications, 2009), 210. See Rev. 22:3–5.

102 Schnackenburg, *St John*, 3:84.

103 Peace is a generally accepted common good of any kinship group. Pedersen (*Israel*, 1:354) states: "Peace of the family is the foundation to everything." See also Leo G. Perdue, "The Household, Old Testament Theology and Contemporary Hermeneutics," in *Families in Ancient Israel*, eds. L. G. Perdue, J. Blenkinsopp, J. J. Collins, and C. Meyers (Kentucky: Westminster John Knox Press, 1997), 238. The "peace" between the Father and the Son is disclosed by their unity and that they act in one accord. Texts like John 8:28–29, "I do nothing on my own but I speak these things the Father taught me ... I always do what is pleasing to him," and 10:30, "I and the Father are one," support that there is harmony and peace between them.

104 On the Father's protection of Jesus' own as fulfilling the protection promised in the OT covenant relationship see DeMeo, *Covenantal Kinship*, 413–416.

Peace was the quintessential effect of the interpersonal communion forged in any covenant. The terms "covenant" and "peace" were not only frequently juxtaposed in the OT but the latter was the expressed content of the former.[105] For example, peace between Isaac and Abimelech was effected by the covenant they made with each other in Beersheba. After sharing a covenant meal (Gen. 26:30), they "took oath with one another; and Isaac set them on their way, and they departed from him in peace" (v. 31). In dealing with the Gibeonites, Joshua "made peace with them, and made a covenant with them, to let them live" (Josh. 9:15). Likewise, in the covenant between Solomon and Hiram, the main content was that "there was peace between" them (1 Kings 5:12). To make a covenant was equivalent to "make peace."[106] Similarly, in Malachi 2:5, God proclaims, "my covenant with him [Levi] was of life and peace."[107] The prophets foretold a future communion and indwelling with God in a "covenant of peace."[108] Therefore, in the OT "the covenant effects a unity which is peace."[109]

Because Jesus' own are "in" him (16:33), they have entered, as children of God, the wholeness of the sphere of his filial life with the Father and their shared communion of peace. As a result, they possess divine peace that goes beyond all expectation. This eschatological peace powerfully signifies a most stable state that prevails in their intimate, interior communion with the Father and Son in this

105 According to Gerhard Von Rad, "the connection between the two words ["peace," שלום and "covenant," ברית] is so strong that in this context שלום seems to have become a kind of official term. The thought may be that the relationship of שלום is sealed by both parties in a covenant. Conversely, it may be that the covenant inaugurates a relationship of שלום." See Von Rad, "εἰρήνη," *Theological Dictionary of the New Testament*, 2:403. See also Pedersen, *Israel*, 1:285.

106 Peace and covenant were so interrelated that if one violated the peace between parties then one subsequently violated the covenant and vice versa. Ps. 55:20 manifests this: "He has put forth his hands against those who were at peace with him; he has violated his covenant."

107 In the OT, covenant peace was closely related to the divine grant of "rest" in the covenant (Gen. 2:2; Exod. 33:14; Deut. 12:10; 3:20; 25:19; 2 Sam. 7:1, 11; Ps. 95:11; 1 Chron. 28:2; Sir. 47:13; Heb. 3:7–4:13). See Gerhard Von Rad, "A Rest for the People of God" in his *The Problem of the Hexateuch and Other Essays*, trans. E. W. Trueman Dicken (New York: McGraw-Hill Book Company, 1966), 94–102; Dennis McCarthy, "II Samuel 7 and Deuteronomic History," *Journal of Biblical Literature* 84 (1965): 132.

108 See Isa. 42:6; 49:8; 54:10; Ezek. 34:25–30; 37:26; Jer. 33:6. See Von Rad, "εἰρήνη," *Theological Dictionary of the New Testament*, 2:403. The covenant God granted to Phinehas was his "covenant of peace" (Num. 25:12).

109 Quell, "διαθήκη," *Theological Dictionary of the New Testament*, 2:115. Kalluveettil concurs: "The word šālôm indicates the wholeness of the relationship of communion between two parties. It is intimately connected with covenant as its object and effect. Men conclude a pact for the sake of šālôm, which brings security, intactness, and orderliness in their life. It sums up the whole content of covenant. The parties oblige each other to live in such a way as does not break the established harmony among them." See Kalluveettil, *Declaration and Covenant*, 34. Also Cross, "Kinship and Covenant," 15; Mendenhall, "Covenant," 1:714, 716, 720; Guinan, "Mosaic Covenant," in *The Anchor Bible Dictionary*, ed. David Noel Freedman (New York: Doubleday, 1992), 1:907; Gerhard Von Rad, *Old Testament Theology* (New York: Harper & Row Publishers, 1962), 1:130.

new covenant. Jesus' gift of peace—this definitive covenant solidarity with their God—is, ultimately, consolation for their hearts.

Consecration

In John 17:17–19, Jesus prays for the consecration of his disciples. It stresses that they are "not out of the world" (17:16), but rather they are "out of God,"[110] set apart as his own. As Jesus is consecrated by his Father[111] and consecrates himself,[112] so in a similar fashion the disciples are consecrated by the Father—who is the origin and source of their consecration as the one who is "Holy Father" (17:11)—as those who are sacred, holy to the Father (17:17).

Furthermore, the disciples are consecrated "in the truth" (17:17a), which, as Jesus goes on to specify, is the Father's word (17:17b). Jesus is himself the Word of God (1:1–2), he speaks the Father's word (14:10, 24; 17:8, 14) which is the truth (8:40). In fact, the Son is himself the truth (8:32, 36; 14:6) and fully discloses his interpersonal communion with the Father. In this manner, "truth" in the gospel essentially refers to the definitive revelation of the Father and his love by the only Son of the Father. It is the unveiling of the sonship of the Son and the fatherhood of the Father, and their interrelation.[113] Consequently, the disciples' consecration "in the truth" signifies their participation in the sonship of the Son and in the fatherhood of the Father. As the prologue states, the disciples are children of God because they have received him who is "full of ... truth" (1:12–14). Thus, their consecration "in the truth" definitively seals their participation in Jesus' filial relation to the Father; it seals their status as "children of God."[114]

Such a consecration is appropriate at the ratification of a covenant. The covenant between God and Israel on Sinai is framed by the divine call for Israel to be a consecrated nation: "keep my covenant ... [and] you shall be to me ... a consecrated nation" (Exod. 19:6). To prepare to enter into covenant with their God, Israel was to perform a divinely instituted ritual of consecration (19:10; also vv. 14, 22, 23).[115] In the "book of the covenant" (Exod. 21–23), the first-born sons of the families of Israel were called to be consecrated (22:29, 31; also 13:1–16). This consecration corresponds to the general consecration of Israel in Exodus 19

110 See John 1:12–13; 8:47; 11:52.

111 John 10:36. See also 6:27, "on him has God the Father set his seal."

112 John 17:19. See also 6:69, "you are the holy one of God.

113 See John 1:14, 18; 8:40; 16:25. See Ignace De la Potterie, *La Vérité dans Saint Jean*, Analecta Biblica 73–74 (Rome: Pontifical Biblical Institute, 1977), 2:1012; Ignace De la Potterie, "I am the Way, the Truth and the Life," *Theological Digest* 16 (1968): 63.

114 See De la Potterie, *La Vérité dans Saint Jean*, 2:782–783. For a similar account of consecration and divine sonship see Heb. 2:11–13 and 1 Pet. 1:14–17.

115 The consecration of the people in Exod. 19:14 is accompanied by a ritual washing. Likewise in John 13–17, the consecration of Jesus' disciples is associated with their feet being washed by Jesus (13:4–16) and "being made clean by the word" (15:3) which Jesus has spoken to them.

since Israel, corporately understood, is God's first-born son (4:22–23). Thus, they are set apart in the Sinai covenant precisely as God's first-born son. Israel's call to be a consecrated nation in a covenant relationship with their God is echoed in Deuteronomy 7:6, "For you are a people consecrated to the Lord your God." The Deuteronomic covenant itself demands that Israel be consecrated to God: "you shall be a people consecrated to the Lord your God" (26:19).

When the Davidic divine covenant was renewed under the Davidic king Hezekiah (2 Chron. 29:1ff.), the act of consecration was central to the covenant ratification rituals. Not only did the covenant renewal call for the Levitical priests to consecrate themselves and to consecrate the temple (29:5; also vv. 15, 17, 19), it also functioned to consecrate the assembly of Israel to their God: "You have now consecrated yourselves (מלאתם ידכם /ἐπληρώσατε τὰς χεῖρας ὑμῶν)[116] to the Lord; come near, bring sacrifices and thank offerings to the house of the Lord" (2 Chron. 29:31). It is through the ratification of the covenant that the consecration of Israel takes place.[117]

In light of the connection between the ratification of the OT divine covenant and the consecration of Israel, the consecration of the disciples in John 17:17–19 functions as a sign that the disciples' new covenant relationship with the Father and the Son is definitively sealed—they are fully and completely Jesus' covenantal "own." More specifically, as with the covenant at Sinai, this consecration in the truth decisively and resolutely sets Jesus' own apart as covenantal children of God.

Glorification

The Johannine meaning of "glory" forcefully reflects common traditions of Israel (especially the Sinai revelations).[118] In the Exodus, the glory of God was a sign[119] of his victorious power over the Egyptian Pharaoh which visibly manifested himself to his people so that they may believe in him (14:31) and so that all shall "know that I am the Lord" (Exod. 14:4; also 14:17-18; 15:1, 6, 11, 21). During the ratification

116 The Hebrew idiom (followed slavishly by the LXX translators) rendered "you (pl.) have filled your hands," implies consecration and usually refers to priestly investiture (see 2 Chron. 13:9). In this context it applies to the whole assembly of Israel. The same idiom is utilized in this wider sense in 1 Chron. 29:5. See J. A. Thompson, *1, 2 Chronicles*, The New American Commentary, vol. 9 (Nashville: Broadman & Holman Publishers, 1994), 349; Hahn, *The Kingdom of God as Liturgical Empire: A Theological Commentary on 1–2 Chronicles* (Grand Rapids: Baker Academic, 2012), 174.

117 In the Second Temple Period 2 Macc. 1:25 relates the tradition of Israel's consecration in connection with their covenant election by God: "You did choose the fathers and consecrate them." Sir. 45:3–6 relates that Moses' election is signified by his consecration: "he consecrated him through faithfulness and meekness; he chose him out of all mankind" (v. 4). He was consecrated so that he could "teach Jacob the covenant" (v. 5).

118 See Keener, *John*, 1050. Tsutserov (*Glory*, 189) argues that the use of "glory" in Exod. 33–34 defines the connotations of the term throughout the gospel.

119 According to Numbers 14:22, God's action in the Exodus (among others) is regarded as a glorious "sign" (σημεῖα).

of the Sinai covenant "the glory of the Lord settled on Mount Sinai" for seven days (24:16). This continuous dwelling in glory visibly manifested in the cloud and devouring fire (vv. 17–18) was a perceptible sign of God's active power to establish a familial communion through the covenant ratified by blood (v. 8).[120] Furthermore, God's power and indwelling presence in the tabernacle was signified in glory (Exod. 40:34–35). As a perceptible sign of the covenant relationship itself, the Ark of the Covenant was often referred to as "the glory."[121]

John 13:31–32 and 17:1, 5 relate that the hour of the mutual glorification of the Father and the Son has come. According to 17:24, the Father gives glory to the Son because he loves him. Their mutual glorification is rooted in their communion of love.[122] Furthermore in 17:22, this glory of the communion of love between the Father and the Son is given to the disciples, who subsequently will be one as the Father and the Son are one (17:22–23). In possessing the Son's glory they recognize and acknowledge that the Father has "loved them even as you [Father] have loved me [the Son]" (v. 23). Lastly, the mutual glorification of the Father, the Son, and the disciples is ordered externally to all future believers (17:20, 22–23). Verse 23c—"so that the world may know that you have sent me and have loved them even as you loved me"—indicates that the glory of the communion of love in which the disciples participate will be a glorious sign to the world which will point to the relation of the Son to the Father ("you have sent me") and, ultimately, to the love of the Father for his Son and for the world. In other words, the disciples' communion of love will be the glorious sign for all future believers to know and recognize the sonship of the Son and the love of the Father. Through this glorious sign, and the consequent belief and knowledge initiated by it, a relation will be generated which essentially concerns the relationship between the Father and the Son and their love, namely, all future believers will be generated as children of God.[123]

---

120 See Varghese, *Imagery*, 318. In a similar manner, the power and presence of God was disclosed in glory amidst the renewal of the Sinai covenant in Exod. 32–34. The glorification between God and his people functioned as a sign of their restored covenant communion: "both I and your people shall be glorified beyond all the nations, as many as are upon the earth" (Exod. 33:16 LXX; see also 33:18, 19, 22; 34:10 LXX).

121 For instance, 1 Sam. 4:21 and 22 state: "'The glory has departed from Israel!' because the Ark of God had been captured." According to the prophetic literature, "glory" is a vital element in Israel's eschatological hopes. It will be associated with the restoration of Israel and Judah, with the forgiveness of sins, the renewal of the covenant, and the return of God's presence to the temple (Jer. 33:9; Ezek. 43:4; 44:4). In the eschatological day, Israel will glory in God's name (Isa. 42:8; Zeph. 10:11). See Chennattu, *Johannine Discipleship*, 136 who cites *Tanhuma* במדבר 20 where God promises, "In the age to come, when I have led my dwelling place [שׁכינה] to Sion, I will reveal myself in my glory [כבוד] to all Israel, and they shall see and live for ever."

122 See Michael Waldstein, "The Mission of Jesus and the Disciples in John," *Communio* 17 (1990): 323. See also Wilhelm Thüsing, *Die Erhöhung und Verherrlichung* (Münster: Aschendorffsche Verlagsbuchhandlung, 1960), 236; Dodd, *Interpretation*, 262; Schnackenburg, *St. John*, 1:234; De la Potterie, *La Vérité dans Saint Jean*, 2:732.

123 This glorious sign of the disciples' communion of love is identical to the sign of love manifest to

The glorification of the Father, Son, and disciples in John 13:31–32 and 17:1–26 ought to be understood in light of its primary background, namely, the exodus event and the Sinai covenant, and as the "natural outworking of the analogy with Moses introduced in 1:14–18."[124] As glory was the visible sign for generating belief and knowledge in the exodus and the visible sign of God's fidelity and love in his covenant with Israel, so in John 13–17: through the communication of the glorious, visible sign of the communion of love of the Father and the Son, all future believers in the world will come to know the Father and the Son and their love given in the new covenant. Jesus is evoking OT traditions for the establishment of a sign by which the covenant relationship can be known, remembered, and shared.[125]

IV. Conclusion: Hermeneutic of Continuity and Fulfillment

It has been argued that the covenant principle, which defines the relationship of God to his people throughout the OT, permeates John 13–17 and is functioning within its theology. Put differently, John 13–17 goes to great lengths to describe the relationship between God and his people—the status, obligations, and the character of interiority—with the distinctive elements of what the biblical record calls a covenant. It is not unique in this regard, for it has followed the long period of biblical history which employed a covenant theology to provide a basic set of theological categories and values for understanding the relationship between God and Israel. John 13–17, therefore, possesses a profound continuity with the covenant theology of the OT.

However, such continuity does not mean equality. Although the covenant theology of John 13–17 is rooted in many traditions of the various OT covenant theologies, it presents itself not only as fulfilling these traditions, but as exceeding them in an unforeseen manner, and, therefore, presents a redefinition of the

---

all men associated with Jesus' new commandment which is given directly after the statement of the mutual glorification of the Father and the Son, and the conferral of the status of children to the disciples (13:31–35; see also 15:8). Notice that St. Cyril of Alexandria, commenting on 17:24, connects the communication of glory and love with the disciples' divine sonship: "to live with Him and to be deemed worthy to see His glory, belongs only to those who have been already united to the Father through Him, and have obtained His love, which He has from the Father. For we are loved as sons, insofar as we are like Him who is actually by nature His Son. Although this love is not dealt out to us in equal measure as to the Son, yet it is a complete semblance of the love the Father has for the Son; it coincides with and manifests the image of the glory of the Son." *Commentary on the Gospel of John*, Bk. 11, ch. 12 [*Commentariorum In Joannem*, Lib. XI, Cap. XII].

124 See Keener, *John*, 1052; Beasley-Murray, *John*, 14; also 217; Moloney, *Gospel of John*, 385. Notice the parallel between 17:24, "Father, I desire that those also, whom you have given me, may be with me where I am, to see my glory, which you have given me because you loved me before the foundation of the world," and *Assumption of Moses* 1:14, "He prepared me before the foundation of the world, that I should be the mediator of His covenant." See Glasson, *Moses in the Fourth Gospel* (Illinois: Allenson Inc., 1963), 77; Brown, *John XIII–XXI*, 781.

125 See Gen. 9:12–13; 17:11; Exod. 24:4; Deut. 27:2, 4; Josh. 24:26–27; 2 Sam. 7:16. See Varghese, *Imagery*, 356.

covenantal people of God. This unexpected fulfillment is disclosed through the eschatological revelation of God as "Father" by Jesus "the Son," who has enabled his disciples to participate in their familial relationship as those "born of the Spirit," as "children of God." This unanticipated realization expresses the significant shift in emphasis that has occurred when progressing through the continuous story of Israel as presented in Scripture's bi-covenantal corpus. The OT frequently and predominately employed the term "covenant" to describe the relationship between God and his people. In contrast, kinship terminology expressing familial relations and obligations in the OT was, for the most part, regulated to the background of God's dealings with his people. Although an extension of divine kinship status was disclosed at vital moments in Israel's history, it was often an implicit part of a future promise.[126] However, the reverse is true when progressing from the OT to its fulfillment in the NT. The term "covenant" has receded into the background while kinship terminology has taken a predominant position and has been employed with such unprecedented frequency and force that it has surpassed all OT expectations.[127]

Thus, there is no substantial discontinuity between the covenant theology of the OT and the covenant theology of the NT. The OT covenant has not been forgotten by the NT, rather it has been fulfilled by the NT. In light of this fulfillment, the language of divine kinship increases, while the explicit use of the term "covenant" predictably decreases. The language of divine kinship, which permeates John's gospel, is not only employed in a structured and systematic manner, but in relation to the OT it is utilized with unparalleled frequency and force. Like several other NT texts, the Fourth Gospel understands the ratification of the new covenant to fulfill the OT covenant relationship between God and his people with a hitherto unexpected escalation of sacred kinship and divine familial communion. In John's gospel there does not exist a sharp break or major departure from the covenant theology revealed in the story of Israel, but rather a fulfillment that exceeds all expectations.

---

126 Baker comments, "The relationship expected as the fruit of biblical covenants is one of family or kinship." Christopher J. Baker, *Covenant and Liberation* (New York: Peter Lang, 1991), 38.

127 Janet Soskice observes this shift: "The main name relation of God to the people in Exodus is covenant, not kinship ... The kinship of God and humankind is both compelled and resisted by the Hebrew scriptures—compelled for reasons of intimacy and resisted for fear of idolatry ... [in the NT] we see the turning of the symbol, the God who is 'not Father' in Exodus ... is revealed in the intimacy of the address of 'Abba' in the books of the New Testament ... the audacity of addressing God as Abba breaks the 'reserve to which the whole Bible testifies ... The audacity is possible because a new time has begun' ... within the Christian texts this movement ... from refusal of the language of physical generation to a word of designation, the 'I Am Who I Am,' and then to the promise of kinship—is a process completed by the audacious address of the Son." *The Kindness of God: Metaphor, Gender, and Religious Language* (Oxford: Oxford University Press, 2007), 75–78.

Letter & Spirit 9 (2014): 153-175

Fulfillment in Christ
The Priority of the Abrahamic Covenant in Paul's Argument Against the Galatian Opponents (Galatians 3:15–18)[1]

~: **Scott W. Hahn** :~

Franciscan University of Steubenville

Introduction

Some scholars hold that the word διαθήκη (*diathēkē*) in Galatians 3:15 should be translated "will" or "testament," an "act by which a person determines the disposition of his or her property after death."[2] Other scholars, almost as equally widespread, hold that the verse, so translated, renders Galatians 3:15–18 unintelligible with respect to both the legal background of the passage and the logic of Paul's argument.

This article will attempt to bring intelligibility and clarity to Galatians 3:15–18. I will show, first, that the meaning of διαθήκη in Galatians 3:15, 17 should be understood in the usual Pauline sense of "covenant," that is, "a legal fellowship under sacral guarantees."[3] Next, and having the interpretation of 3:15–18 now guided by the concept of "covenant" rather than by "will" or "testament," the

---

1 This article is a revision of my earlier treatment of Gal. 3:14–18, "Covenant, Oath, and the Aqedah: Διαθήκη in Galatians 3:15–18," *Catholic Biblical Quarterly* 67 (2005): 79–100. In this present article I take into account, among other things, responses to my initial article from Don Garlington, *An Exposition of Galatians: A Reading from the New Perspective* (3rd Ed.; Eugene, Oregon: Wipf & Stock, 2007); Thomas R. Schreiner, *Galatians*, Exegetical Commentary on the New Testament 9, ed. Clinton E. Arnold (Grand Rapids: Zondervan, 2010); Jerome Murphy O'Connor, *Keys to Galatians: Collected Essays* (Collegeville: Liturgical Press, 2012).

2 See Hans D. Betz, *Galatians: A Commentary on Paul's Letter to the Churches in Galatia* (Hermeneia; Fortress, 1979), 155; Richard N. Longenecker, *Galatians*, Word Biblical Commentary 41 (Dallas: Word, 1990), 128; James D. G. Dunn, *The Epistle to the Galatians* (London: A & C Black, 1993), 180–183; J. Louis Martyn, *Galatians: A New Translation with Introduction and Commentary*, Anchor Bible 33A (New York: Doubleday, 1997), 344–345. The definition is from *Merriam-Webster's Collegiate Dictionary*, 11th edition (Springfield, Mass.: Merriam-Webster, 2003), 1291a.

3 See Gottfried Quell and Johannes Behm, "διατίθημι, διαθήκη," *Theological Dictionary of the New Testament*, trans. G. Bromiley, eds. G. Kittel and G. Bromiley (Michigan: Eerdmans, 1964) [hereafter, *TDNT*] 2.104–134, here at 112 (Quell). For διαθήκη as "covenant" in Gal. 3:15 see J. B. Lightfoot, *The Epistle of St. Paul to the Galatians* (London: Macmillan, 1866), 141–142; Ernest De Witt Burton, *A Critical and Exegetical Commentary on the Epistle to the Galatians*, International Critical Commentary 35 (Edinburgh: T&T Clark, 1920), 496–505; Hermann N. Ridderbos, *The Epistle of Paul to the Churches of Galatia*, New International Commentary on the New Testament (Grand Rapids: Eerdmans, 1953), 130–131; and John J. Hughes, "Hebrews IX 15ff. and Galatians III 15ff.: A Study in Covenant Practice and Procedure," *Novum Testamentum* 21 (1976–77): 27–96, espec. 66–91.

identification of a *specific Old Testament covenant-making narrative* underlying Paul's argument will appear—Genesis 22:15–18, the covenant with Abraham ratified by divine oath after the Aqedah (the binding of Isaac). Once it has been determined that the specific narrative Paul has in mind in Galatians 3:15–18 is the covenant-oath of the Aqedah, his theological argument emerges. The thrust of the entire unit (3:15–18) is that the Abrahamic covenant enjoys historical priority and theological primacy over the Mosaic covenant at Sinai.

The coherence of Paul's argument in Galatians 3:15–18, though subtle, is recognizable when we follow sound lexicography, employ contextual sensitivity, and engage biblical texts with a typological reading.

I. Διαθήκη *as "Covenant" in Galatians 3:15*

Although the most basic meaning of διαθήκη seems to have been "a disposition," from διατίθημι, "to dispose, determine, distribute, establish," this meaning is rarely attested and only in older texts.[4] Over time the term became particularized to one specific kind of disposition, namely, "a final testamentary disposition in view of death":[5]

> The law shall run as follows: Whosoever writes a will (διαθήκη) disposing of his property, if he be the father of children, he shall first write down the name of whichever of his sons he deems worthy to be his heir. …[6]

Within Hellenistic Judaism, however, the development of the term followed a different trajectory. The translators of the Septuagint [hereafter, LXX], with almost complete consistency, chose διαθήκη to render the Hebrew ברית, "covenant." This translational choice has elicited some scholarly discussion, since the usual Greek term for "covenant," outside of the LXX, is συνθήκη.[7] Yet there is no reason to think that the LXX translators misunderstood ברית as "last will and testament." Rather, "it may be assumed that where LXX uses διαθήκη the intention is to mediate the sense and usage of ברית."[8] "Testament" makes no sense in the contexts in which the LXX uses διαθήκη, for example, "So Abraham took sheep and oxen and gave them to Abimelech, and the two men made a covenant (διαθήκη)" (Gen.

---

4 Behm, *TDNT* 2.125.

5 Behm, *TDNT* 2.104–105.

6 Plato, *Laws*, XI, 923c, trans. from Tufts University online "Perseus" edition: http://www.perseus. tufts.edu/cgi-bin/ptext?doc=Perseus:text:1999.01.0166:section=923c.

7 Behm, *TDNT* 2.126. Aristophanes uses διαθήκη as "covenant" once: "Not I … unless they make a covenant with me (ἢν μὴ διάθωνταί γ' οἵδε διαθήκην ἐμοι) …" (*Av.* 440).

8 Quell, *TDNT* 2.107.

21:27). For the most part, later Second Temple literature also employed διαθήκη to mean "covenant."[9]

It scarcely needs demonstration that a testament is a quite different sort of legal institution from a covenant. A testament provided for the distribution of an individual's estate shortly before or after his or her death, whereas a covenant was a legally-binding relationship of obligation—which could take a wide variety of forms—ratified by an oath between one party and one or more others, which seldom concerned the distribution of goods after one's death *per se*.[10]

Usually, which of the two senses διαθήκη bears is clarified by the context, but Galatians 3:15 is a difficult case:

> 'Αδελφοί, κατὰ ἄνθρωπον λέγω· ὅμως ἀνθρώπου κεκυρωμένην διαθήκην οὐδεὶς ἀθετεῖ ἢ ἐπιδιατάσσεται.
>
> Brothers and sisters, I give an example from daily life: once a person's will has been ratified, no one adds to it or annuls it. (NRSV)

Like the translators of the NRSV, most contemporary commentators agree that διαθήκη here should be taken in the secular sense of "will" or "testament." This consensus remains strong despite three serious difficulties:

First, Paul always employs διαθήκη as "covenant" in his other writings.[11] The same is true for the LXX translators, as well as for the other NT writers and the Apostolic Fathers.[12] With one possible exception, there is not a single instance where διαθήκη means "testament" in any of the above.[13]

Second, the reference to a Hellenistic "testament" in v. 15 would represent a lapse in the coherence of Paul's argument. Both before and after v. 15 he proceeds strictly within the conceptual sphere of Jewish (not Greco-Roman) law. Since the

---

9 Behm, *TDNT* 2.127.

10 On the definition of "covenant" (בְּרִית), see Quell, *TDNT* 2.106–124; and Gordon P. Hugenberger, *Marriage as a Covenant: A Study of Biblical Law & Ethics Governing Marriage, Developed from the Perspective of Malachi*, Vetus Testamentum Supplements 52 (Leiden: Brill, 1994), 168–215.

11 See Rom. 9:4, 11:27; 1 Cor. 11:25; 2 Cor. 3:6, 14; Gal. 3:17, 4:24; compare Eph. 2:12.

12 For the LXX, see Quell, *TDNT* 2.106–107; for the NT, see Behm, *TDNT* 2.131–134, espec. 134: "In both form and content the NT use of διαθήκη follows that of the OT." See Matt. 26:28, Mark 14:24, Luke 1:72; 22:20, Acts 3:25; 7:8, Heb. 7:22; 8:6, 8–10; 9:4, 15–17, 20; 10:16, 29; 12:24; 13:20; Rev. 11:19; *1 Clem.* 15:4, 35:7; *Let. Barn.* 4:6–8; 6:19; 9:6, 9; 13:1, 6; 14:1–3, 5, 7. Only in Gal. 3:15 and Heb. 9:16–17 is the sense "testament" a possibility.

13 See Hughes, "Hebrews IX 15ff.," 66–71. The exception is Heb. 9:16–17 (see Harold W. Attridge, *The Epistle to the Hebrews: A Commentary on the Epistle to the Hebrews*, Hermeneia [Philadelphia: Fortress, 1989], 253–256). But even here I would read "covenant." See Scott W. Hahn, "A Broken Covenant and the Curse of Death: A Study of Hebrews 9:15-22," *Catholic Biblical Quarterly* 66 (2004): 416–436.

dispute at hand concerns the interpretation of the Jewish Torah (νόμος), it is difficult to imagine what rhetorical force or relevance either Paul or his opponents would see in an analogy drawn from the secular court.

Third (and most seriously), if Paul intends διαθήκη to be understood as "testament" in v. 15, his statement "no one adds to or annuls [a διαθήκη]" is simply erroneous.[14] It is widely acknowledged that all known Greek, Roman, or Egyptian "testaments" could be annulled (ἀθετέω) or supplemented (διατάσσομαι) by the testator.[15] Legal practice in the first century directly contradicts what Paul seems to be claiming. This has led to an exegetical impasse.[16]

In an attempt to get beyond this impasse, some scholars suggest that Paul's statement οὐδεὶς ἀθετεῖ ἢ ἐπιδιατάσσεται means "no one [other than the testator] can annul or supplement [it]." It is then supposed that Paul holds God to be the "testator" of the Abrahamic "testament," whereas *angels* give the Mosaic law (Gal. 3:19).[17] Since the angels are not the "testators," their law cannot annul or supplement the original testament.

This interpretation strains the sense of v. 19. Burton remarks: "δι' ἀγγέλων ("through angels") does not describe the law as proceeding from the angels, but only as being given by their instrumentality, and the whole argument of vv. 19–22 implies that the law proceeded from God."[18] It was a commonplace in Second Temple Judaism that God gave the Sinaitic law by means of angels.[19] If Paul had intended to say something more radical—that is, that the angels were acting independently of God—then one would have expected him to clarify his meaning.

Other attempts around the impasse have concentrated on finding some contemporary legal instrument that *does* fit Paul's description of a διαθήκη in v. 15. Greer Taylor suggests that Paul refers to the Roman *fidei commissum*.[20] Ernst Bammel states that Paul has the Jewish מתנת בריא in view.[21] While these suggestions can-

14 Burton, *Galatians*, 502.

15 See Hughes, "Hebrews IX 15ff.," 83–91, Longenecker, *Galatians*, 128–130, Betz, *Galatians*, 155.

16 See Longenecker, *Galatians*, 130.

17 See Martyn, *Galatians*, 366–367; Hans J. Schoeps, *Paul: The Theology of the Apostle in the Light of Jewish Religious History*, trans. Harold Knight (Philadelphia: Westminster, 1961), 182–183. To the contrary, Longenecker, *Galatians*, 130.

18 Burton, *Galatians*, 503. Compare with Paul N. Tarazi, *Galatians*, Orthodox Biblical Studies (Crestwood, NY: St. Vladimir's Seminary Press, 1994), 152; and Longenecker, *The Triumph of Abraham's God: The Transformation of Identity in Galatians* (Edinburgh: T&T Clark, 1998), 59.

19 See Josephus, *A.J.* 15.5.3 §136 ("through angels [δι' ἀγγέλων] *sent by God*"), Acts 7:38, 53; Heb. 2:2.

20 Greer M. Taylor, "The Function of ΠΙΣΤΙΣ ΧΡΙΣΤΟΥ in Galatians," *Journal of Biblical Literature* 85 (1966): 58–76.

21 Ernst Bammel, "Gottes ΔΙΑΘΗΚΗ (Gal III 15–17) und das jüdische Rechtsdenken," *New Testament Studies* 6 (1959–60): 313–319. For a critique of Bammel, see Hughes, "Hebrews IX 15ff.," 72–76.

not be ruled out, there is no positive evidence that Paul's Galatian audience would have been familiar with either of these legal institutions. Furthermore, neither was called a διαθήκη.[22] How could Paul have expected his readers to understand that by διαθήκη he meant neither "covenant" nor "testament" but a lesser-known legal instrument not called by that name?[23]

A better interpretation results if one understands διαθήκη according to Paul's normal use of the word, that is, as "covenant." This has two advantages over the previously-mentioned proposals: First, "covenant" is the only sense of διαθήκη used by Paul elsewhere in Galatians and in his other letters (not to mention the LXX and the other NT documents). If we may assume that the Galatian congregation was familiar with Paul and his manner of speaking, it seems likely that they would have understood Paul's use of διαθήκη according to his usual meaning.[24] Second, since a covenant was irrevocable even by its maker (as I will show immediately below), Paul's statement οὐδεὶς ἀθετεῖ ἢ ἐπιδιατάσσεται ("no one sets aside or adds to [it]") rings true without nuance.[25]

A. The Covenant as Inviolable Legal Institution

The covenant institution had a life of its own in antiquity quite apart from its particular religious significance in Judaism and Christianity. Frank Moore Cross offers the following working definition: "Oath and covenant, in which the deity is witness, guarantor, or participant, is ... a widespread legal means by which the duties and privileges of kinship may be extended to another individual or group."[26] Covenants were widely used to regulate human relationships on the personal, tribal, and national levels throughout ancient Mesopotamian, Anatolian, Semitic, and classical (Greek and Latin) cultures.[27] The Bible itself attests to the widespread use of covenants: at least *twenty-five* different covenants between two human parties—always rendered by διαθήκη in the LXX—are mentioned in the Hebrew Scriptures: for example, between Abraham and Abimelech (Gen. 21:27–32), Laban and

22 Ben Witherington III, *Grace in Galatia: A Commentary on Paul's Letter to the Galatians* (Edinburgh: T&T Clark/Grand Rapids: Eerdmans, 1998), 242–243.

23 See Betz, *Galatians*, 155. The מתנת בריא was distinguished from a דייתיקי (διαθήκη) in Jewish law (see Longenecker, *Galatians*, 129–130; Betz, *Galatians*, 155).

24 As Martyn (*Galatians*, 344–345) admits. See also Burton, *Galatians*, 504: "Paul is replying to the arguments of his judaising opponents, and is in large part using their terms in the sense which their use of them had made familiar to the Galatians."

25 On the covenant as irrevocable, see Quell, *TDNT* 2.114; Burton, *Galatians*, 505.

26 Frank Moore Cross, *From Epic to Canon: History and Literature in Ancient Israel* (Baltimore: Johns Hopkins University Press, 1998), 8.

27 See Moshe Weinfeld, "The Common Heritage of Covenantal Traditions in the Ancient World," in *I trattati nel mondo antico: forma, ideologia, funzione*, ed. L. Canfora et al. (Rome: L'Erma di Bretschneider, 1990), 175–191.

Jacob (Gen. 31:44), David and Jonathan (1 Sam. 18:3), David and Abner (2 Sam. 3:12–13), and many others.[28]

Of particular relevance to Paul's point in Galatians 3:15 is the narrative of the covenant between the Israelites and Gibeonites in Joshua 9 (and the epilogue of the story in 2 Sam. 21:1–14), which illustrates the binding nature of a human covenant. In Joshua 9 we have a covenant between two human parties (Israelites and Gibeonites): "Joshua made peace with them and made a covenant (διαθήκη [LXX]) with them, to let them live, and the elders of the congregation swore to them" (Josh. 9:15). Significantly, the text explicitly states that the covenant, once sworn, could not be annulled, even when it comes to light that it was made on the basis of a deception:

> But all the leaders said to all the congregation, "We have sworn to them by the LORD, the God of Israel, and now we may not touch them. ... Let them live, lest wrath be upon us, because of the oath which we swore to them." (Josh. 9:19–20)

This passage illustrates the point that even a human διαθήκη—indeed, one made without consulting the LORD (Josh. 9:14)—is inviolable, a point brought home even more poignantly in 2 Samuel 21:1–14, where, even after the passing of several generations, Saul's breech of the covenant with the Gibeonites still results in three years of famine on Israel and must be atoned for by the death of seven representatives of his family.

Also of significance for Paul's use of διαθήκη is that in the late 2nd century B.C. the author of 1 Maccabees used the word to describe secular covenants between human parties:

> In those days lawless men came forth from Israel, and misled many, saying, "Let us go and make a covenant (διαθήκη) with the Gentiles round about us, for since we separated from them many evils have come upon us." (1 Macc. 1:11)

---

28 See Gen. 26:28 (covenant between Isaac and Abimelech); 1 Sam. 11:1 (Nahash the Ammonite and the men of Jabesh-gilead), 20:8 (David and Jonathan), 23:18 (the same); 2 Sam. 5:3 (David and the elders of Israel); 1 Kings 5:12 (Solomon and Hiram), 15:19 (Asa and Ben-hadad/Baasha and Ben-hadad), 20:34 (Ahab and Ben-hadad); 2 Kings 11:4 (Jehoidada and the captains of the guards); Isa. 33:8 (human covenants in general); Jer. 34:8 (Zedekiah and the people of Jerusalem); Ezek. 17:13 (Zedekiah and Nebuchadnezzar), 30:5 (an international treaty); Hos. 12:1 (Israel and Assyria); Amos 1:9 (Edom and Tyre); Obad. 1:7 (Edom and surrounding nations); Mal. 2:14 (husband and wife); Ps. 55:20 (psalmist and his friend); Dan. 9:27 (the "prince" and "many"); 2 Chron. 16:3 (Asa and Ben-hadad/Baasha and Ben-hadad); 23:3 (Joash and the "assembly"), 16 (Jehoiada, people, and king). Paul Kalluveettil has examined these human (or "secular") covenants in *Declaration and Covenant: A Comprehensive Review of Covenant Formulae from the Old Testament and the Ancient Near East*, Analecta Biblica 88 (Rome: Pontifical Biblical Institute, 1982).

Later in the book we read:

> [King Ptolemy] sent envoys to Demetrius the king, saying, "Come, let us make a covenant (διαθήκη) with each other, and I will give you in marriage my daughter who was Alexander's wife, and you shall reign over your father's kingdom. (1 Macc. 11:9)

Obviously, διαθήκη in 1 Maccabees 1:11 and 11:9 cannot refer to a "last will and testament." Thus, the author of 1 Maccabees provides us an example of a Hellenistic Jew, writing not so very long before Paul, who understood διαθήκη in the sense of ברית or "covenant" and applied the term in that sense to relatively recent human affairs.

Those scholars who work with biblical and non-biblical covenant texts point out that a covenant *was always ratified by an oath.*[29] The close relationship between a covenant and its ratifying oath can be seen in the narrative of Joshua 9 (esp. vv. 15, 18–20) cited above. Gordon P. Hugenberger states, "the *sine qua non* of 'covenant' in its normal sense appears to be its ratifying oath."[30] For this reason, the terms "oath" (אלה, ὅρκος) and "covenant" (ברית, διαθήκη) are frequently associated and at times functionally equivalent in the Bible (both testaments), OT psuedepigrapha and Apocrypha, Qumran literature, Targums, ancient Near Eastern documents, and classical Greek literature.[31]

The oath that ratified a covenant generally took the form of an implicit or explicit self-curse in which the gods were called upon to inflict punishments upon the covenant-maker should he violate his commitment.[32] Because a covenant was ratified by oath before the gods (or God), the obligations to which the parties had sworn could not be subsequently annulled or supplemented by either party.[33] Gottfried Quell summarizes the legal status of an oath-sworn covenant as follows:

---

29 Quell, *TDNT* 2.115; Weinfeld, "ברית *bᵉrîth*," *Theological Dictionary of the Old Testament*, eds. G. Johannes Botterweck and Helmer Ringgren (Grand Rapids: Eerdmans, 1974) [hereafter, *TDOT*], 2.256; Cross, *Epic*, 8.

30 Hugenberger, *Marriage as a Covenant*, 4, 182–184.

31 For the juxtaposition of "oath" (שבע אלה, ὅρκος, ὁρκισμός) with "covenant" (ברית, διαθήκη, συνθήκη), see Gen. 21:31–32; 26:28; Deut. 4:31; 7:12; 8:18; 29:12, 14; 31:20; Josh. 9:15; Judg. 2:1; 2 Kings 11:4; Ps. 89:3; Ezek. 16:8, 59; 17:13, 16, 18, 19; Hos. 10:4; CD 9:12; 15:6, 8; 16:1; 1QS v.8, 10; 4QD^b (4Q267) 9 i.7; 4QD^f (4Q271) 4 i.11; Wis. 18:22, 12:21; *Jub.* 6:10-11; *Pss. Sol.* 8:10; *Ass. Mos.* 1:9, 2:7, 3:9, 11:17, 12:13; Josephus *A.J.* 10.4.3 §63; Luke 1:72–73; and Heb. 7:21-22. For a fuller listing of Hebrew evidence see Hugenberger, *Marriage as a Covenant*, 183–184. For "covenant and oath" as a hendiadys ("one [idea] from two [words]") in Hittite, Akkadian, and Greek literature, see Weinfeld, "Common Heritage," 176–177; in the Targums, see Robert Hayward, *Divine Name and Presence: The Memra*, Oxford Centre for Postgraduate Hebrew Studies (Totowa, N.J.: Allanheld, Osmun & Co., 1981), 57–98, at 57, where Hayward states that the Targumists "understand the covenant as an oath sworn by God to the Fathers."

32 Hugenberger, *Marriage as a Covenant*, 194.

33 So F. C. Fensham, "The Treaty Between Israel and the Gibeonites," *Biblical Archaeologist* 27

> The legal covenant ... makes the participants brothers of one bone and one flesh. ... Their relationship as thus ordered is *unalterable, permanent, ... and inviolable,* and thus makes supreme demands on the *legal* sense and responsibility of the participants. There is no firmer guarantee of *legal* security ... than the covenant. Regard for the institution is made a religious duty by means of the oath taken at its establishment.[34]

Thus, if διαθήκη is taken as "covenant" in Galatians 3:15, Paul's statement that "no one annuls or supplements even a human διαθήκη once it is ratified" makes excellent sense. Paul, like the translators of the LXX and the author of 1 Maccabees, has employed διαθήκη as the equivalent of ברית to describe covenants both human and divine.

B. Coherence with the "Covenant Logic" of Galatians 3:6–18.

Two other aspects of the covenant institution integrate smoothly into Paul's argument in Galatians 3:6–18.

First, as Cross has indicated (see above), the covenant was a legal means of extending kinship privileges to outsiders. It is precisely the extension of the privilege of sonship—both divine and Abrahamic—to the Gentiles that is of paramount concern to Paul in Galatians 3–4 (see 3:7, 26-29, 4:1–7, 21–31). Even when Paul speaks of the outpouring of the Spirit on the Gentiles (3:2–3, 5, 14), he is speaking of *the Spirit of the Son* (4:6) which imparts sonship (4:5) to the recipients.

Second, as numerous biblical and ancient Near Eastern covenant documents attest, covenants transmit blessings and curses.[35] It is precisely the interplay between covenantal curses and blessings that concerns Paul in the dense discussion of the Mosaic law and Abrahamic blessing in Gal 3:10-14.

Third, since covenants created kinship ties, they could also order the transmission of property (see Gen. 15:18–21), or an "inheritance" (κληρονομία), a concept Paul mentions in Galatians 3:18. In fact, Abraham's "inheritance" was given to him by God via a promise incorporated into a covenant oath (see Gen. 15:1–21, especially vv. 18–21).[36]

(1964): 96–100, espec. 98–99, and Walther Eichrodt, *Theology of the Old Testament,* Old Testament Library; (Philadelphia: Westminster, 1975), 2.69.

34 Quell, *TDNT* 2.114–115 (my emphasis).

35 See, for example, Lev. 26, Deut. 28, J. B. Pritchard (ed.), *Ancient Near Eastern Texts Relating to the Old Testament* (Princeton, N. J.: Princeton University Press, 1969), 201a, 205b, 206b, 532–541.

36 Thus, *pace* Jerome Murphy-O'Connor (*Keys to Galatians,* 113–114), it should not be argued that the discussion of "inheritance" in Gal. 3:18 is only compatible with διαθήκη as "will" and not as "covenant."

Thus, not only does the inviolable covenant fit the precise statements of Paul in v. 15, but Paul's thinking throughout chapters 3 and 4 is deeply shaped by the covenant institution, such that one could describe it as "covenant logic."[37]

C. *Arguments for "Testament" Critiqued*

If διαθήκη as "covenant" fits the context of Galatians 3:15 so well, why is the term so widely understood as "will" or "testament"? Usually it is proposed that either (1) the presence of "technical legal terms" (κυρόω, αθετέω, επιδιατάσσομαι [ratify, set aside, add to])[38] or (2) the introductory statement κατὰ ἄνθρωπον λέγω ["I am speaking in human terms"[39]] suggests that Paul is using διαθήκη in its Hellenistic sense.[40]

First, with respect to the legal terminology in v. 15, Johannes Behm's assessment is typical: "The many legal terms used in the passage make it clear that he is here using the word διαθήκη in the sense of Hellenistic law," that is, in the sense of "testament."[41] Unfortunately, Behm presupposes a false dichotomy between the "legal" sense of διαθήκη as "testament" and the "non-legal" sense of διαθήκη as "covenant." Rather, as we have seen above, a "covenant" is just as much a legal instrument as a "testament," only of a different kind. Legal terminology is equally applicable to both.[42] Indeed, Paul uses "legal" terminology throughout Galatians 3, yet always within the context of Israel's religious law and covenantal history.[43]

Moreover, Behm and others exaggerate the extent to which the terms used in v. 15 are associated specifically with the secular court.[44] For example, the verb κυρόω is not used as an exclusively legal term, as can be seen from 2 Corinthians 2:8 and 4 Maccabees 7:9. Significantly, Paul applies the variant forms προκυρόω and ακυρόω to διαθήκη in Galatians 3:17, but no one for that reason suggests that διαθήκη as used *there* (v. 17) means "testament." The verb αθετέω is even less restricted to the legal sphere; observe the use of the word in Mark 6:26, 7:9; Luke 7:30, 10:16; 1 Corinthians 1:19, 2:21; 1 Thessalonians 4:8; 1 Timothy 5:12; Hebrews 10:28; and Jude 8. The verb δικαιόω likewise has a wide range of uses, only some of which

---

37 Witherington, *Grace in Galatia*, 243.

38 See Dunn, *Galatians*, 182; Betz, *Galatians*, 156; Martyn, *Galatians*, 338.

39 This phrase will be discussed at length below.

40 See Longenecker, *Galatians*, 128; and F. F. Bruce, *The Epistle to the Galatians: A Commentary on the Greek Text*, New International Greek Testament Commentary (Grand Rapids: Eerdmans, 1982), 169.

41 Behm, *TDNT* 2.129.

42 See Quell, "The Covenant as Legal Institution," *TDNT* 2.111–118.

43 For example, see διαθήκη (3:17), νόμος (3:2, 5, 10–13, 17, 19, 21, 23–24), δικαιόω (3:8, 11, 24), προκυρόω (3:17), ἀκυρόω (3:17), κληρονομ- (3:18, 29), προστίθημι (3:19), and διατάσσω (3:19).

44 See Hughes, "Hebrews IX 15ff," 68–69.

are legal.[45] The form of the verb used by Paul in v. 15 (ἐπιδιατάσσομαι) is a *hapax legomenon* in Greek literature, legal or otherwise; Paul seems to be coining the term.[46] Therefore, none of the words Paul uses in Gal 3:15 is so exclusive to the secular court as to require διαθήκη to be taken in the sense of "testament."

Second, as Charles H. Cosgrove has shown, the all-too-common rendering of κατὰ ἄνθρωπον λέγω as "I cite an example from everyday life" cannot be substantiated by similar phraseology in contemporary Greek literature.[47] A better translation would be "I speak according to human standards." Paul is introducing the lesser, human element (prime analogate) in his lesser-to-greater (*a fortiori*) argument, with the greater, divine element introduced in v. 17. His argument runs as follows: if, according to human standards of justice, it is illegal to alter the obligations of a covenant after one has ratified it by oath (v. 15), how much more so according to divine standards, when God himself ratifies a covenant (v. 17)?[48] In order for Paul's argument to be valid, the central term, διαθήκη, must bear the same meaning (covenant) in each analogate (vv. 15 and 17).

Therefore, neither the presence of legal terminology nor the phrase κατὰ ἄνθρωπον λεγω supports understanding διαθήκη as "testament" rather than "covenant."

---

45 See Liddell-Scott-Jones, *Greek-English Lexicon*, 414b.

46 See Longenecker, *Galatians*, 128; Bruce, *Galatians*, 171; Burton, *Galatians*, 180. The oft-quoted definition of the word given by Bauer, "to add a codicil to a will," can only have been derived from Gal. 3:15, and so begs the question regarding the meaning of διαθήκη in the verse (see W. Bauer, W. F. Arndt, and F. W. Gingrich (3d ed.; rev. by F. W. Danker), *Greek-English Lexicon of the NT* [Chicago: Chicago University Press, 2000], s.v. ἐπιδιατάσσομαι). Compare the more judicious definition in Johannes P. Louw and Eugene A. Nida, *Greek-English Lexicon of the New Testament Based on Semantic Domains*, 2 vols., 2nd ed. (New York: United Bible Societies, 1988), 603a, §59.73: "to add to." The middle διατάσσομαι is used in the NT with the same force as the active διατάσσω (see, for example, Acts 7:44, 20:13, 24:23; 1 Cor. 7:17, 11:34; Titus 1:5) and never in a juridical setting.

47 Charles H. Cosgrove, "Arguing Like a Mere Human Being: Galatians 3. 15-18 in Rhetorical Perspective," *New Testament Studies* 34 (1988): 536–549. Compare with Witherington, *Grace*, 241; Burton, *Galatians*, 504: "To take [this expression] as meaning 'I am using terms in a Greek, not a Hebrew sense' … is quite unjustified by the usage of that expression."

48 On the inviolability of human covenants, in addition to Josh. 9:3–27 and 2 Sam. 21:1–14 mentioned above, see Ezek. 17:11–18; Mal. 2:14–15; and Fensham, "Treaty," 96–100. Paul may have had this biblical background in mind, and/or the notion that commitments ratified by oath are inviolable in human culture generally—certainly in first-century Hellenistic culture. See Joseph Plescia, *The Oath and Perjury in Ancient Greece* (Tallahassee: Florida State University Press, 1970); Peter Karavites and Thomas E. Wren, *Promise-Giving and Treatment-Making: Homer and the Near East*, Mnemosyne, bibliotheca classica Batava Supplementum 119 (Leiden: E. J. Brill, 1992), 48–81, 116–200; and John T. Fitzgerald, "The Problem of Perjury in a Greek Context: Prolegomena to an Exegesis of Matthew 5:33; 1 Timothy 1:10; and *Didache* 2.3," in *The Social World of the First Christians: Essays in Honor of Wayne A. Meeks*, ed. L. Michael White and O. Larry Yarbrough (Minneapolis: Augsburg Fortress, 1995), 156–177.

II. *The* Διαθήκη *of Galatians 3:15, 17 as the Covenant-Oath of the Aqedah*

If, by διαθήκη, Paul means "covenant" in Galatians 3:15, can one determine a specific διαθήκη from which Paul draws his analogy to a "human covenant"? Although commentators often describe vv. 15 and 17 as speaking of "*the* Abrahamic covenant" in general, some scholars have recently noted that Genesis records at least two distinct covenant-making episodes in the life of Abraham (Gen. 15:17–21 and 17:1–27).[49] While these are often read as doublets of the same event narrated by different redactors (J and P), Paul would have read them synchronically, as two separate covenants.[50] Furthermore, in addition to Genesis 15:17–21 and 17:1–27, it is likely that Paul, like other first-century Jews, recognized another episode in the Abrahamic narrative as the ratification of a covenant: namely, the divine oath at the Aqedah (Gen. 22:15–18).

A. The Oath of the Aqedah as "Covenant" in Second Temple Judaism

Several texts from late Second Temple Judaism witness to the identification of the oath of the Aqedah as a covenant with Abraham.

Luke 1:72–73 tells of Zechariah praying to the Lord "to remember his holy covenant, the oath which he swore to our father Abraham." The "holy covenant" (διαθήκης ἁγίας) is thus identified with "the oath which he swore to Abraham" (ὅρκον ὃν ὤμοσεν πρὸς Ἀβραὰμ), a reference to Genesis 22:15–18, the only explicit divine oath made to Abraham in Scripture.[51] The identification is confirmed by Luke 1:74, which speaks of "being rescued from the hands of our enemies," a reflection of the promises of Genesis 22:17: "And your offspring shall possess the gate of their enemies."

In Acts 3:25, Peter refers to "the covenant (διαθήκη) which God gave to your fathers, saying to Abraham, 'And in your seed (ἐν τῷ σπέρματί σου) shall all the families of the earth be blessed.'" (my translation). Since only in Genesis 22:18 does God swear a covenant with Abraham that the blessing of the Gentiles shall be "in your seed" (ἐν τῷ σπέρματί σου), Acts 3:25b again identifies the "covenant" with the oath of the Aqedah.

Assumption (Testament) of Moses 3:9 reads, "God of Abraham…remember your covenant (διαθήκη) which you made with them, the oath *which you swore to*

49 See Paul R. Williamson, *Abraham, Israel, and the Nations: The Patriarchal Promise and Its Covenantal Development in Genesis*, Journal for the Study of the Old Testament Supplements 315 (Sheffield: Sheffield Academic Press, 2000), 1–25.

50 Carol K. Stockhausen ("2 Corinthians 3 and the Principles of Pauline Exegesis," in *Paul and the Scriptures of Israel*, ed. Craig A. Evans and James A. Sanders, Journal for the Study of the New Testament Supplements 83, Studies in Scripture in Early Judaism and Christianity 1[Sheffield: Sheffield Academic Press, 1993], 143–164, here 159–161) shows that Paul noticed significant differences between the covenant in Gen. 15 and the one in chapter 17.

51 Joseph A. Fitzmyer, *The Gospel According to Luke I–IX: Introduction, Translation, and Notes*, Anchor Bible 28 (Garden City: Doubleday, 1981), 384.

them by yourself," which can only refer to Genesis 22:15–18, the only time God swears by himself to any of the patriarchs. The phrase "covenant and oath" occurs elsewhere in the book as a reference to the oath of the Aqedah.[52]

Although its date is uncertain, the *Fragmentary Targum* of Leviticus 26:42 speaks of "the covenant oath which I swore with Isaac on Mount Moriah" in reference to Genesis 22:15–18.[53]

Many contemporary scholars recognize the virtual equivalence of the oath in Genesis 22:15–18 to the establishment of a διαθήκη. John Van Seters, for example, observes the correspondence between "oath" and "covenant" in Genesis: "The expression 'I will establish ... my covenant', (17:7) corresponds to ... 'I will establish ... the oath' (26:3), since oath and covenant are equivalent terms here."[54] T. Desmond Alexander applies Van Seters' observation—confirmed by the equivalence of "covenant" and "oath" in Genesis 21:22–34, 26:26–33, and 31:43–54—to Genesis 22:16–18 and the relationship of these verses to earlier promises made to Abraham, concluding, "Following the successful outcome of his testing of Abraham, God confirms with an oath in 22:16–18 what he had earlier promised. *It is this oath which ratifies or establishes the covenant.*"[55]

Alon Goshen-Gottstein notes a shift between Genesis and Deuteronomy in the terms used to describe the patriarchal covenant:

> The term "covenant" [in Deuteronomy] is replaced by the term "oath" to the Patriarchs. This occurs with every mention of the patriarchal covenant in Deuteronomy .... The covenant with the Patriarchs is understood as an oath, the oath to the Patriarchs taking the place of the covenant with the Patriarchs.[56]

In sum, the ancient readers of Deuteronomy came to associate the patriarchal "covenant" with God's "oath," pointing back to Genesis 22:16–18, the only oath God explicitly swears to any patriarch.[57]

---

52 On this, see Betsy Halpern-Amaru, *Rewriting the Bible: Land and Covenant in Postbiblical Jewish Literature* (Valley Forge, Penn.: Trinity Press International, 1994), 56–58.

53 See Hayward, *Divine Name*, 72–73, 80–81.

54 John Van Seters, *Abraham in History and Tradition* (New Haven: Yale University Press, 1975), 283.

55 T. Desmond Alexander, *Abraham in the Negev: A Source-Critical Investigation of Genesis 20:1–22:19* (Carlisle, Cumbria, U.K.: Paternoster, 1997), 110 (my emphasis). See also Alexander, *Abraham in the Negev*, 87–89.

56 Alon Goshen-Gottstein, "The Promise to the Patriarchs in Rabbinic Literature," in *Divine Promises to the Fathers in the Three Monotheistic Religions: Proceedings of a Symposium Held in Jerusalem, March 24-25th, 1993*, ed. Alviero Niccacci, OFM, Studium Biblicum Franciscanum Analecta 40 (Jerusalem: Franciscan Printing Press, 1995), 65. See Deut. 1:8, 4:31, 7:12, 8:18, 29:12; Josh. 2:1; 1 Chron. 16:16; and Ps. 105:9.

57 See Keith N. Grüneberg, *Abraham, Blessing and the Nations: A Philological and Exegetical Study*

B. To Which Abrahamic Covenant Text Does Paul Refer in Galatians 3:15–18?

In looking for Paul's specific source-text for the Abrahamic covenant in Galatians 3:15–18, Genesis 22:15–18 is the most likely candidate as it fits far more agreeably into the context of Paul's remarks in Galatians 3:6–18 than the other two covenant-making episodes in the Abrahamic narratives—those of Genesis 15:17–21 and 17:1–27.

A close reading of the context of Galatians 3:15–18 reveals three salient characteristics of the διαθήκη of v. 17: (1) It is *"ratified by God"* (προκεκυρωμένην ὑπὸ τοῦ θεοῦ, v. 17), not by a human (ἄνθρωπος, v. 15). (2) It is made with *Abraham and his "seed"* (σπέρμα, vv. 16, 18).[58] (3) It guarantees a divine *blessing* (εὐλογία) *to the Gentiles* (τὰ ἔθνη, v. 14).[59] Since neither Genesis 15:17–21 nor 17:1–27 promise blessing to the Gentiles, Genesis 22:16–18 is the only potential source-text with all three characteristics.[60] The passage reads:[61]

> By myself I have sworn (κατ᾽ ἐμαυτοῦ ὤμοσα), says the LORD, because you have done this, and have not withheld your son, your only son,[62] I will indeed bless you (εὐλογῶν εὐλογήσω σε), and I will multiply your seed (σπέρμα) as the stars of heaven and as the sand which is on the seashore. And your seed shall inherit

---

of Genesis 12:3 and its Narrative Context, Beihefte zur Zeitschrift für die alttestamentliche Wissenschaft 332 (Berlin: Walter de Gruyter, 2003), 228–235.

58 Verses 16 and 18 speak of a promise(s) (ἐπαγγελία[ι]), and v. 14 of a blessing (εὐλογία). Some suggest that Paul equates the "covenant" (vv. 15, 17) with the "promise(s)" in vv. 16, 18 (for example, Frank J. Matera, *Galatians*, ed. Daniel J. Harrington, Sacra Pagina 9 [Collegeville, MN: Liturgical Press, 1992], 128; Jeffrey R. Wisdom, *Blessing for the Nations and the Curse of the Law: Paul's Citation of Genesis and Deuteronomy in Gal 3.8-10*, Wissenschaftliche Untersuchungen zum Neuen Testament 133, 2nd series [Tübingen: Mohr Siebeck, 2001], 147–148), and the "promise" with the "blessing" in v. 14 (Wisdom, *Blessing*, 143, 145; Martyn, *Galatians*, 323). But the proper relationship is this: Paul is describing a *covenant* containing a *promise* of *blessing*.

59 See previous note. Significantly, v. 14a is an interpretive reworking of Genesis 22:18. See Niels A. Dahl, *Studies in Paul: Theology for the Early Christian Mission* (Minneapolis: Augsburg, 1977), 171; Jon D. Levenson, *The Death and Resurrection of the Beloved Son* (New Haven: Yale University Press, 1993), 212–213; Geza Vermes, *Scripture and Tradition in Judaism: Haggadic Studies*, Studia postbiblica 4, 2nd ed. (Leiden: Brill, 1973), 221.

60 Wisdom (*Blessing*, 23 *et passim*) and Martyn (*Galatians*, 339) point out that, of the three patriarchal promises of land, descendants, and blessing to the nations, only the promise of blessing to the nations concerns Paul in Gal 3. Gen. 15:17–21 and 17:1–27 promise only land and descendants. Other considerations that work against Gen. 15:17–21 or 17:1–27 are: (1) In Gen. 17:1–27, *God* does not ratify the covenant (Alexander, "Genesis 22 and the Covenant of Circumcision," *Journal for the Study of the Old Testament* 25 [1983]: 17–22; Williamson, *Abraham*, 69–71). *Abraham* does, through circumcision (see Hugenberger, *Marriage*, 196). (2) Neither Gen. 15:17–21 nor 17:1–27 describe Abraham as receiving "blessing" (εὐλογία). But compare Gal. 3:14a (ἡ εὐλογία τοῦ Ἀβραὰμ) with Gen. 22:17a (εὐλογῶν εὐλογήσω σε).

61 The translation is mine, highlighting what may have been important nuances to Paul.

62 The MT has יְחִידְךָ, "your one/only"; the LXX, ἀγαπητός, "beloved." But Paul is aware of the MT, as will be shown below.

> the gate of his enemies[63] and by your seed shall all the nations (πάντα τὰ ἔθνη) of the earth be blessed ...

Here all three elements occur—(1) *ratification by God* with a solemn oath of a covenant containing a promise (2) *to Abraham and to his "seed"* concerning (3) *blessing of the Gentiles* (ἐνευλογηθήσονται ... πάντα τὰ ἔθνη, v. 18a).[64] It is reasonable to conclude that the specific διαθήκη Paul has in mind in Galatians 3:17 is the Abrahamic covenant in its final form, as ratified most solemnly by God's oath after the Aqedah (Gen. 22:15–18).

C. *Supporting Evidence: Allusions to the Aqedah in the Near Context*

The conclusion that in Galatians 3:15–18 Paul has the Aqedah and its subsequent oath in mind is strengthened by evidence in the near context.

In Galatians 3:8, Paul alludes to the covenant-oath of the Aqedah by forming a conflated quotation of Genesis 12:3 and 22:18.[65] The text reads:

> ἡ γραφὴ ... προευηγγελίσατο τῷ Ἀβραὰμ ὅτι ἐνευλογηθήσονται ἐν σοὶ πάντα τὰ ἔθνη.

> ...the scripture...preached the gospel beforehand to Abraham, saying, "In you shall all the nations be blessed."

The phrase ἐνευλογηθήσονται ἐν σοὶ ("in you shall be blessed") must be taken from Genesis 12:3, but πάντα τὰ ἔθνη ("all the nations") as the object of the blessing comes from Genesis 22:18, the only place those words are spoken to Abraham.[66]

More significant than the brief allusion to Genesis 22:18 in Galatians 3:8, however, is the substantial relationship between the Aqedah and vv. 13–14. This text reads:

> 13 Χριστὸς ἡμᾶς ἐξηγόρασεν ἐκ τῆς κατάρας τοῦ νόμου γενόμενος ὑπὲρ ἡμῶν κατάρα, ὅτι γέγραπται· ἐπικατάρατος πᾶς ὁ κρεμάμενος ἐπὶ ξύλου, 14 ἵνα εἰς τὰ ἔθνη ἡ εὐλογία τοῦ Ἀβραὰμ γένηται ἐν Χριστῷ Ἰησοῦ, ἵνα τὴν ἐπαγγελίαν τοῦ πνεύματος λάβωμεν διὰ τῆς πίστεως.

---

63 MT has איביו, "his enemies," singular to agree with זרה, "seed."

64 On ratification by oath, see Alexander, *Abraham in the Negev*, 85: "The divine oath of chap. 22 marks the ratification of the covenant ...." The covenant in Gen 17:1-27 is not ratified by God; see n. 60 above.

65 So Richard B. Hays, *Echoes of Scripture in the Letters of Paul* (New Haven/London: Yale University Press, 1989), 106, 108; and C. J. Collins, "Galatians 3:16: What Kind of Exegete Was Paul?," *Tyndale Bulletin* 54 (2003): 75–86, espec. 80–86.

66 Gen. 18:18 is not the source for πάντα τὰ ἔθνη, since unlike Gen. 22:18 this verse is not spoken to Abraham, and Gal. 3:8 says, "ἡ γραφὴ ... προευηγγελίσατο τῷ Ἀβραὰμ."

> 13 Christ redeemed us from the curse of the law by becoming a curse for us—for it is written, "Cursed is everyone who hangs on a tree"— 14 in order that in Christ Jesus the blessing of Abraham might come to the Gentiles, so that we might receive the promise of the Spirit through faith. (NRSV)

Several scholars have suggested that in v. 13 Paul works with an Isaac/Christ typology, juxtaposing the Aqedah with the passion. Paul's quotation is from Deuteronomy 21:23, ἐπικατάρατος πᾶς ὁ κρεμάμενος ἐπὶ ξύλου ("cursed is everyone who hangs on a tree"), and primarily has the crucifixion of Christ "on a tree" in view (see Acts 5:30, 10:39, 13:29; 1 Pet. 2:24). But one hears echoes of an earlier near-death experience "upon the wood" (ἐπάνω τῶν ξύλων):

> καὶ ᾠκοδόμησεν ἐκεῖ Αβρααμ θυσιαστήριον καὶ ἐπέθηκεν τὰ ξύλα καὶ συμποδίσας Ισαακ τὸν υἱὸν αὐτοῦ ἐπέθηκεν αὐτὸν ἐπὶ τὸ θυσιαστήριον *ἐπάνω τῶν ξύλων* (Gen. 22:9 LXX)

> ...and Abraham built an altar there and laid the wood in order. He bound his son Isaac, and laid him on the altar, *on top of the wood*. (Gen 22:9 NRSV)

Paul has apparently linked Deuteronomy 21:23 with Genesis 22:9 via the analogy of ἐπάνω τῶν ξύλων ωιτη ἐπὶ ξύλου. Max Wilcox argues that "behind the present context in Galatians 3 there is an earlier midrashic link between Gen. 22:6–9 and Deut. 21:22–23 by way of the common term עץ (ξύλον, קיסא)," citing *Gen. Rab.* 56:4 and (Ps.)-Tertullian, *Adv. Iudaeos* 10:6 as evidence.[67]

By itself the link between Deuteronomy 21:23 and Genesis 22:9 via the hook-word ξύλος would not be conclusive. But when Paul's thought is followed into the next verse (v. 14), one finds an undeniable textual relationship with the Aqedah. As mentioned above, v. 14a is essentially a reworking of Genesis 22:18a.[68] The phrase εἰς τὰ ἔθνη ἡ εὐλογία ... γένηται ("to the nations the blessing...might be") in Galatians 3:14a corresponds to ἐνευλογηθήσοντα ... πάντα τὰ ἔθνη ("all the nations will be blessed") in Genesis 22:18a; ἐν Χριστῷ Ἰησου ("in Christ Jesus"—Gal. 3:14a) corresponds to ἐν τῷ σπέρματί σου ("in your seed"—Gen. 22:18a). Here Paul implicitly equates the "seed" of Abraham with Jesus Christ, as he will do explicitly in v. 16.[69]

Thus, the sense of vv. 13–14 is that the death of Christ ἐπὶ ξύλου ("on a tree") allows the blessing of Abraham given after the Aqedah (Gen. 22:18) to flow to the

67 Max Wilcox, "'Upon the Tree'—Deut 21:22-23 in the New Testament," *Journal of Biblical Literature* 96 (1977): 85–99, at 98.

68 Dahl, *Studies*, 171; Levenson, *Beloved Son*, 212–213; Vermes, *Scripture*, 221.

69 See Wilcox, "Upon the Tree," 97; and Cosgrove, "The Mosaic Law Preaches Faith: A Study of Galatians 3," *Westminster Theological Journal* 41 (1977): 146–164, espec. 150–151.

ἔθνη ("nations") through Jesus Christ (ἐν Χριστῷ Ἰησου). The movement of v. 13 to v. 14 is structured on the Aqedah itself, where the binding of Isaac ἐπάνω τῶν ξύλων ("upon the wood [collective idea]" or, literally, "upon the trees") merits from God a covenant oath to bless the ἔθνη (nations) through Abraham's "seed."[70]

The typology of the Aqedah has not been lost on Jewish scholars of Paul. Geza Vermes notes the implicit comparison of the death of Christ and the self-offering of Isaac, commenting: "In verses 13 and 14 [Paul] obviously has Genesis xxii. 18 in mind .... In developing his theological interpretation of the death of Christ, Paul ... followed a traditional Jewish pattern."[71] Jon D. Levenson also recognizes how Aqedah-typology controls much of the argument here: "The equivalent for Jesus of the binding of Isaac is, once again, his crucifixion. It is undoubtedly this that underlies Paul's citation of Deuteronomy 21:23 (Gal. 3:13)."[72] For Levenson, Galatians 3:13–14 is Paul's reapplication of the model of the Aqedah—the father sacrificing his son to release blessing to the nations—to Jesus' sacrifice on the cross. Thus, "In the juxtaposition of Gal. 3:13 and 3:14, we can thus hear a recapitulation of the whole movement of Pauline salvation history."[73] Since Paul has the Aqedah in mind in the verses 13–14—immediately preceding his discussion of the Abrahamic διαθήκη (vv. 15–18)—it is all the more likely that the specific form of the Abrahamic διαθήκη discussed in vv. 15–18 is that of Genesis 22:16–18.

Even the example of a human διαθήκη in v. 15 itself may have been inspired by Paul's meditation on the near context of the Aqedah. Strikingly, the Aqedah (Gen. 22:1–19) is directly preceded by the first account of the making of a *human covenant* recorded in Scripture, that between Abraham and Abimelech (Gen. 21:22–34). Since Paul engages the pericope of the Aqedah (Gen. 22:1–19) in Galatians 3:15–18 and the pericope of the expulsion of Ishmael (Gen. 21:8–21) in Galatians 4:21–31, he cannot have failed to notice the narrative of a human covenant (Gen. 21:22–34) sandwiched between them.[74]

D. The Significance of the Aqedah and its Covenant-Oath to Paul

The ratification of the covenant at the Aqedah is not simply one of three covenant-making texts (Gen. 15:17–21, 17:1–27, or 22:15–18) from which Paul could have drawn his argument. Rather, as the *final* ratification of the covenant with Abraham, it is the "last word," the definitive form of that legal bond. For Paul, the Aqedah

70 See Joseph P. Braswell, "'The Blessing of Abraham' Versus 'The Curse of the Law': Another Look at Gal 3:10-13," *Westminster Theological Journal* 53 (1991): 73–91, at 89 n. 46.

71 Vermes, *Scripture*, 220–221.

72 Levenson, *Beloved Son*, 212–213.

73 Levenson, *Beloved Son*, 213.

74 Carol Stockhausen remarks that "when the constitutive presence of Abraham's story in Paul's argument" is recognized, "then segments of Galatians not generally seen to relate to Paul's scriptural argument ... become less isolated and problematic" ("2 Corinthians 3 and Pauline Exegesis," 150). The relationship between Gen. 21:22–34 and Gal. 3:15 may be a case in point.

is the occasion on which the Abrahamic covenant takes on its greatest theological significance, where Abraham's *faith* and God's *promise* reach their quintessential expressions (see James 2:21–24). God's promise (ἐπαγγελία) and Abraham's faith (πίστις) are, as it were, the two strands from which Paul weaves his theology here (Gal. 3:6–29) and elsewhere (for example, Rom. 3–4). Although the word "faith" (πίστις) is not used in the LXX of Genesis 22:1–14, clearly in this narrative Abraham's faith successfully undergoes its most severe test, as Second Temple literature attests.[75] As a result of Abraham's demonstration of faith, the divine blessings, given in the form of promises alone in Genesis 12:1–3, are raised to the level of legally-binding covenant stipulations ratified by solemn oath (Gen. 22:16–18).[76] The Aqedah brings to perfection both Abraham's faith and the consequent divine promise to bless all nations.

III. The Interpretation of Galatians 3:15–18

Granted that Paul has the covenant-oath of the Aqedah in mind in his discussion of the "διαθήκη ratified beforehand by God" in vv. 15 and 17, how does this insight illuminate Paul's theological argument in Galatians 3:15–18?

A. The Legal Form of Paul's Argument in Galatians 3:15–18

Paul's argument in vv. 15–18 is a *legal* argument (thus the legal terminology) in the *qal wāhomer* (*a fortiori*, or lesser-to-greater) form.[77] Since even in the lesser sphere of human justice it is illegal to change the conditions of a covenant after one has sworn to it (v. 15), it is more so in the sphere of divine justice, when God unilaterally swears to bless all the Gentiles through Abraham's seed (v. 17).

Paul's argument is also a *reductio ad absurdum*: he shows that his opponent's position leads to an unacceptable conclusion. The Judaizers argue that obedience to the Mosaic Law is necessary for the Abrahamic blessing to reach the Gentiles, that is, for them to become children of God and children of Abraham. In Paul's view, this concept would be tantamount to placing the Mosaic Law as a condition for the fulfillment of God's covenant with Abraham to bless the nations through his "seed" (Gen. 22:16–18). Since, at the Aqedah, God put himself under a unilaterally binding oath to fulfill his covenant with Abraham, this would be nonsense. To suppose that God added conditions (the Mosaic Law) to the Abrahamic covenant

75 Sir. 44:19–21; 1 Macc. 2:52; Heb. 11:17; James 2:21–24; Longenecker, *Triumph of Abraham's God*, 131.

76 See Rabbi Hirsch, quoted by Meir Zlotowitz and Nosson Scherman, *Bereishis = Genesis: A New Translation with a Commentary Anthologized from Talmudic, Midrashic, and Rabbinic Sources* (New York: Mesorah, 1978), 2.809.

77 Matera (*Galatians*, 131) and Burton (*Galatians*, 141) recognize Paul's *kal va-homer* argument in vv. 15, 17; but unless διαθήκη is taken with the same meaning ("covenant") in both verses, the argument's logic fails, and apologies must be made for it (for example, Dunn, *Galatians*, 181–182; Longenecker, *Galatians*, 127–130).

long after it had been unilaterally sworn by God would imply that God acted *illegally*, reneging on a commitment in a way not tolerated even with human covenants. This would be an utterly unacceptable conclusion. Therefore, the premise that obedience to the Mosaic law had become the condition for the inclusion of the Gentiles in the blessings of the Abrahamic covenant must be rejected.

B. Paul's Argument in Galatians 3:16: The One "Seed" is Christ

If the Aqedah is indeed the background for the discussion in Galatians 3:15–17, light is shed on Paul's puzzling argument based on the singular "seed" of Abraham in v. 16, a notorious *crux interpretum*.[78] The narrative context of the Aqedah enables Paul to lay another subtle but significant plank in his argument against his Judaizing opponents.

It is not coincidence that the narrative of Genesis 22 stresses three times that Isaac is the *one* or *only* son of Abraham (יחיד ["one, only"] vv. 2, 12, 16; see Gal. 3:16, ἐφ ἑνός ["to one"]), pointedly excluding Ishmael (see Gen. 17:18–21) and any other progeny (see Gen. 25:1–5) from view. Moreover, the covenantal blessing in Genesis 22:18, unlike similar ones in 12:3 and 18:18, is only through Abraham's "seed," which in context is Isaac. Thus, Paul's point about the promise not being to "seeds" but to the one "seed" has some justification from the narrative of Genesis itself.[79]

If Paul had simply made the point that the "seed" in the context of Genesis 12–22 is primarily one individual, Isaac, there would be no controversy. However, Paul identifies the one "seed" as Christ. Why Christ and not Isaac? The most satisfying explanation is that Paul is engaged in an Isaac/Christ typology.[80] What Paul has in view is probably Isaac's singular claim to Abrahamic sonship in Genesis 22, precisely as a result of the expulsion and disinheritance of Abraham's other "seed," Ishmael, in Genesis 21. This expulsion/replacement theme becomes explicit in Galatians 4:21–31, the climax of Paul's argument.[81] Miguel Pérez Fernández comments:

> Throughout Paul's entire argumentation and in the typological representation that he makes of Isaac, the term with which

---

78 See discussion in Witherington, *Grace*, 244. Because v. 16 contains καὶ τῷ σπέρματί σου ("and to your seed"), Gen. 17:8 is usually considered the referent. But καὶ τῷ σπέρματί σου ("and to your seed") also occurs in Gen. 13:15, 24:7, 26:3, 28:4, 28:13, 35:12; and 40:4. Collins ("Galatians 3:16") sees v. 16 as a reference to Gen. 22:18a: "καὶ ... ἐν τῷ σπέρματί σου ..." ("and...in your seed").

79 See Levenson, *Beloved Son*, 210–211; Witherington, *Grace*, 244–245; Dunn, *Galatians*, 184–185.

80 Levenson (*Beloved Son*, 211) denies an Isaac-Christ typology. But Wilcox ("Upon the Tree," 96–99) interprets Gal. 3:16 as a *pesher* on the Aqedah.

81 Betz (*Galatians*, 19–22, 238–240) argues that the epistolary *probatio* (main argument) extends from Gal. 3:1–4:31. Thus 4:21-31 is not an afterthought but a climax.

> Isaac is denominated in Gen. 22.2.12.16 in the chapter about the *Akedah* is fundamental ... Paul ... translate[s] the concept of *yaḥid* with the Greek numeral *heis* ["one" or "only"]. The whole argumentation of chapter 3 of Galatians is based on the following equivalence: Isaac is *heis*, Jesus is *heis*, God is *heis*, believers are called to overcome their differences [cf. Gal. 3:28] ... by being *heis* in Christ.[82]

But more is involved in Paul's Isaac/Christ typology than the motif of "only" (יחיד, εἷς) sons: he sees Christ's passion as the fulfillment of Isaac's binding.

Isaac indeed carries the wood of his death up the mountain and is affixed to it in sacrifice, the "only" beloved son of his father, offering himself in obedience to God's command. But ultimately the sacrifice is abortive: it is, after all, the *Aqedah* and not the *'olah* (whole burnt offering) of Isaac. The sacrifice is incomplete, and the divine promises (Gen. 22:16–18) are not actualized in Isaac.

When and through whom was Isaac's abortive sacrifice completed and the promises actualized? In Paul's view, through Christ at Golgotha. There, the "only beloved son" (see Rom. 8:32; John 3:16) bore the wood of his death up the mountain, was affixed to it, and died in obedience to the command of the Father. Now through him the promised blessing of the Gentiles (Gen. 22:18)—that is, the outpouring of the Holy Spirit (Gal. 3:2, 5, 14)—had come to pass. For Paul, Abraham's binding of Isaac not only merited the blessing of the Gentiles through Abraham's "seed" (Gen. 22:18), but in fact *prefigured* and *pre-enacted* the sacrifice of the only beloved Son, which would release that same blessing.[83]

Galatians 3:16 is not the only evidence that Paul reads the Abrahamic narratives typologically.[84] An implicit Isaac/Christ typology of the Aqedah has been recognized by Vermes, Levenson, and others in Galatians 3:13–14, as noted above. Moreover, at the climax of the epistolary *probatio* in Galatians 4:21–31, Paul draws an explicit typological allegory based on Genesis 21, in which the exclusion of Ishmael from the Abrahamic covenant blessing and the exclusive identification of Isaac as Abraham's heir figure prominently. Paul intends his readers to link the Gentiles who accept circumcision with Ishmael, who received circumcision as an adult (Gen. 17:25) but was nonetheless disinherited (Gen. 21:10). Uncircumcised converts are meant to be associated with the late-in-coming Abrahamic son of promise, Isaac, who was designated heir while still uncircumcised (Gen. 17:19).

Galatians 3:16 may be seen as anticipating Galatians 4:21–31. As Galatians 3:16 sees Isaac as a type of Christ in Genesis 22, so Galatians 4:21–31 sees Isaac

---

82 Miguel Pérez Fernández, "The Aqedah in Paul," in *The Sacrifice of Isaac in the Three Monotheistic Religions: Proceedings of a symposium on the interpretation of the scriptures held in Jerusalem, March 16-17, 1995*, ed. Frédéric Manns, Studium Biblicum Franciscanum Analecta 41 (Jerusalem: Franciscan Printing Press, 1995), 81–98, at 90. See Wilcox, "Upon the Tree," 96–99.

83 Gordon J. Wenham, *Genesis 16–50*, Word Biblical Commentary 2 (Waco: Word, 1994), 117.

84 On Gal. 3:16 as typology, see Pérez Fernández, "Aqedah in Paul," 88–89.

in Genesis 21 as a type of Christians. The typologies are intimately related, since believers are "one in Christ Jesus ... Abraham's offspring, heirs according to the promise" (Gal. 3:29).[85]

C. The Conclusion of Paul's Argument: The Priority of the Abrahamic Covenant

Understanding the covenant oath of the Aqedah as the background for Galatians 3:6–18 clarifies Paul's argument concerning the relationship between the Abrahamic and Mosaic covenants, as well as their fulfillment in Christ's curse-bearing death on the "tree."

Paul sees the historical *priority* of the Abrahamic covenant vis-à-vis the Mosaic covenant as revealing the theological *primacy* of God's sworn obligation to bless all nations, over and against Israel's sworn obligation to keep the Sinaitic Torah (Gal. 3:17). In other words, Paul argues that since the Mosaic covenant is *subsequent* to the Abrahamic, God's purpose in binding Israel at Sinai to keep the law (that is, as Abraham's seed) must be legally *subordinated* to his purpose in binding himself at the Aqedah to bless all the nations (that is, through Abraham's seed). What God promised to Abraham was not negated by what happened at Sinai. Yet the Sinai legislation did serve a pedagogical function, as a divine accommodation to Israelite transgressors, that is, the backsliding descendants and heirs of the Abrahamic promise (Gal. 3:19, 23–24).

The oath of the Aqedah ensured the success of God's plan to bless all the nations through Abraham's seed despite their backsliding. By swearing the oath, God subjected himself to a curse should Abraham's seed fail to convey that blessing to the Gentiles.[86] After Israel had sworn a covenant with God at Sinai (Exod. 24:1–8)—which they promptly transgressed (Exod. 32:1–8)—the covenant curse-of-death was triggered (Exod. 32:10).[87] This curse was averted only when Moses appealed to God to keep his *own* covenant oath, sworn to Abraham's seed at the Aqedah (Exod. 32:13). God's oath to Abraham preserved the life of rebellious Israel on that and other occasions (Num. 14:16, 23). Still, the Mosaic law stipulated many covenant curses (Deut. 28:15–68), all of which were borne collectively by Israel as a nation, with the notable exception of one singular curse-bearing provi-

85 For a fuller discussion of Gal. 3–4 and the covenants with Abraham, see Scott W. Hahn, *Kinship by Covenant: A Canonical Approach to the Fulfillment of God's Saving Promises*, Anchor Yale Bible Reference Library (New Haven & London: Yale University Press, 2009), 238–277.

86 An oath always entailed at least an implicit self-curse: "The fact that אָלָה (originally meaning "curse")... is used [to mean "covenant"] serves to emphasize the hypothetical self-curse which underlies biblical oaths" (Hugenberger, *Marriage as a Covenant*, 194, 200–201).

87 On death as the usual penalty for covenant transgression, see John Dunnill, *Covenant and Sacrifice in the Letter to the Hebrews*, Society for New Testament Studies Monograph Series 71 (Cambridge: Cambridge University Press, 1992), 249; and O. Palmer Robertson, *The Christ of the Covenants* (Grand Rapids: Baker, 1980), 11–12.

sion that was only applied to certain individuals—namely, being hung on a tree for a crime punishable by death (Deut. 21:23).[88]

Paul's citation of that notable exception in the immediately preceding context (Gal. 3:13) indicates the covenantal form of the legal logic behind his typological argument, by which he proves the salvific efficacy of God's sworn covenant to Abraham at the Aqedah over and against Israel's sworn (and transgressed) covenant at Sinai. The covenant consequences of Christ's death are revealed: On the one hand, Christ's willing consent to crucifixion—prefigured by Isaac—uncovers the deepest dimension of the Aqedah, that is, the pre-enactment of what God alone must do to bring about "the blessing of Abraham" for Israel and the nations, even if it calls for his own sacrificial self-identification with Abraham's "seed" (and "only beloved son"). On the other hand, Christ's curse-bearing impalement "on a tree"—also prefigured by Isaac—reveals God's preemptive strategy and merciful resolution to remove the legal impediment of the Deuteronomic curses that hang over unfaithful Israel (Gal. 3:13).[89] In sum, the laws and curses of the Mosaic covenant will not cause—or prevent—the promises and sworn blessings of the Abrahamic covenant from reaching Israel and the nations.

IV. Conclusions

A. Paul was a Contextually Sensitive Exegete

What kind of exegete was Paul?[90] Scholarly opinion on this question falls across a wide spectrum. Some argue that Paul routinely disregards the context of his Old Testament Scriptural quotations and deploys *rhetorically* effective but *logically* incoherent arguments.[91] Others—at least those who are willing to accept his understanding of the inspiration and authority of the Scriptures of Israel—find

88 See Kjell A. Morland, *The Rhetoric of Curse in Galatians: Paul Confronts Another Gospel*, Emory Studies in Early Christianity 5 (Atlanta: Scholars Press, 1995), 220: "Deut. 21:23 ... is the only law in the deuteronomic law corpus that has a curse as a sanction. It may thus easily be drawn together with the curses of Deut. 27. It is also the only deuteronomic law that denotes individual persons as cursed in a metonymic way [that is, as *becoming* a curse].... It may thus easily be drawn together with the other metonymic expressions of Israel as cursed in the Deut. 27–30 tradition." See also Morland, *Rhetoric of Curse*, 70–71.

89 Having "become" a curse according to Deut. 21:23, Christ serves as an expiatory sacrifice on behalf of the people. See discussion in Morland, *Rhetoric of Curse*, 221–223; Helmut Merklein, "Die Bedeutung des Kreuzestodes Christi für die paulinische Gerechtigkeits- und Gesetzesthematik," in *Studien zu Jesus und Paulus*, Wissenschaftliche Untersuchungen zum Neuen Testament 43 (Tübingen: Mohr/Siebeck, 1987), 1–106.

90 C. J. Collins raised this question with respect to Gal. 3 over a decade ago: "Galatians 3:16: What Kind of Exegete Was Paul?" *Tyndale Bulletin* 54 (2003): 75–86.

91 Heikki Räisänen gained notoriety for adopting a strong form of this position: see his *Paul and the Law*, WUNT 29 (Tübingen: Mohr-Siebeck, 1987). Mika Hietanen is less rhetorically aggressive, but similarly faults Paul at a number of places for fallacious argumentation: *Paul's Argumentation in Galatians: A Pragma-Dialectical Analysis*, European Studies on Christian Origins; LNTS [JSNTS] 344 (London: T & T Clark, 2007).

his use of Scriptural quotations profoundly sensitive to the Old Testament context, and his logic compelling.[92]

In an essay published over two decades ago, Carol Stockhausen proposed several principles concerning Paul's exegesis, among them that the "narrative texts of the Pentateuch are usually at the core of his arguments," that "he is extremely concerned with the stories themselves," and that he pays "consistent attention to the context of cited passages."[93] Stockhausen also states that "a fundamental awareness of the constitutive presence of Abraham's story in Paul's argument requires that Paul's arguments in the whole of Galatians be seen ... [as having] the primary goal of correctly interpreting the story of Abraham itself."[94] This article confirms Stockhausen's observations. We have shown that, far from employing a hermeneutical and rhetorical slight-of-hand, in Galatians 3–4, Paul engages in a thoughtful and exacting meditation on the theological implications of the Abrahamic narrative—especially the account of the Aqedah—for the Gospel and for the Church.

B. The Priority of the Abrahamic Covenant in Paul's Argument in Galatians 3

It was demonstrated above that διαθήκη in Galatians 3:15 should be taken as "covenant," which accords well with the actual statements of the verse and the "covenant logic" of the context. In particular, the διαθήκη Paul has in mind in vv. 15, 17 is the covenant oath sworn by God at the Aqedah with Abraham and his "seed" (Gen. 22:16–18). The example of a "human covenant" (Gal. 3:15) itself may have been prompted by the record of a human covenant immediately preceding the Aqedah (Gen. 21:22–34). A pattern of allusion to the Aqedah and its context is evident throughout Galatians 3:6–18.

In the heart of the unit, vv. 15–18, Paul uses a *kal va-homer* argument—only valid if διαθήκη means "covenant" in *both* v. 15 and v. 17—to demonstrate that

92 The origin of the "contextual" approach to Pauline scriptural citation may be C. H. Dodd, *According to the Scriptures: The Sub-Structure of New Testament Theology* (New York: Charles Scribner's Sons, 1953). More recent discussion (pro and con) may be found in the following: M. D. Hooker, "Beyond the Things That are Written? St. Paul's Use of Scripture," *New Testament Studies* 27 (1981-82): 295–309; D. A. Carson and H. Williamson (eds.), *It is Written: Scripture Citing Scripture* (New York: Cambridge University, 1988); R. B. Hays, *Echoes of Scripture in the Letters of Paul* (New Haven: Yale, 1989); G. K. Beale, "Did Jesus and His Followers Preach the Right Doctrine From the Wrong Texts? An Examination of the Presuppositions of Jesus' and the Apostles' Exegetical Method," *Themelios* 14 (1989): 89–96; Carol Stockhausen, "2 Corinthians 3 and the Principles of Pauline Exegesis," in *Paul and the Scriptures of Israel*, ed. C. A. Evans and J. A. Sanders (Sheffield: Journal for the Study of the Old Testament Press, 1993), 143–164; G. K. Beale (ed.), *Right Doctrine From Wrong Texts?* (Grand Rapids, MI: Baker, 1994).

93 Stockhausen, "2 Corinthians 3 and Pauline Exegesis," 144–145.

94 Stockhausen, "2 Corinthians 3 and Pauline Exegesis," 150.

the Mosaic covenant cannot possibly supplement or alter the conditions of the covenant oath of the Aqedah, in which God took upon himself the responsibility to bless the Gentiles through Abraham's seed. The background of the Aqedah also elucidates the obscure argument in v. 16: Paul sees Isaac, the "only son" of Abraham, as a type of the Christ, the "one seed" of Abraham *par excellence*, whose self-sacrifice would be completed and serve to actualize the promised blessing of the Gentiles merited at the Aqedah.

The thrust of the entire unit (vv. 15–18) is that the Abrahamic covenant enjoys historical priority and theological primacy over against the Mosaic covenant at Sinai. The coherence of Paul's argument in Galatians 3:15–18, though subtle, is recognizable when we acknowledge his contextual use and typological reading of biblical texts.

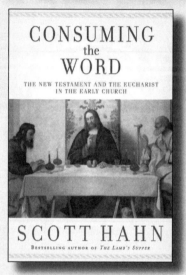

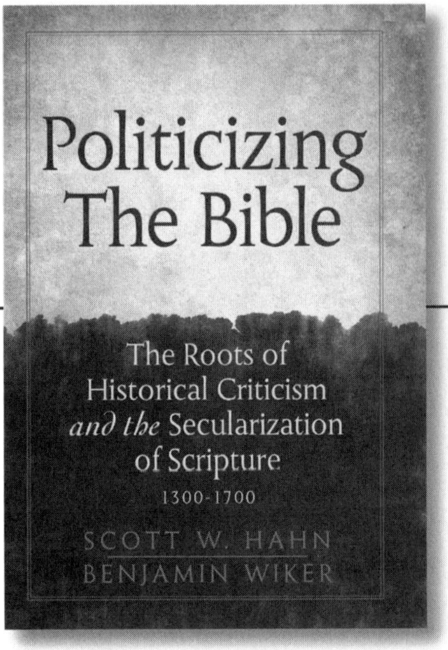

ARCHBISHOP AUGUSTINE DINOIA

Secretary of the Vatican Congregation for Divine Worship

"Historical criticism has its own history, and its development should be subject to the scrutiny of historical method, as it is in these pages."

HADLEY ARKES

Edward N. Ney Professor of Jurisprudence and American institutions, Amherst College

"Hahn and Wiker have not only given us a notable work in theology, but one of the most compelling histories of political philosophy. I cannot recall any book that achieves that combination as arrestingly as this one. It is, altogether, the most remarkable of works."

FRANCIS J. BECKWITH

Professor of philosophy and Church-State Studies, Baylor University

"This is an important work that will force its readers to readjust, and in some cases totally reject, what they had been taught about the objectivity and neutrality of contemporary approaches to God's Word."

JACOB NEUSNER

Professor of religion and senior fellow of the Institute of Advanced Theology at Bard College

"Hahn and Wiker show how the study of Scripture was transformed by centuries of conflict over the fundamentals of Western civilization. They demonstrate their thesis in minute detail. The Bible clearly emerges as the foundational document of western civilization and its academy."

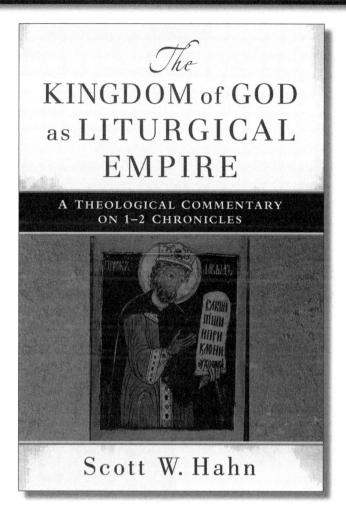

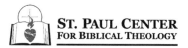